Accelerated
NetWare 5 CNE
Study Guide

Accelerated
NetWare 5 CNE
Study Guide

Dorothy Cady

McGraw-Hill
New York • San Francisco • Washington, D.C. • Auckland • Bogotá
Caracas • Lisbon • London • Madrid • Mexico City • Milan • Montreal
New Delhi • San Juan • Singapore • Sydney • Tokyo • Toronto

McGraw-Hill

A Division of The McGraw·Hill Companies

Copyright © 1999 by The McGraw-Hill Companies, Inc. All rights reserved. Printed in the United States of America. Except as permitted under the United States Copyright Act of 1976, no part of this publication may be reproduced or distributed in any form or by any means, or stored in a data base or retrieval system, without the prior written permission of the publisher.

The views expressed in this book are solely those of the author, and do not represent the views of any other party or parties.

1 2 3 4 5 6 7 8 9 0   AGM/AGM   9 0 3 2 1 0 9 8

ISBN 0-07-134531-0

The sponsoring editor for this book was Judy Brief and the production supervisor was Clare Stanley. It was set in Dante by Patricia Wallenburg.

Printed and bound by Quebecor/Martinsburg.

McGraw-Hill books are available at special quantity discounts to use as premiums and sales promotions, or for use in corporate training programs. For more information, please write to the Director of Special Sales, McGraw-Hill, 11 West 19th Street, New York, NY 10011. Or contact your local bookstore.

 This book is printed on recycled, acid-free paper containing a minimum of 50% recycled, de-inked fiber.

Acknowledgments

Many people contribute to the creation of a book, from those who inspired it to those who made sure every aspect of its layout and printing as well as its distribution was successfully completed. For the latter, McGraw-Hill's staff gets the credit. For the former, Judy Brief at McGraw-Hill gets the credit. As for everything in between, well, my family (Raymond, Shana, and Ray) gets credit for their patience and understanding, and my friend Nancy Cadjan gets the credit for ensuring I didn't stray too far from the intent of the book, or leave out anything of importance.

To each of these people, as well as to all of those who helped me to finish this book on time, I give my thanks and appreciation.

Contents

Introduction

NetWare 5 is the world's largest networking software, with almost four million NetWare servers supporting more than 80 million nodes in the world today. Its design makes it easier for developers to produce third-party applications, and therefore helps to ensure that network clients have access to a wide variety of easy-to-manage network resources, including easy access to the Internet.

NetWare 5 provides the best network management capabilities of any server operating system. As a network operating system, NetWare 5 has proven to be reliable, scalable, and secure. It also provides the best platform for deploying Java-based applications, and is built on open protocols and standards.

But what does all of this mean to you? As a NetWare 5 Certified Novell Engineer (CNE) candidate, you need to understand not only the basics of NetWare 5, but the more advanced features, applications, and other programs associated with it. To learn the basics about NetWare 5, you should already have read this book's companion: the *Accelerated NetWare 5 CNA Study Guide*. Its contents cover that information you must know in order to pass the official Novell authorized NetWare 5 Advanced Administration test, #050-413. That same test, in addition to the NetWare 5 Advanced Administration test, #50-640, is required in order to obtain your NetWare 5 CNE certification. This book, the *Accelerated NetWare 5 CNE Study Guide*, is designed to help you quickly, and with limited amounts of time, learn enough about the advanced features of NetWare 5 so that you can successfully pass the NetWare 5 Advanced Administration test.

Who Should Read This Book

If you need to learn about NetWare 5 and become certified in a short period of time, this book was designed for you. To learn the needed information and pass the required tests for certification, you may find it necessary to study whenever snatches of time are available. This means you need learning tools that are portable, small, and to-the-point. This *Accelerated NetWare 5 CNE Study Guide* was designed to meet those requirements.

What This Book Covers

This book covers the information you need to know to pass the NetWare 5 Advanced Administration test. It is divided into ten chapters. Each chapter concentrates on an area of NetWare 5 such as remote network access, or on a major task such as upgrading a NetWare 3 or NetWare 4 network to a NetWare 5 network.

- Chapter 1, *Planning a NetWare 5 Network*, provides an overview of the NetWare 5 server, and explains how to plan and prepare for your NetWare 5 upgrade. It discusses such topics as the server console, NLMs, console command, minimum requirements for upgrading, methods of upgrading, and what steps to take in order to prepare for the upgrade.
- Chapter 2, *Creating a NetWare 5 Network*, discusses the process of upgrading NetWare 3 and NetWare 4 servers to NetWare 5. It also discusses how to install other products and programs, and how to provide GUI and JAVA support, as well as how to add JAVA programs and applets to the NetWare 5 server.
- Chapter 3, *Completing the Upgrade*, delves into the after-upgrade tasks, at least some of which must be completed in order to successfully complete the installation of a NetWare 5 network. It gives you information on which post-upgrade tasks you can perform. It also tells you how to customize and configure server setup, how to set up NDS security, how to secure your NetWare 5 file server, and how to use Novell's Enhanced Sbackup software once you have completed the upgrade.
- Chapter 4, *Working With the NetWare 5 Console*, concentrates on familiarizing you with the file server console. It shows you how to use

ConsoleOne, NetWare's new GUI-based server administration tool. It also shows you how to set up and use remote access to the console. In addition, it shows you how to run the Monitor NLM at the server console so you can gather performance statistics and other information about the NetWare 5 server.

- Chapter 5, *Understanding and Establishing Network Printing*, shows you how to set up network printing so that users can access and print to printers on the network. It explains queue-based as well as NDPS-based network printing. In addition, it shows you how to set up, enable, and manage network printing.

- Chapter 6, *Enabling Remote Network Access*, explains NIAS and RADIUS, two methods of remote access. It also discusses relevant information to help you enable and configure remote access, and to establish a remote connection.

- Chapter 7, *Understanding and Using DNS and DHCP Services*, explains what DNS and DHCP services are, how to install and configure them on NetWare 5 servers, and how to set up workstations to use DNS. It also explains how to start DNS.

- Chapter 8, *Installing and Configuring Netscape FastTrack and FTP Servers*, explains what Netscape FastTrack and FTP Servers are, as well as how to install and configure each of them.

- Chapter 9, *Maintaining and Optimizing a NetWare 5 Network*, shows you how you can take advantage of features in NetWare 5 to better manage and administer your network, as well as to make it run more smoothly and seamlessly for your network users. This chapter discusses memory and memory management, methods for optimizing disk space and usage, improving communications using LIP and packet burst, using applications, and maintaining NDS.

- Chapter 10, *Enhancing the Network with Other Novell Services*, covers other services NetWare 5 provides. It discusses other available services, and explains how to integrate Border Manager, NDS for NT, GroupWise, and ManageWise on the network.

Each chapter in this book also contains a Practice Test Questions section. Going through these questions is designed to help further your knowledge of NetWare 5. In addition, these are designed to help you become comfortable with answering test questions so that you will be more relaxed and do better on the actual certification test than you might otherwise have done.

Novell's certification tests are presented in electronic format at a certified testing center. Each question is chosen from a database of test questions which have themselves been tested for validity, and in many instances, for level of difficulty. Although most test questions are multiple choice, more than one correct answer may be possible. Where more than one correct answer is possible, you are told to choose more than one answer.

For example, a test question may include instructions which tell you to choose the two best answers. In this case, you must provide the two correct choices, or you will not receive any credit for answering the question. (Sorry, but the test is not designed to give you partial credit if you get part of the answer right.)

While the format of the practice test questions is designed to emulate the types of questions you see on Novell's tests, these test questions are for practice purposes only, and in no way should be construed as being the actual test questions contained within the Novell authorized database of test questions for the NetWare 5 CNA or CNE certification exams.

To ensure you understand which concept each of the sample test questions were designed for, the correct answers for the practice test follows the practice test questions. Use the answers to help you see what concept or detail you may need to study further.

What This Book Does Not Cover

Like the *Accelerated NetWare 5 CNA Study Guide*, this book concentrates on teaching you what you need to know about Novell's NetWare 5 network operating system and accompanying utilities and features. It assumes that you have a basic understanding of computers, as well as a basic understanding of and some experience with operating systems such as DOS, Windows 95, and Windows NT. It also assumes that you either have basic knowledge of NetWare 5 from job-related work, or from having studied the *Accelerated NetWare 5 CNA Study Guide*. Therefore, it does not cover hardware or software associated with computers, except where that information is relevant to using a computer as a network workstation or file server.

For More Information

Although this book is designed to help you pass the Novell NetWare 5 CNE Advanced Administration test without additional assistance, you may find that there are certain aspects of NetWare 5 about which you would like more information. As previously noted, you may also want to pick up and read McGraw-Hill's *Accelerated NetWare 5 CNA Study Guide*, also by this author. It will help prepare you to take the NetWare 5

Administration test, which you must also pass if you want to become a NetWare 5 CNE.

If you want to get your CNE or just learn more about networking technologies and NetWare, you may also want to pick up one of McGraw-Hill's other excellent books such as *The CNA/CNE Study Guide Intranetware Edition* by Mueller and Williams. The Mueller and Williams book covers NetWare 4 rather than NetWare 5, but is an excellent reference for learning about those features of NetWare 5 which existed in NetWare 4. In addition, it covers the information contained in several of the other courses whose certification exams you must pass in order to obtain your CNE. The Mueller and Williams book contains 900 pages of information. It is designed to aid new CNE candidates obtain their certification, so it provides information the candidate needs in order to pass other certification tests required of a new CNE candidate. (Unfortunately, just passing the NetWare 5 Administration and NetWare 5 Advanced Administration tests is not all you need to do to get a CNE.) Thus, for the individual who is just beginning their CNE program, this Mueller and Williams book also will be a valuable resource.

While the Mueller and Williams book is based on Novell's NetWare 4 operating system software, many of the concepts and basic features of NetWare 4 (such as NDS, security, and so on) are the same for NetWare 5.

Once you have access to a NetWare 5 network, you can also take a look at Novell's online documentation for more information about NetWare 5. Their online documentation is presented in HTML format and shipped with the Netscape browser for viewing. While you can read it using almost any Internet browser software, the included Netscape browser software has a powerful search engine and printing capabilities not available with other browsers.

No inexperienced individual can become a NetWare network administrator and a CNE overnight. But if you have experience with a previous version of NetWare, particularly NetWare 4, or you've been working in the field for some time, you will find that this *Accelerated NetWare 5 CNE Study Guide* will help you to learn what you need to know as quickly as possible in order to pass Novell's authorized NetWare 5 Advanced Administration certification test and to obtain your NetWare 5 CNE certification. It's designed to let you learn in short snatches of time, and to let you test your knowledge using the Practice Test Questions section provided in each chapter. So take this book with you wherever you go so that you can make the best possible use of your time.

Good luck, and welcome to the *Accelerated NetWare 5 CNE Study Guide*.

CHAPTER 1

Planning a NetWare 5 Network

Planning a NetWare 5 network requires some understanding of what NetWare 5 is, how it works, how to access a NetWare 5 server, and what is involved in installing and upgrading or migrating NetWare 3 and NetWare 4 servers. You already know what a network is, what a file server is, what clients are, and so on. This chapter helps you to better understand the NetWare 5 server.

Understanding NetWare 5 and the Server

It is the NetWare 5 operating system running in the computer's RAM which makes the computer a NetWare 5 file server. You load the NetWare operating system software into the computer's RAM by running a program called **Server.exe**. Once loaded, the NetWare 5 server's main job is to regulate communication between network devices and services, and to manage the transmission of data between itself, workstations, and various storage devices such as hard disks.

Overview of the NetWare Server

The NetWare 5 operating system, like earlier versions of NetWare, is modular in design, consisting of three major areas of importance:

- Kernel
- Console
- NLMs

To understand the NetWare 5 server, its functions and purposes, as well as how best to manage it, you will first need to understand these three areas of the network operating system, the first of which is the kernel.

The kernel is the heart of the Netware 5 operating system. It is responsible for supporting the computer's microprocessor. In NetWare 5, the kernel can support multiple microprocessors on the same server. NetWare 5's kernel is called the NetWare Multi-Processor Kernel (MPK) because it is both a uniprocessor kernel and a multiprocessor kernel.

The kernel is also responsible for:

- **Providing memory protection.** This feature allows potential problematic applications to run without interfering with or damaging other application programs, or without crashing the file server.
- **Providing virtual memory.** Virtual memory lets the server swap from real memory to the hard disk that information which currently qualifies as "least used" to make sufficient room in memory for processing programs larger than the computer's physical memory. When the larger program no longer needs the memory space, or the "least used" information or program software is needed again, it is swapped back into real memory from the hard disk. The actual amount of memory a server needs can be reduced because of NetWare's virtual memory capability.
- **Balancing the network's processing load.** On a server with multiple processors, this feature lets processing tasks be balanced between the processors.
- **Scheduling processing.** The NetWare server lets the administrator determine how processing time should be scheduled to ensure more important applications receive a greater amount of processing time.
- **Preempting processes.** The NetWare 5 OS can take control of the processing and preempt it to take advantage of the scheduling processing capability and ensure that the applications scheduled for the greater amount of processing time receive that time.

The other two aspects of the NetWare server are the console and NetWare Loadable Modules (NLM).

The Server Console

The server console is the interface by which you access and control the NetWare server. It provides a console prompt from which you enter commands and run network server utilities. You access the console from the server itself, but you can also access the console from a remote workstation, using special remote control software.

You access the console to perform various server management and analysis tasks. For example, you will use the console to send a message to all logged in users when you are ready to upgrade a NetWare 4 server to NetWare 5. You can also access the server console to:

- monitor traffic on the network
- modify server configuration parameters
- modify server configuration and batch files
- load and unload programs
- start up and shut down the server

Console Commands and NLMs

To perform these and other tasks at the file server requires that you use either console commands or NLMs. Which you choose to use depends on the function or task you want to perform.

KEY CONCEPT

Console commands and NLMs are the two major categories of NetWare server utilities. Console commands are NetWare server commands you enter at the file server console much as you enter DOS commands at any other computer's DOS prompt. Like many DOS commands which are part of the DOS operating system software, console commands are part of the NetWare operating system software.

DOS commands let you perform tasks at the computer's DOS prompt. For example, you can use DOS commands to perform such tasks as checking the status of the hard disk, viewing directories and files, and assessing how much space is left on the hard disk.

Console commands let you perform tasks such as sending messages to users who are currently logged in to the network. To view a list of available console commands, you can enter the **Help** command at the console prompt. Figure 1-1 shows a sample of the display you see when you enter the **Help** console command.

You can also use console commands to change the default server configuration parameters. Using the **SET** console command, you specify what parameter you want to change, and specify the value you want to change that parameter to. The format you follow to use the **SET** command is: **SET parameter = value**. Replace parameter with the specific

#	;	ABORT REMIRROR
ADD NAME SPACE	ALERT	ALIAS
APPLET	APPLETVIEWER	BIND
BINDERY	BROADCAST	CLEAR STATION
CLS	CONFIG	CPU CHECK
CSET	DISABLE TTS	DISABLE LOGIN
DISMOUNT	DISPLAY IPX NETWORKS	DISABLE IPX SERVERS
DISPLAY INTERRUPTS	DISPLAY PROCESSORS	DISPLAY ENVIRONMENT
DISPLAY MODIFIED ENVIRONMENT		
DOWN	ECHO OFF	ECHO ON
ENABLE TTS	ENABLE LOGIN	ENVSET
FILE SERVER NAME	HELP	IPX INTERNAL NET
JAF	JAV	CGI

FIGURE 1-1 Sample of the various console commands you can enter at a NetWare 5 file server console.

configuration parameter you want to change, and value with what you want to change the current setting to.

For example, you can change the maximum number of buffers for incoming packets to 200 using the **SET** command at the console prompt by typing: **SET MaximumPacketReceiveBuffers = 200**. You should be aware, however, that any settings you change using the **SET** command at the file server console are effectively temporary. The next time you bring the server down and restart it, the setting returns to the default. If you want to make a setting permanent, you can enter that **SET** command into the appropriate startup configuration file, such as the **Startup.ncf** file.

NOTE

You can also set parameters using server utilities such as Monitor.

You can also use console commands to load into file server RAM other types of NetWare utilities called NLMs. NLMs or NetWare Loadable Modules are programs that run on and become part of the NetWare operating system once they are loaded (see Figure 1-2).

There are different types of NLM programs including:

- **Disk drivers (.ham or .cdm)**. Disk drivers control communication between the file server and its storage devices. NetWare 5 supports two types of disk drivers: HAM (Host Adapter Module), which supports the host adapter (bus), and CDM (Custom Device Module), which supports the hardware devices attached to the bus.
- **LAN drivers (.lan)**. LAN drivers control communication between the NetWare 5 operating system and the network boards in the file server.
- **Name space support modules (.nam)**. Name space modules allow non-DOS filenames to be stored on NetWare volumes. Three name

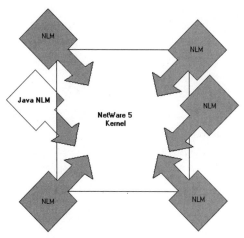

FIGURE 1-2 Diagram showing NLMs becoming part of the NetWare operating system's kernel as they are loaded.

support modules ship with NetWare 5: **Mac.nam**, **Long.nam**, and **NFS.nam**.

■ **Management utilities and server applications modules (.nlm).** Management utilities and server application modules allow services not included in the operating system to be run on the NetWare server. Several management utilities and server application modules are included with NetWare 5, while others can be purchased as upgrades from other companies as well as from Novell.

NetWare 5 ships with several NLMs. Even NDS is a network service provided by NLMs, as are security, authentication, printing, remote server console, and the Java Virtual Machine. One NLM you may find yourself using frequently is the Monitor NLM.

To add any NLM to a NetWare 5 server, you load it into the server's memory. With previous versions of NetWare, you typed the **Load** command followed by the name of the nlm at the console prompt. For example, to load the Monitor NLM, type **Load Monitor** at the file server console. With NetWare 5 you no longer have to use the **Load** command. You can load Monitor on the NetWare 5 server by typing only the name of the NLM at the server console.

You can also remove an nlm from the file server by typing **Unload** followed by the name of the NLM. For example, to unload Monitor, you type **Unload Monitor** at the file server console.

Planning Your NetWare 5 Network

When planning your NetWare 5 network you should take into consideration five specific areas:

- meeting minimum requirements
- choosing the upgrade method
- choosing which protocol you will implement
- planning the network file system
- determining whether you will implement NSS (Novell Storage Services)

Minimum Requirements

Depending on what you are planning to include on your NetWare 5 server, there are different minimum requirements to be met. You must meet the basic hardware requirements for a NetWare 5 server. In addition, you may want to meet the minimum requirements for Java support.

BASIC HARDWARE REQUIREMENTS FOR A NETWARE 5 SERVER

To run NetWare 5, you must meet the following basic hardware requirements for a NetWare 5 server:

- A PC with a Pentium processor
- 64 MB of RAM
- 30 MB DOS partition
- 200 MB free disk space for the Sys volume
- A network board

HARDWARE REQUIREMENTS FOR JAVA SUPPORT

Java applications that present a GUI interface require the following minimum hardware requirements:

- 48 MB of RAM on the server (64 MB is recommended)
- Microsoft PS/2 mouse (if you will use a mouse at the server)
- A video card which conforms to the VESA 1.2 specification (ISA, EISA, and PCI video cards are supported as well, but better Java GUI presentation exists with a VESA 1.2 video card)

Upgrade Methods

In addition to being able to install NetWare 5 on a new server, you can also upgrade previous versions of NetWare to NetWare 5. You have two upgrade options (see Figure 1-3):

- **In-place upgrade.** Use this method when you want to convert an existing NetWare server to NetWare 5. Use the NetWare 5 server installation software for an in-place upgrade.
- **Across-the-wire upgrade.** Use this method when you want to move the file system and NetWare bindery or NDS from a server running an earlier version of NetWare to another server running NetWare 5. Use the Novell Upgrade Wizard for an across-the-wire upgrade.

Use the in-place upgrade if your current NetWare server is running NetWare 3.1x, NetWare 4.x, IntranetWare, or IntranetWare for Small Business. You can also use this method to upgrade a NetWare 2 server, but only if you first upgrade the NetWare 2 server to either a NetWare 3 or NetWare 4 server.

KEY CONCEPT

Choosing the in-place upgrade method lets you use suballocation and disk compression on your NetWare volumes if you choose to do so. Choose the **Upgrade From 3.1x or 4.1x** option in the NetWare 5 installation program.

Use the across-the-wire upgrade if you have a NetWare 3.1x file server whose bindery and volume information you want to migrate to an existing NetWare 5 server. Migrating the bindery and volumes also migrates passwords and security rights.

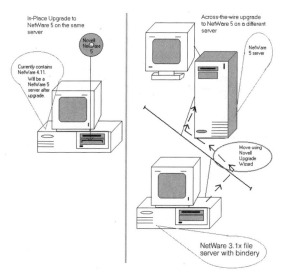

FIGURE 1-3 NetWare 5 Upgrade Options.

KEY CONCEPT

There are several advantages to using the across-the-wire upgrade method on a NetWare 3.1x server. First, you can use the graphical modeling capabilities of the Novell Upgrade Wizard to ensure the design of the network is what you want it to be before you migrate. Second, even a power shortage won't destroy your data, as it remains on the original file server. In addition, you can migrate the server one part at a time if you choose to, and you can migrate multiple servers to a single NetWare 5 server. Finally, conflict checks and options for correcting them before you migrate are available with the Novell Upgrade Wizard.

Available Protocols

NetWare 5 lets you choose to implement your network using the IPX (Internet Packet Exchange) protocol, the IP (Internet Protocol) protocol, or both protocols. Networks running versions of NetWare prior to NetWare 5 generally ran IPX, at least on part of their network. With companies seeking to improve business, communications, and knowledge through the Internet, more companies are interested in running their network using the same IP protocol as the Internet. By giving companies the option to run only IPX, only IP, or a combination of both protocols on their network, Novell makes it easier for companies to convert to IP without giving up their investment in their current IPX-based network.

If you choose to run IP, you must have:

- An IP address
- A subnet mask
- A router or gateway address

When you choose to run your network as a pure IP network, any IPX data currently used on your network is encapsulated by the IP protocol. It can then be transmitted across a pure IP network. This allows you to continue to use applications and services which are IPX-based.

When you choose to run your network as a pure IPX network, you can continue to use all of the IPX applications your network currently has. NetWare automatically loads and binds each IPX frame type it detects for your network boards. By default, it will load and bind Ethernet_802.2.

When you choose to run your network as a combined IP/IPX network, NetWare will support both IP and IPX on the same network. Those network nodes which are IP can communicate with IPX-based nodes, and those nodes which are IPX can communicate with IP-based nodes. In addition, you can bind both protocols to a single network board.

Plan the Network File System

Access to shared programs, files, and directories is an important capability of a network. Being able to find what you need in those files and directories is also important. To be able to find the files and directories users need requires that the file system be logically arranged and organized. NetWare divides the file system into volumes and directories. Some volumes and directories are created automatically when you install NetWare 5; you can choose to have other volumes and directories created as well.

Regardless of how you plan to organize the server's file system structure, consider that the file system structure should be:

- Easy to use
- As simple and quick as possible to maintain
- Set up to simplify file system security
- Designed to best meet users' needs

Default Directory Structure

Before you install NetWare, you should plan your network file structure. You will also want to know what directory structure is automatically created for you by NetWare when you install NetWare 5.

KEY CONCEPT

By default, the NetWare 5 installation process creates one volume called **Sys**, and 16 directories whose function is to maintain normal server and network operations. It also installs several files.

The 16 directories installed by default when you install NetWare 5 are:

- **Cdrom$$.rom.** Stores an index of the contents of a CD-ROM once it has been mounted as a NetWare volume.
- **Deleted.sav.** Holds deleted files which have not been purged.
- **Etc.** Contains sample TCP/IP configuration files.
- **Java.** Contains support files for Java.
- **Javasave.** Stores other Java-related files.
- **License.** Holds files related to licensing.
- **Login.** Contains programs and related files for logging in to the network.
- **Mail.** Stores user login script and print files in individual subdirectories if the NetWare 5 server was upgraded from a previous version of NetWare.

- **Ndps.** Holds Novell Distributed Print Services files.
- **Netbasic.** Contains support files for NetBasic.
- **Ni.** Holds NetWare installation files.
- **Perl.** Holds files related to Perl scripts.
- **Public.** Contains the commands and utilities available to all network users.
- **Readme.** Stores readme files.
- **System.** Contains the NLMs and files used by the NetWare operating system, and by the network administrator.
- **Temp.** Holds temporary files needed by NetWare. (This directory is only created if needed and may not exist the first time you look at the installation-created directories.)

You should never move, rename, or delete the **Sys** volume or any of the directories or files which are installed during the NetWare 5 installation process. You can, however, add directories and volumes.

Suggested Directory Structure Additions

KEY CONCEPT

Novell recommends that you structure your file system to include home directories, Z.E.N.works profile directories, application directories, and shared data directories. Give each of these directories a name that makes the directories content at least somewhat self-evident.

Create home directories so that each user has a location on the network where they can store their files. As a rule, you do not want users storing their files in the same directory as the application programs they run. You can also create a shared user directory into which multiple users can put files for all users to access. And, you can create Z.E.N.works profile directories to store the profiles you create using Z.E.N.works, and application directories to store the program and related files for each application.

KEY CONCEPT

The benefit of creating application, home, and other directories is that it not only organizes your directory structure to make finding needed information and maintaining the directory structure easier, but it also makes administering network security simpler.

Sample Directory Structures

The smaller the network, the less complexity can exist in the file system. In a network with 50 or fewer users, for example, you may want to keep only one volume (**Sys**), and set up a single main Home directory into which you put an individual home directory for each user (See Figure 1-4).

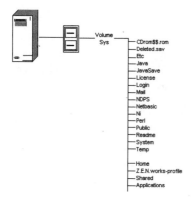

FIGURE 1-4 A sample directory structure for a small network which relies on a single volume.

If your network has more than 50 users or you need to keep user access to the **Sys** volume to a minimum, you may want to create a second volume when you install the NetWare 5 file server. By adding a second volume, you can provide greater security for application programs and protect volume **Sys** from becoming overcrowded. If volume **Sys** runs out of disk space, you will have problems running your file server. Figure 1-5 displays a sample file system for a larger network.

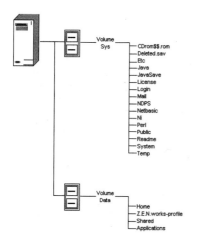

FIGURE 1-5 A sample directory structure for a larger network which relies on multiple volumes.

Prepare to Implement NSS

In addition to the traditional file system structure provided by NetWare 5 and earlier versions of NetWare, NetWare 5 also provides you with the ability to use Novell Storage Services (NSS) on your network. NSS is an enhanced high-performance file storage and access system that is independent of the default NetWare file system structure, but is also completely compatible with it. While NSS provides many enhancements, it still creates and uses the standard structure of a NetWare file system: volumes, directories, and files. NSS has been referred to as the file system of the future because it provides many advantages not found in the traditional file system. NSS does have its drawbacks, however, so you should consider both when planning and implementing NSS.

KEY CONCEPT

In order to provide the benefits that NSS provides, it uses an NSS provider, a consumer, and a storage group. The provider is responsible for scanning storage devices and locating free storage space. The consumer manages that free space by creating a deposit object to represent the free space, establishing access to the free space, and registering its ownership of the free space to prevent other consumers from accessing it. The storage group is an object that represents all of the logical space regardless of how many and which storage devices it resides on. A storage group is organized into NSS volumes that can be mounted and function the same way a standard NetWare volume is mounted and functions.

BENEFITS OF IMPLEMENTING NSS

If you choose to implement NSS on your NetWare file server, your network and users will be able to take advantage of the following benefits (see Figure 1-6):

- Storage of large files (up to 8 TB)
- No effective limit on the number of files in a single directory
- Much quicker access to data
- Faster volume mounting and repair
- Low memory requirements (32 MB RAM minimum)
- Support for most kinds of storage devices, either now or in the future
- Free space on multiple storage devices can be used as a single volume
- Enhanced support for CD-ROMs as volumes
- Four NetWare partitions allowed per disk
- No limit on the number of volumes per NetWare partition

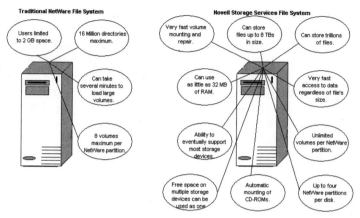

FIGURE 1-6 Benefits of NSS.

DRAWBACKS OF IMPLEMENTING NSS

While adding NSS provides many advantages over the traditional file system, it cannot replace it because it cannot create its own **Sys** volume. In addition, it does not support all of NetWare's features, including:

- Transaction Tracking System (TTS)
- Disk striping or mirroring
- Hierarchical storage management (HSM)
- Real-Time Data Migration (RTD)
- File compression
- Vrepair

SETTING UP NSS

If you are setting up NSS on a server with hard disks that are already fully partitioned, you can use the NSS In-Place Upgrade Utility to convert existing NetWare file system volumes (but not volume **Sys** or volumes which have TTS enabled on them) to NSS-controlled volumes. You can also choose to enable NSS when you install a new NetWare server, or you can repartition an existing server's hard disk. If you repartition an existing server's hard disk, first ensure it has sufficient free space available.

To create NSS components on your NetWare 5 server, there are several available utilities, including the NSS Advanced Configuration utility. To create an NSS volume using the NSS Advanced Configuration utility, follow these steps:

1. Type **Nwconfig** at the file server console to load the configuration utility. The Configuration Options menu opens.

2. Choose **NSS Disk**. The NSS Options screen opens displaying the Available NSS Options menu.
3. Choose **Storage**. The Available NSS Storage Options menu opens.
4. Choose **Assign Ownership**. The Available Free Space is displayed.
5. Press **Enter**. The Consumer Deposit Configuration screen opens (see Figure 1-7) and provides a field titled Enter Size in Meg(s).
6. Type the number of megabytes you want to assign to the NSS volume, then press **Enter**. You must assign at least 10 MB. The Confirm Action screen opens.
7. Press **Enter** to confirm the action. The Available NSS Storage Options menu redisplays.
8. Choose **Return to Previous Menu**. The Available NSS Options menu redisplays.
9. Choose **NSS Volume Options**. The Directory Services Login/ Authentication screen opens.
10. Log in to NDS. Supply a complete full name (such as **.CN=Admin.O=SSSCo**), and the password. A message box stating that you are logging in to NDS displays, and then the Available NSS Volume Options menu opens.
11. Choose **Create**. The Select Create Option menu opens.
12. Choose **Storage Group**. The Select a Managed Object menu opens.
13. Press **Enter** on the highlighted Media Type. The Confirm Action screen opens.
14. Press **Enter** to confirm the action. The Select Create Option menu reopens.
15. Press **Esc** three times to return to the Configuration Options menu.
16. Choose **Exit**, then choose **Yes** when prompted to Exit Nwconfig.

FIGURE 1-7 The Consumer Deposit Configuration screen.

Preparing for the Upgrade

You can upgrade NetWare 3 file servers as well as NetWare 4 file servers to NetWare 5. Before starting any upgrade tasks, regardless of which server you are upgrading, there are some basic steps you should perform first. This section discusses those steps. In addition, it provides details about using **Sbackup** to back up your NetWare 3 or NetWare 4 server before upgrading it to NetWare 5.

What Steps to Take

The exact pre-upgrade steps you take depend on whether you are using the NetWare 5 Install software to upgrade a NetWare 3 server or a NetWare 4 server, or the Novell Upgrade Wizard to migrate a NetWare 3.1x server. The process of migrating a NetWare 3.1x server to a NetWare 5 server is a little more complex for two reasons. First, the NetWare 3 server is bindery-based, while the NetWare 5 server is based on NDS. Second, the migration process requires that you move your NetWare 3 bindery and volumes to another file server. This process involves additional steps including updating your NetWare 3 server's NLMs. Because the upgrade and migrate processes differ, so too do the pre-upgrade steps.

PREPARING TO USE NETWARE 5 INSTALL TO
UPGRADE A NETWARE 3 OR NETWARE 4 SERVER

These are the steps you must take to prepare a NetWare 3 or NetWare 4 server to upgrade it to Netware 5:

1. Determine whether the server you are upgrading first contains the master replica of the [Root] partition. If not, consider upgrading the server which does contain the master replica of the [Root] partition first, or convert this server so that it contains the master replica of the [Root] partition. Otherwise, you may experience database schema conflicts.
2. Using a backup software compatible with NetWare 3 or NetWare 4, as well as with NetWare 5, make two or more backups of your existing bindery or NDS Directory, and each network volume and its contents. Sbackup is the recommended backup software. It was included with NetWare 3 and NetWare 4, and an **Enhanced Sbackup** is included with NetWare 5.
3. Locate information about the server's network board. Specifically, you need to know what its current settings are (such as the IRQ and I/O port).

4. Send a broadcast message to all users logged in to the network telling them that the server will be upgraded, and requesting that they log out. If you are not doing the upgrade immediately, let them know when you will be doing it, and specify when and for how long they need to log out.

5. Determine whether any of the current NLMs, disk drivers, or LAN drivers used by this server are compatible with NetWare 5.

NetWare 5 requires a HAM driver for each host bus adapter. It does not support DSK drivers.

NOTE

PREPARING TO USE NOVELL UPGRADE WIZARD TO MIGRATE A NETWARE 3.1x SERVER

Following are the steps you must take to prepare to migrate a NetWare 3.1x server to a Netware 5 server:

1. Because you migrate NetWare 3.1x information into an existing NDS tree, make a backup of the existing NDS Directory and each network volume.

2. Make a list of information you need for the upgrade, including the name of the tree into which you will be migrating the NetWare 3.1x server, the server's proposed context, and the administrator user's name and password.

3. If more than one server is being migrated, consolidate users' names (when one user has different login names on different 3.1x servers), and verify that no two users whose user account will be in the same context have the same login name.

4. Upgrade the clients to the latest Novell client (or at least to version 2.2 for Windows 95 workstations and 4.11 for Windows NT workstations).

5. Ensure you have Supervisor or equivalent rights to both servers, or Supervisor to the NetWare 3.1x server and console operator rights to the NetWare 5 server.

6. Either disable SAP filtering on each server affected by the migration, or ensure all affected servers are on the same network segment.

7. Update the NetWare 3.1x server's NLMs using the migration NLMs that were installed into the following directory when you installed the Novell Upgrade Wizard: **c:\programfiles\novell\upgrade\ products\nw3x**.

8. Using the **Unload** command at the NetWare 3.1x file server, unload the following files in this exact order:

- Tsa311.nlm or Tsa312.nlm
- Smdr.nlm
- Smdr31x.nlm
- Spxs.nlm
- Tli.nlm
- After311.nlm
- Clib.nlm
- A3112.nlm
- Streams.nlm

9. Type **Load Tsa312.nlm** at the NetWare 3 file server to update the NLM programs.

10. Load and add name spaces to the NetWare 5 file server for any NetWare 3.1x servers which contain files using non-DOS naming conventions.

11. Decide what you will migrate (bindery only, one or more volumes only, or both bindery and volumes).

Back Up the Server

Backing up the NetWare 3, NetWare 4, or NetWare 5 server as appropriate is an important task to complete before you begin the upgrade or migration process. Once the upgrade or migration is started, unexpected events (such as a power failure or corrupted files) can cause severe and sometimes irreparable damage to your network data. Backing up the bindery, NDS, and network volumes before you begin the upgrade or migration is the only security you have that your network will be restorable to its original condition. Also, because you may need to go from one NetWare server to another (such as from a NetWare 4 to a NetWare 5 server) with that backup, you need to use a backup software that is compatible with each of the different NetWare versions. Therefore, when you back up your NetWare 3 or NetWare 4 server, you should consider using the Sbackup software that shipped with these products. Also, when you back up your NetWare 5 server, consider using the Enhanced Sbackup software in NetWare 5.

To back up NDS and the file system information on a NetWare 5 server from a Windows 95 workstation, first add the Client for Microsoft Network to your Windows 95 workstation as outlined in the following procedure. If you will be working from a Windows NT workstation, you do not need to add the Client for Microsoft Network.

ADD THE CLIENT FOR MICROSOFT NETWORK TO A WINDOWS 95 WORKSTATION

Complete the following steps to add the Client for Microsoft Networks to your Windows 95 workstation:

1. Right-click **Network Neighborhood**.
2. Click **Properties**.
3. Verify that the TCP/IP Protocol has been installed.
4. Click **Add**.
5. Double-click **Client**.
6. Click **Microsoft**.
7. Click **Client for Microsoft NetWorks**.
8. Click **OK**.
9. Verify that Novell NetWare Client is displayed in the Primary Network Logon field.
10. Click **TCP/IP**.
11. Click **Bindings**.
12. Make sure the **Client for Microsoft Networks** and **Novell NetWare Client** boxes are checked.
13. Click **OK** in the TCP/IP Properties window.
14. Click **OK** in the Network window.
15. If prompted, provide the path to the Windows 95 Installation CD.
16. When prompted, reboot the workstation, then log back into the network as an Admin user.

BACK UP THE NETWARE SERVER

To back up NDS and the file system, complete these steps:

1. Load the device driver for your system's backup device.
2. Verify that a print queue object dedicated to and configured for backup operations exists.
3. Load the TSA500 NLM on the NetWare 5 server from which the backup will be running (the host server), as well as on the NetWare 5 server whose NDS will be backed up (the target server). If the target server has a replica on it, also load the TSANDS NLM on it.
4. Load the NetWare Backup/Restore NLMs on the host server (Smsdi, Qman, Sbsc, and Sbcon).
5. Run **sys:\public\Nwback32.exe** on your workstation.
6. Specify what information is to be backed up on the target, where the information is to be backed up to, and the type of backup.
7. Set the schedule and rerun interval, provide a description, and submit the job.
8. Insert the backup media (tape, etc.), then continue. Add tapes as prompted.
9. When the backup is complete, press **Esc** until you return to the backup menu.
10. Unload the backup engine and backup device NLMs in reverse order from the way you loaded them.

Chapter Summary

This chapter introduced you first to the NetWare 5 operating system, explaining that it runs in the computer's RAM to make the computer a NetWare 5 file server. You load the NetWare operating system software into the computer's RAM by running a program called **Server.exe**. Once loaded, the NetWare 5 server's main job is to regulate communication between network devices and services, and to manage the transmission of data between itself, workstations, and various storage devices such as hard disks.

Overview of the NetWare Server

The NetWare 5 operating system, like earlier versions of NetWare, is modular in design. It consists of three major areas of importance:

- **Kernel.** The kernel is the heart of the NetWare 5 operating system. It is responsible for supporting the computer's microprocessor.
- **Console.** The server console is the interface by which you access and control the NetWare server. It provides a console prompt at which you enter commands and run network server utilities.
- **NLMs.** NetWare Loadable Modules are programs that run on and become part of the NetWare operating system once they are loaded. The different types of NLMs are: Disk drivers (.ham or .cdm), LAN drivers (.lan), Name space support modules (.nam), and Management utilities and server applications modules (.nlm).

This chapter also discussed minimum hardware requirements for installing NetWare 5 and adding Java support, as well as methods by which you can upgrade existing NetWare servers to NetWare 5. For example, to run NetWare 5, you must meet the following basic hardware requirements for a NetWare 5 server:

- PC with a Pentium processor
- 64 MB of RAM
- 30 MB DOS partition
- 200 MB free disk space for the Sys volume
- Network board

To support Java applications, the server must meet the following minimum hardware requirements:

- 48 MB of RAM on the server (64 MB is recommended)
- Microsoft PS/2 mouse (if you will use a mouse at the server)

- Video card which conforms to the VESA 1.2 specification (ISA.EISA, and PCI video cards are supported as well, but better Java GUI presentation exists with a VESA 1.2 video card)

To upgrade an existing NetWare server to NetWare 5, there are two upgrade options:

- **In-place upgrade.** Use this method when you want to convert an existing NetWare server to NetWare 5. Use the NetWare 5 server installation software for an in-place upgrade.
- **Across-the-wire upgrade.** Use this method when you want to move the file system and NetWare bindery or NDS from a server running an earlier version of NetWare to another server running NetWare 5. Use the Novell Upgrade Wizard for an across-the-wire upgrade.

This chapter also discussed planning and organizing the server's file system structure, and suggested that when planning it you consider that the file system structure should be:

- Easy to use
- As simple and quick as possible to maintain
- Set up to simplify file system security
- Designed to best meet users' needs

It also discussed the default directory structure created when NetWare 5 is installed, recommended that you never move, rename, or delete the **Sys** volume or any of the directories or files which are installed during the NetWare 5 installation process. It also suggested that you consider adding directories and volumes as appropriate.

The default structure includes one volume called **Sys**, and 16 directories whose function is to maintain normal server and network operations. It also installs several files. The 16 directories installed by default when you install NetWare 5 are: **Cdrom$$.rom, Deleted.sav, Etc., Java, Javasave, License, Login, Mail, Ndps, Netbasic, Ni, Perl, Public, Readme, System**, and sometimes **Temp**.

This chapter also stated that Novell recommends that you structure your file system to include home directories, Z.E.N.works profile directories, application directories, and shared data directories. Name each of these directories with a name that makes its content at least somewhat self-evident.

In addition, information about implementing NSS volumes on your NetWare 5 server was provided, and explained that in order to provide the benefits that NSS provides, it uses an NSS provider, a consumer, and a storage group. The provider is responsible for scanning storage devices and locating free storage space. The consumer manages that free space by creating a deposit object to represent the free space, establishing access to the free space, and registering its ownership of the free space to prevent other consumers from accessing it. The storage group is an object which represents all of the logical space regardless of how many and which storage devices it resides on. A storage group is organized into NSS volumes, which can be mounted and otherwise function the same way as a standard NetWare volume.

The steps to take to prepare for the upgrade were discussed, and identified the fact that the exact pre-upgrade steps you take depend on whether you are using the NetWare 5 Install software to upgrade a NetWare 3 server or a NetWare 4 server, or the Novell Upgrade Wizard to migrate a NetWare 3.1x server. The process of migrating a NetWare 3.1x server to a NetWare 5 server is a little more complex than upgrading either a NetWare 3 or NetWare 4 server for two reasons. First, the NetWare 3 server is bindery-based, while the NetWare 5 server is based on NDS. Second, the migration process requires that you move your NetWare 3 bindery and volumes to another file server. This process involves additional steps, including updating your NetWare 3 server's NLMs. Because the upgrade and migrate processes differ, so too do the pre-upgrade steps.

Finally, this chapter discussed the importance of backing up your NetWare servers before beginning the upgrade, and recommended that you use a backup software compatible with the all of the versions of NetWare you would be migrating from, as well as NetWare 5. That way, you should have no problems if you need to restore what you have backed up. NetWare 5 ships with an Enhanced Sbackup software you can use.

Practice Test Questions

1. The program file which loads the NetWare 5 server software is:
   a. **Nwserver.exe**
   b. **NetwareS.exe**
   c. **Server.exe**
   d. **NetServ.exe**

2. The NetWare 5 server's three major modular pieces are:
   a. Kernel
   b. Server
   c. Console
   d. NLM

3. Memory protection is provided by the NetWare 5:
   a. Kernel
   b. Server
   c. Console
   d. NLM

4. The interface for running commands or loading applications is the:
   a. Kernel
   b. Server
   c. Console
   d. NLM

5. What three methods can you use to configure server parameters?
   a. Kernel
   b. Set
   c. Startup.ncf
   d. Monitor

6. The two disk drivers supported by NetWare 5 are:
   a. Ham
   b. Dsk
   c. Nam
   d. Cdm

7. Of the following, which is *not* a NetWare 5 minimum requirement?
   a. Pentium
   b. 64 MB RAM
   c. 30 MB DOS partition
   d. 100 MB hard disk space

8. If you want to convert an existing NetWare Server to NetWare 5, use:
   a. Across-the-wire upgrade
   b. In-place upgrade
   c. NetWare 5 install
   d. A and B
   e. B and C

9. The default installed directory that holds the NetWare installation files is:
   a. Ndps
   b. Ni
   c. Public
   d. System

10. Which of the following is not a Novell-recommended directory?
    a. Home
    b. Z.E.N.works profile
    c. Application
    d. Working
    e. Shared

11. The enhanced, high performance file storage system provided by NetWare 5 is:
    a. NSS
    b. NDPS
    c. NMS
    d. NI

12. Which of the following is *not* associated with NetWare 5's enhanced high performance storage system?
    a. Consumer
    b. Provider
    c. Resident
    d. Storage group

13. The largest file size that the enhanced high performance storage system can handle is:
    a. 2 MB
    b. 10 MB
    c. 4 TB
    d. 8 TB

14. The smallest size volume you can create for an enhanced high performance storage system is:
    a. 2 MB
    b. 10 MB
    c. 4 TB
    d. 8 TB

15. When preparing to upgrade a NetWare 3 or 4 server to NetWare 5, you should:
    a. Upgrade a server containing the master replica
    b. Upgrade the server to NetWare 2 first
    c. Load Ham and Dsk drivers before upgrading
    d. None of the above

Answers to Practice Test Questions

1. c	6. a, d	11. a
2. a, c, d	7. d	12. c
3. a	8. e	13. d
4. c	9. b	14. b
5. b, c, d	10. d	15. a

CHAPTER 2

Creating a
NetWare 5 Network

To establish a NetWare 5 network, you can install all new NetWare
5 servers, or you can upgrade existing NetWare 3.1 or NetWare 4
servers. This chapter explains the process of upgrading a NetWare
3.x server and a NetWare 4 server to NetWare 5, and shows you how to
install other products and programs on a NetWare 5 server.

Upgrading a NetWare 3 Server
(Across-the-Wire Upgrade)

You use the Novell Upgrade Wizard to upgrade a NetWare 3 server to a
NetWare 5 server (see Figure 2-1). You run an across-the-wire upgrade,
which means that you install NetWare 5 on another server, then you connect
to the two servers and migrate the bindery and file system (including passwords and security rights) on the NetWare 3 server to the NetWare 5 server.

One of the advantages of the Novell Upgrade Wizard is that it lets
you determine how the bindery information should fit into the existing
NDS structure before you actually migrate the bindery into NDS. This
feature allows you to see potential problems or inconsistencies before
you commit yourself to the design and migration. This graphical modeling feature of the Novell Upgrade Wizard helps you head off potential
problems before they begin.

FIGURE 2-1 The Novell Upgrade Wizard main window.

Once you start the migration, the Novell Upgrade Wizard again helps prevent problems before they occur. It has the ability to perform a conflict and security check before it actually migrates the contents of the NetWare 3 bindery. It looks for and identifies to you any conflicts it finds, such as name conflicts. You then have the opportunity to resolve those conflicts before you migrate the bindery.

In NetWare 3, you can have the same user name on multiple file servers because the user logs in to a single file server. Effectively, other NetWare servers on the network are unaware of the user who has logged in to another NetWare 3 server. These other servers only become aware of this user when the user attempts to log in or attach to them. In NetWare 3, a user account has a single identifier, the user account (or login) ID. Because the login ID is applicable only to the file server on which it is stored (in the bindery), it is automatically unique.

The process in NetWare 5 with NDS is different, however. In NetWare 5, all network resources and services are tracked as individual objects in NDS and stored in a single database, referred to as the Directory. Each object in NDS has a name based on the name assigned to the object, and the location of the object within the Directory (referred to as the object's context). For example, a User object (the equivalent of the user's login name in NetWare 3) in NDS has a name assigned to it which identifies it as a specific User object within a specific NDS context. That is known as the object's complete context. In NetWare 5, NDS recognizes a User (account) object by its *complete context*. This NDS design is the reason a user can log in from any workstation to a NetWare 5 network and have access to all resources for which they have rights, regardless of where on the network those resources are located. Figure 2-2 depicts the difference between NetWare 3's bindery-based user login and NetWare 5's NDS-based login.

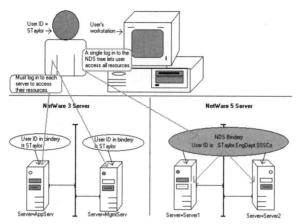

FIGURE 2-2 NetWare 3 (bindery) versus NetWare 5 (NDS) login.

To use the Novell Upgrade Wizard to migrate (perform an across-the-wire upgrade) a NetWare 3.1x server to a NetWare 5 server, complete the following steps:

1. Perform all of the preparation steps necessary, as discussed in the section titled "Preparing for the Upgrade" in Chapter 1. If you have not already done so, install the Upgrade Wizard to your administrator's workstation. To install the Upgrade Wizard, run the **upgrdwzd.exe** file in the **\products\upgrdwzd** directory on the *NetWare 5 Operating System CD*. This is a self-extracting file. Follow the prompts to run it.

2. Log in to the NetWare 5 server from a Windows 95 workstation.

3. Click **Start**, then click **Programs**.

4. From the Programs menu, click **Novell**, then click **Novell Upgrade Wizard**, and click **Novell Upgrade Wizard** again. The Startup dialog opens.

5. Click **Create New Upgrade Project**, then click **OK**.

6. Type a name for this upgrade in the Project Name field, and browse to find the location where you want to store this project. Then click **Next**.

7. Specify the source NetWare 3.1x server and the destination NetWare 5 server using the drop-down lists provided by the arrows next to each option, then click **Create**. The Project window opens.

8. In the Project window, use drag-and-drop to move volumes and the bindery from the source server side of the window to the destination side of the window. Be sure to drop each volume or bindery into the

location where you want it to be added to the Directory tree on the destination side of the Project window.

9. Click **Project**, then click **Verify Project**. The Overview page opens.

10. Read the Overview page, then click **Next**.

11. Run the verification process to ensure the upgrade can take place. To run the verification process, specify whether print information is to be upgraded, an object creation template is to be used, and which categories are to be verified. Also, provide the passwords for the source server and destination tree. When you have completed the verification setup, click **Next** to start the verification process.

12. Specify what should occur for each conflict the verification process finds, then click **Next**. For example, you might choose to let the wizard automatically rename an object when a naming conflict exists. You can also choose not to migrate the object, or to merge the duplicate objects, maintaining either the bindery properties or the NDS properties.

13. Finish resolving all conflicts, then click **Next**. The verification summary displays.

14. Click **Finish**.

15. Click **Project**, then click **Upgrade** on the toolbar.

16. Read the Overview page, then click **Next**. The verification process runs again. Any remaining conflicts are displayed, and you must resolve them before you can complete the upgrade.

17. Click **Upgrade** to start the upgrade process. A progress bar shows the progress of the upgrade.

18. When the upgrade is complete, view the error log by clicking **View Error Log**, click **Close** to complete the upgrade, then exit the Novell Upgrade Wizard.

Upgrading a NetWare 4 Server

If you want to upgrade an existing NetWare 4 server to NetWare 5 (install NetWare 5 on the same computer as the existing NetWare 4 server), first ensure the NetWare 4 server hardware meets the minimum requirements for a NetWare 5 server. Then, complete the following steps.

1. At the NetWare 4.11 server console, type **Down**, press **Enter**, then type **Exit** and press **Enter**.

2. Change to the drive containing the NetWare 5 installation files, then type **Install** and press **Enter**. The licensing agreement screen opens.

3. Read the licensing agreement, then press **F10**.

4. From the menu bar, click **Options**, then click **Modify**.

5. Click **Upgrade From 3.1x or 4.1x**, then press **Tab** to toggle to the Options window, and click **Continue**. (If you want to modify any of the advanced settings, press **F2**.)

6. Select the mouse type and video driver for your server. The installation program begins copying files to the hard disk.

7. Verify that the correct storage adapter and device are selected, then click **Continue**. The installation program mounts volume **Sys** and presents information about the network board it automatically selected and configured.

8. Verify that the network board is configured correctly, then click **Continue**. The installation program copies additional files to the hard disk, loads the Java virtual machine, and displays the Java console.

9. If prompted, click **Next** in the Configure File System window. The Mount Volumes window opens.

10. Click **No, Mount Volumes Now**, then click **Next**. The Protocols window opens.

11. Click the **Network Board** icon.

12. Click **IP**, fill in the required information (IP address, subnet mask, and router information), then click **Next**.

13. Enter the administrator's Admin Object's Name and Context, then click **Next**. The License screen opens.

14. Click the **Browse** button, click the appropriate .NLF file, then click **OK** and click **Next**. The window to install additional products and services opens.

15. Click **Deselect All**, then click to check those services and products you want to install, and click **Next**. The Summary screen opens.

16. Review the Summary screen, then click **Finish**. The installation program begins to copy files to the server.

17. If prompted to replace files, choose to do so then click **Yes** to complete the installation process.

Installing Other Products and Programs

When you initially install NetWare 5, you have the option of choosing to also install various other products and programs. However, doing so during installation does not mean you can't install them later. The NetWare GUI allows you to run the install program again, and choose only to install additional products. You do not need to reinstall the NetWare 5 server.

Install Other Novell Products

To run the install program and install other products, complete the following steps:

1. Click the **Novell** button in the lower left corner of the Novell GUI window on the NetWare file server. The GUI menu opens (see Figure 2-3).
2. Click **Install**. A list of previously installed NetWare products opens.
3. Click **New Product**. You are prompted for the path to the location of the product files.
4. Provide the path to the files for the product you want to install, then click **OK**. The Additional Products and Services window opens.
5. Click the product or products you want to install, then click **Next**. If prompted for configuration information, follow the prompts to provide the needed information. The Summary window opens.
6. Click **Customize** if you need to customize the installation of any of the products you chose.
7. Click **Finish**. The file copy begins. Once complete, follow the prompts and reboot the server.

Provide GUI and JAVA Support

Until NetWare 5, NetWare administrators had no option but to use text-based network management applications (NLMs) on the NetWare server. NetWare 5, however, supports not only text-based applications at the file server, but also Java-based applications with a GUI interface you can run using a mouse or the keyboard.

To take advantage of the Java-based server applications, your NetWare 5 network must first meet the minimum hardware requirements. Chapter 1, *Planning a NetWare 5 Network*, discussed the hardware requirements for running GUI Java-based applications on the NetWare 5 server.

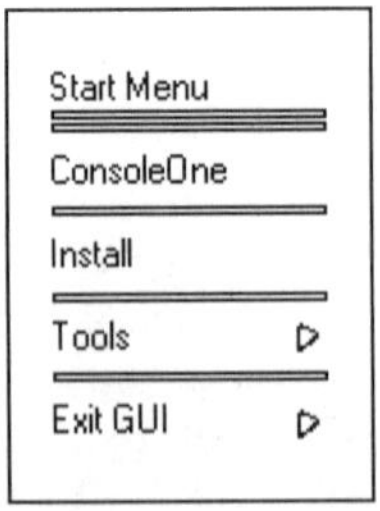

```
Start Menu
ConsoleOne
Install
Tools        ▷
Exit GUI     ▷
```

FIGURE 2-3 The GUI Install menu.

Once you have ensured the minimum hardware requirements have been met, you can then load Java GUI support on the server as needed. You can also free up memory by unloading it when you do not need the GUI support.

NOTE   To ensure applications will run on the NetWare server, Novell requires developers to write their server applications to conform to the Java AWT. NetWare GUI server implementation currently runs on the X-Windows platform, the platform currently used to display Java programs conforming to Java AWT.

To load GUI support on the NetWare 5 server, either type **Startx.ncf** at the server console prompt, or load a Java class or Java applet that requires GUI support. Loading the class or applet automatically launches **Startx.ncf**. To unload GUI support, type **Unload Startx.ncf** at the file server prompt.

Add JAVA Classes and Applets

Java-based applications are either Java classes or Java applets. A *Java class* is any complete Java-based application, while a *Java applet* is a Java program designed to run inside a Java-compatible browser such as Netscape Navigator. NetWare 5 supports both Java classes and Java applets through the Java.nlm.

To run Java applications or Java programs inside a Java-compatible browser requires that you first load the Java NLM on the NetWare 5 file server. You can then run any Java applications from the server console by typing: **Java [-options] path_to_java_class**. Replace [**-options**] with any appropriate Java run-time options (see Figure 2-4), and **path_to_java_class** with the path on the server where the Java application is stored.

NOTE   Java class names are case sensitive and require long name space support.

NetWare 5 includes an applet viewer that runs any Java applet defined as part of an HTML document. This is used primarily to view HTML-based help and HTML-based Internet documents. This applet viewer is made accessible when you load the Java NLM on the server, and type **Applet HTTP://URL**, replacing **URL** with the actual path and name of the HTML document. Loading the Java NLM then typing the **Applet** command runs the Java applet specifically defined as such (contained

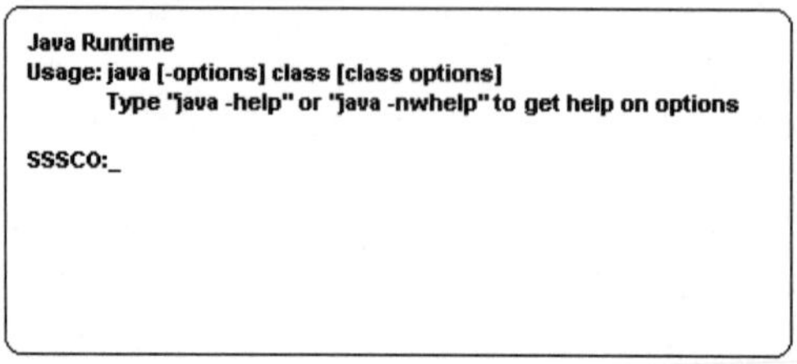

```
Java Runtime
Usage: java [-options] class [class options]
       Type "java -help" or "java -nwhelp" to get help on options

SSSCO:_
```

FIGURE 2-4 The Java.nlm help screen showing available options.

between the **<applet>** and **</applet>** commands in the HTML code) in the associated URL.

Chapter Summary

To establish a NetWare 5 network you either install all new NetWare 5 servers, upgrade existing NetWare 3.1 or NetWare 4 servers, or a combination. This chapter explained how to upgrade existing NetWare 3.x and NetWare 4 server to NetWare 5. It also showed you how to install other products and programs on a NetWare 5 server.

This chapter explained how to use the Novell Upgrade Wizard to upgrade a NetWare 3 server to a NetWare 5 server using an across-the-wire upgrade process. This method lets you migrate the bindery and file system (including passwords and security rights) on the NetWare 3 server to an existing NetWare 5 server.

This chapter also discussed the advantages of the Novell Upgrade Wizard, the primary advantage being that it lets you determine how the bindery information should fit into the existing NDS structure before you actually migrate the bindery into NDS. Using the graphical modeling feature provided as part of the Novell Upgrade Wizard lets you see potential problems or inconsistencies before you commit yourself to the design and migration of your NetWare 3 server.

Upgrading a NetWare 4 server to NetWare 5 was also discussed in this chapter. You use the Novell NetWare 5 Installation program to upgrade NetWare 4 to NetWare 5. You also use the New Product Install option in the NetWare 5 server GUI to add products to the NetWare 5 server. If necessary, you can load GUI support on the NetWare 5 server, either by typing **Startx.ncf** at the server console prompt, or by loading a Java class or Java applet that requires GUI support. Loading the class or applet automatically launches **Startx.ncf**.

This chapter also discussed how NetWare 5 supports both Java classes and Java applets through the Java.nlm, and how to run Java applications or Java programs inside a Java-compatible browser. It explained that running Java applications or Java programs requires that you first load the Java NLM on the NetWare 5 file server. It also discussed the fact that NetWare 5 includes an applet viewer that runs any Java applet defined as part of an HTML document that is used primarily to view HTML-based help and HTML-based Internet documents.

Practice Test Questions

1. You use what to move the bindery and file system from a NetWare 3 server to a NetWare 5 server?
   a. Novell Upgrade Wizard
   b. Novell Upgrade Wizard
   c. In-Place Upgrade Wizard
   d. NetWare 5 Install, Upgrade NetWare 3 to NetWare 5 option

2. The feature of the Wizard that lets you view how the NetWare 3 bindery fits into the NetWare 5 directory structure is:
   a. GUI interface
   b. Modeling
   c. Upgrade interface
   d. None of the above

3. The menu from which you choose Novell Upgrade Wizard is:
   a. Install
   b. Upgrade
   c. Programs
   d. NetWare 5

4. When upgrading a NetWare 3 server, which is used?
   a. Object template
   b. Object designer
   c. Object verifier
   d. Object resolver

5. To upgrade a NetWare 4.11 server, you must first:
   a. Mount the NetWare 5 volume
   b. Read and agree to the licensing agreement
   c. Install the NetWare 5 installation files
   d. Down the NetWare 4.11 server

6. To upgrade a NetWare 4.11 server to NetWare 5, you must first do what before you can install the licensing file?
   a. Verify that the correct storage adapter and device are selected
   b. Mount the volums
   c. Provide an IP address
   d. All of the above
   e. None of the above

7. To install products once the initial installation of NetWare 5 is complete, you:
   a. Click the **Novell** button on the Novell GUI window
   b. Restart the NetWare 5 install and answer yes this time when prompted to install other products
   c. Click the **New Product** button on the Novell GUI window
   d. None of the above

8. What must you type at the NetWare 5 server console in order to load GUI support on a NetWare 5 server?
   a. **Load Install**
   b. **Install**
   c. **Startx.ncf**
   d. **Load StartGUI**

9. To view HTML-based Java help on a NetWare 5 server, you must:
   a. Take advantage of the Java applet viewer included with NetWare 5
   b. Type **Load Applet** at the NetWare 5 server
   c. Run Java_class
   d. None of the above

10. A complete Java-based application is known as a/an:
    a. Java applet
    b. Java class
    c. Java browser
    d. Java NLM

Answers to Practice Test Questions

1. b	6. d
2. b	7. a
3. c	8. c
4. a	9. a
5. d	10. b

CHAPTER 3

Completing the Upgrade

Once you upgrade an existing NetWare server to NetWare 5, there are other tasks you may find useful to complete. Some tasks you must perform after you upgrade a server to NetWare 5. Other tasks are optional, though often recommended. For example, you don't have to upgrade your existing queue-based printing to NetWare 5's NDPS print services, but you will find it beneficial to do so. You will also want to complete the following tasks:

- Modify container and user login scripts
- Upgrade NetWare clients as needed
- Customize configuration files
- Setup NDS security
- Secure the file system
- Use Enhanced Sbackup (or other backup software)

The processes of modifying container and user login scripts and of upgrading NetWare clients is covered in the companion to this book: *Accelerated NetWare 5 CNA Study Guide*. See Chapter 6, *Setting Up and Customizing Network Access for Users* for information on modifying container and user login scripts, and on upgrading NetWare clients. The four other configuration tasks are discussed in this chapter.

Customizing Configuration Files

Configuration files let you control the NetWare server just as DOS configuration files let you control a computer. **Autoexec.bat** and **Config.sys** are the configuration files used by an IBM or compatible PC. **Startup.ncf** and **Autoexec.ncf** are the startup files used by the NetWare file server.

There are many different tasks you can perform using these two configuration files. For example, just as you can use the computer's **Autoexec.bat** file to load **Server.exe** and start the NetWare 5 file server, you can configure the **Startup.ncf** and **Autoexec.ncf** configuration files to performs various NetWare server tasks.

KEY CONCEPT

Some tasks on a NetWare server must be run before other tasks. **Startup.ncf** runs before **Autoexec.ncf**, so put files which must run first (files which must run while **Server.exe** is loading such as the server's disk drivers, name spaces, and some SET parameters) into the **Startup.ncf** file. Commands in the **Autoexec.ncf** file are files used to guide the server during the boot process. For example, time zone and bindery context commands are placed into the **Autoexec.ncf** file, as are LAN drivers, network board settings, commands which bind the protocol to the installed drivers, and load commands for starting other NLM programs (see Figure 3-1).

Some commands are placed into configuration files by default when you install NetWare 5. Other commands can be added later by modifying the server configuration files.

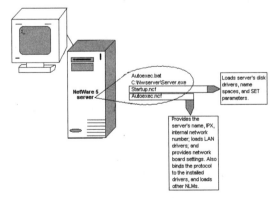

FIGURE 3-1 The NetWare 5 server loading process using configuration files.

Modifying Server Configuration Files

When created initially, server configuration files are stored either on the DOS partition in the **C:\Nwserver** boot directory (**Startup.ncf**), or in the server's **Sys:System** directory (**Autoexec.ncf**). The **Startup.ncf** file contains commands such as those needed to load disk drivers, while the **Autoexec.ncf** file contains commands such as those needed to identify the name and internal network number of the NetWare server. If you make changes to the server, such as adding another hard disk requiring the use of a different disk driver, you can modify the configuration file to accommodate the change.

KEY CONCEPT

To modify the **Startup.ncf** or **Autoexec.ncf** files, load **Nwconfig.nlm** or **Edit.nlm** on the server, or use any other text editor. You can even use a text editor to create an alternative **Startup.ncf** file which you can use when you need to perform maintenance or repair on the server. To load the alternative file, type **Server –s \path/filename** at the **C:\Nwserver** DOS directory, replacing **path/filename** with the location and name of the alternative **Startup.ncf** file. You can also load the server without using either the **Startup.ncf** or **Autoexec.ncf** file by typing **Server –ns** or **Server –na** at the **C:\Nwserver** DOS prompt.

You may find it useful to know what commands exist in these startup files before modifying them. In addition, it is an important part of a network administrator's tasks to keep track of the commands in these files. You should copy these files to a separate file which can later be printed and kept as part of the network's documentation.

To write the server's current parameter settings to a file stored in **sys:\system\setcmds.cp**, complete the following steps:

1. At the server console prompt, type **Monitor** and press **Enter**.
2. Choose **Available Options**. A menu of available options opens.
3. Choose **Server Parameters**. A list of server parameters is displayed (see Figure 3-2).
4. Press **F3**. The current parameter values are copied to the **sys:\ system\setcmds.cp** file.
5. Copy the file to a workstation. Then, using a text editor or other software that can handle a basic DOS text file, print the file.

To create or modify a text file on either a DOS or NetWare partition, you can also use **Edit.nlm** from the NetWare server console. To start **Edit.nlm**, type **Edit** at the server console. If needed, provide the path to

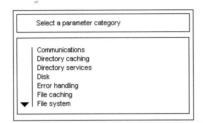

Select a parameter category

Communications
Directory caching
Directory services
Disk
Error handling
File caching
▼ File system

FIGURE 3-2 Server parameters list.

the **Edit.nlm** (if it isn't stored in **Sys:system**). Press **Insert** to display a browse window where you can locate and choose the file you want to edit. If the file you want to edit does not already exist, the program displays a prompt asking if the file should be created. Whether you create it or not depends on whether you believe one already exists. If it does, you have probably specified the wrong path to the file. Try again to find the file to be edited, then make the needed changes.

Creating Server Script Files

You can also create script files which run at the server and automatically perform tasks or procedures that you would manually do from the server console. For example, you can create a server script file to display information about the server.

KEY CONCEPT

You use the Edit NLM to create or modify server script files just as you use the Edit NLM to create or modify server configuration files. The important thing to remember is that the server cannot run a server script file unless it recognizes it as a configuration file. In order for the server to run the script file you create, you must store the file where it can find it by default, such as in **Sys:system**, and the file must have a **.ncf** filename extension.

To create a server configuration file, type **Edit filename.ncf** at the server console, replacing **filename.ncf** with the file's actual name (**.ncf** as the extension is required). When prompted to create the file, choose **Yes**, then add needed commands to the file, and save it by pressing **Esc** then choosing **Yes**. Exit the Edit NLM.

You can use any commands in the script file that NetWare will recognize. For example, you can use the following commands, and many more:

- **CLS**—this clears the server's monitor screen of all text, displaying only the prompt.
- **VERSION**—this displays the NetWare server's version information.
- **SPEED**—this identifies the speed at which the server's processor is functioning.
- **PAUSE**—this stops the script file from executing, awaiting a keyed response from the user (such as pressing the server console's **Enter** key).
- **VOLUME**—this specifies information about the server's volumes.

When you create a server script file, put the name of the server script file into the **Autoexec.ncf** file so it runs automatically when the server boots. You can also run the file any time by typing the file's name at the server console prompt. For example, if you create a server script file called **Info.ncf**, type **Info** at the server console and press **Enter**. The **Info.ncf** file runs.

Modifying Video, Keyboard, and Background Settings

Although NetWare server settings are initially established to optimize the NetWare 5 server, you may want to modify those settings. For example, if you put an upgraded monitor on your NetWare server—one which supports a video resolution greater than 640 x 480 pixels—you will want to configure the video's resolution to take advantage of this upgraded monitor.

 With past versions of NetWare there has been no real reason to upgrade the server's monitor, as all displays were text based. With NetWare 5, however, various utilities use graphical displays. Upgrading the server monitor makes it easier to view these GUI-based utilities.

NOTE

In addition to modifying the video's resolution, you may also want to modify keyboard property settings, or the background graphics which display when you are using NetWare graphics on your server's monitor. To modify the monitor's video resolution or background graphics, or to modify the keyboard's configuration, use ConsoleOne to complete the following steps:

1. Click the **Novell** button in the lower left corner of the ConsoleOne GUI. The Novell menu opens.
2. Click **Tools**. The Tools menu opens (see Figure 3-3).

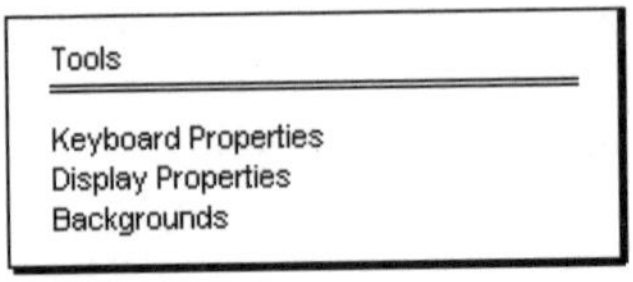

```
┌──────────────────────────────┐
│ Tools                        │
│ ═══════════════════          │
│ Keyboard Properties          │
│ Display Properties           │
│ Backgrounds                  │
└──────────────────────────────┘
```

FIGURE 3-3   The Tools menu, from which you choose what configuration you want to modify (video resolution, keyboard, or background graphic).

3. Depending on what you want to change (video resolution, keyboard configuration, or the background graphic), click one of the following to open the associated list:
   - Keyboard Configuration
   - Display Properties
   - Backgrounds

4. Make changes to the settings as needed, then click **Test** (if you changed video resolution or background graphic) to verify that the changes are acceptable, or **Apply** (if you made keyboard property changes) to activate the changes.

5. Complete the setting change by clicking **OK** one or more times as prompted. In some instances (specifically when configuring the video resolution), you may have to restart ConsoleOne to see the change.

Setting Up NDS Security

Basic NDS security information you should be familiar with includes the following terms:

- **Trustees.** Any object with rights to access a network resource.
- **Rights.** Assigned ability to access or manipulate a network resource.
- **Effective rights.** The combination of rights that determines what network resources an object can access or manipulate.
- **Inheritance.** The ability of rights granted to one object to apply to all objects below that level in the Directory tree
- **IRF (Inherited Rights Filter).** A process which restricts or prevents rights from one container from flowing down the Directory tree to other containers.

You should also understand that while both NDS and file system security are actively engaged on a NetWare 5 network, NDS security and file system security are separate. There are three specific ways in which NDS security differs from file system security (see Figure 3-4):

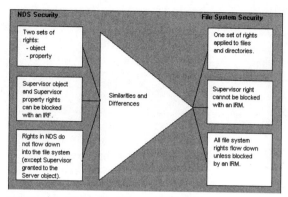

FIGURE 3-4 The similarities and differences between NDS security and file system security rights.

- NDS security has two sets of rights (object and property), while the file system has only one set which applies to directories and files.
- In NDS, the Supervisor object and property right can be blocked by the IRF, but in file system security, the Supervisor right cannot be blocked by the IRM.
- While rights which are not blocked by the IRM in the file system flow down through the file system structure, rights in NDS (with one exception) do not flow into the file system structure. That exception is that rights granted to the Server object in NDS do flow down into the file system structure, but can be blocked using an IRM.

Table 3-1 shows the types of NDS rights, identifies whether the right is an object right or a property right, and provides a brief description of what the associated right allows the trustee to do.

TABLE 3-1 NDS rights and their function.

NDS Right	Type of Right	Description
Supervisor	Object and Property	As an object right, it gives unrestricted access to the object as well as to all of its properties. As a property right, it gives unrestricted access to the values of all properties to which it is assigned.

continued on next page

TABLE 3-1 continued

NDS Right	Type of Right	Description
Browse	Object	Allows trustees to see this object in the Directory tree.
Create	Object	Gives trustees the right to add leaf objects and other container objects to the object, if the object is a container object. Does not apply to leaf objects.
Delete	Object	Allows the trustee to remove this object from the Directory tree.
Rename	Object	Lets the trustee change the name of this object.
Compare	Property	Allows the value of one property to be compared to the value of another property, returning either a True or False to indicate whether the properties are the same.
Read	Property	Grants the trustee the right to read the values associated with the property to which it applies.
Write	Property	Lets the trustee add, change, or delete the values associated with this property.
Add or Delete Self	Property	Allows the trustee to add its User object to or remove its User object from a property when the property's value is a list of object names.

Default NDS Rights

During various events, certain default rights are assigned to different trustees. Which rights are assigned to which trustee and why they are assigned are shown in Table 3-2.

TABLE 3-2 Default rights assignments for various trustees.

Trustee	NDS Right	Purpose
[Public]	[B]Browse Object rights to root (inherited) [R]Read (to messaging server property)	Ensures all users can see the NDS tree and objects in it. Lets network clients see the messaging server assigned to this server.
Admin	[S]Supervisor Object rights to root (inherited)	Allows user Admin to manage the NDS tree.
Container	[R]Read (Login Script property and Print Job Configuration property)	Ensures container's users can run the container login script, and read the container's print job configuration.
Server	[S]Supervisor object rights to itself	Lets the server modify its own parameters when needed.
User	[R]Read (Network Address, Group Membership, Default Server, All Properties, Login Script, and Print Job Configuration) [W]Write (Login Script, and Print Job Configuration)	Ensures users can modify and run their own user login script and print job configuration, as well as view information related to their User object, create print jobs and send them to the printer, and determine their default server.

Guidelines for Implementing NDS Security

To successfully implement NDS security, remember to:

■ Start with the basics all users need. For example, all users should be able to view the directory tree structure and have access to shared files and applications on the network.
■ Avoid using the All Properties option for assigning rights, since it gives the trustee access to all properties of the object. Although you may want some users to have access to some of an object's properties, when the value associated with some of the properties is sensitive or confidential, you may not want the trustee to be able to even view the information.

- Assign specific rights using Selected Properties to avoid security problems. Give the user the right to modify their own User login script, but don't give them the right to change things such as their User object's name.
- Be cautious when assigning the Write property right to the object's Trustee. If you assign this right to the Trustee, the Trustee can then make anyone on the network a Supervisor.
- Be cautious when assigning the Supervisor object right to a Supervisor object. Doing so gives full access to all files and directories in the file system.
- When assigning the Supervisor object right, consider its implications. Assigning the Supervisor object right grants the Supervisor right for all properties to the Trustee to whom you gave the Supervisor right.
- Be aware that the Supervisor object right can be filtered out. If you filter out the Supervisor object right in a section of the NDS tree, you will no longer be able to manage that section of the Directory tree.

In addition to the basic guidelines for implementing NDS identified in the section of this chapter titled, "Setting Up NDS Security," you should also consider following several guidelines for administering NDS security:

- Provide users with access to resources in multiple contexts by creating Directory Map objects, and granting the appropriate rights to the Directory Map object (Read right to the Path property or to All Properties).
- Create Profile objects and create a login script for them, granting users the appropriate right (Read property) to the Login Script property.
- Assign each individual object right and all property rights to all users who are to be administrators of the network to prevent these users from having their access to the Server object blocked through an Inherited Rights Filter (IRF).
- Rename the Admin user object to a name which isn't published as an Admin user, making it more difficult for someone to obtain Admin rights even if they manage to guess a user's login name.
- Avoid using the security-equivalent option to provide administrative rights to other users, as the administrator's rights are lost for all security-equivalent users if the administrator's user is deleted.
- Configure the Administrator's (and other users') passwords to require frequent password changes so that known passwords will not grant rights for very long.

Centralized versus Distributed Administration

There are two methods for administering a network (see Figure 3-5). All administration of the entire tree can be done by a single administrative user (centralized administration), or can be divided up among several network users for various branches (containers) of the network tree (distributed administration). There are benefits and drawbacks to both processes, but the important issue is that centralized administration may not always be practical.

In large networks with thousands of users and hundreds of containers, centralized network administration can require more hours than there are in a day. Centralized administration can also be impractical when the network's tree is geographically dispersed. However, some tasks should be centrally administered whenever possible, including:

- Creating or renaming the NDS tree
- Managing partitioning, replication, and time synchronization
- Assigning and distributing network administration responsibilities

Even if you have your network set up for mostly centralized administration, some tasks are often better handled within a distributed administration framework. You might want to consider implementing distributed administration for:

- Creating and configuring user accounts, workgroup managers, and print services
- Managing user passwords
- Adding file servers to the network and managing file system security
- Backing up and restoring network data and NDS

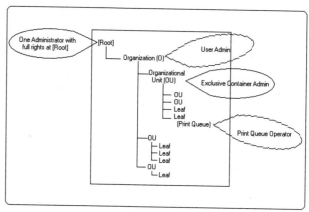

FIGURE 3-5 Distributed versus central administration.

Administrative Roles and Rights Assignments

To distribute network management responsibility means that you must set up the environment (the NDS tree) to make distributed network management possible. To set up the environment you must:

- Create exclusive container administrators (a single user with Supervisor object rights within a specified container) or Organizational Role objects (if more than one administrator will be given administrative responsibility over the same part of the NDS tree) within the container to be administered.
- Make the exclusive container administrator or the Organizational Role object a trustee of the container they are to administer.
- Assign explicit NDS rights ([SBCDRI]) to the container for the exclusive container administrator or the Organizational Role object.
- If Organizational Role objects are created, assign users to those Organizational Role objects.
- If needed, assign rights to the file system for exclusive container administrators or Organizational Role objects.

KEY CONCEPT

Be certain to assign the Inheritable [I] right for the container object to the trustee. If you do not, rights assignments to the objects and containers below the level in the Directory tree at which you assigned the initial NDS rights will not flow down the Directory tree for the trustee. The administrator will not be able to manage any container other than the one to which the trustee assignment was initially made.

If you want to use exclusive container administrators and prevent other network administrators from having access to a container and its objects, you can implement and Inherited Rights Filter (IRF) to block rights for other administrators from flowing down into the container. Use the IRF to block all rights except the Browse [B] object right and the Read [R] property right.

KEY CONCEPT

Before implementing an IRF on a container, be sure to make an explicit trustee assignment of Supervisor [S] and Inheritable [I] rights, or no one will be able to administer that part of the NDS tree and all containers below it.

Once you ensure that the exclusive container administrator can access their assigned container (portion of the NDS tree), remove any explicit trustee assignments to this portion of the NDS tree that was originally granted to any other administrator. Now only the exclusive container administrator will have administrative rights to this portion of the NDS tree.

In addition to the exclusive container administrator, you may want to consider creating an Enterprise NDS Administrator. This administrator would be the default Admin user object, would have to have [S] and [I] rights to [Root] (which are assigned by default to user Admin when this User object is created), and would be responsible for:

- Installing the first server, naming the NDS tree, and creating the upper levels of the NDS tree.
- Managing partitioning, replication, and time synchronization.
- Creating and assigning responsibilities, rights, and users to exclusive container administrators and Organizational Role objects.
- Assigning the initial auditor password.
- Upgrading network servers, clients, and applications, and otherwise performing general network maintenance tasks when they apply to the entire NDS tree and not just a single container.

Other roles and assignments you might choose to make include:

- **Password Manager.** The person(s) assigned to this role would be responsible for resetting users' passwords as needed, setting password restrictions and requirements, and otherwise managing the properties associated with user passwords. The user assigned to this role needs the [RWI] property rights to the Password Management property of the container to which they have been given password management responsibility.
- **Print Server Operator** (for queue-based printing). The person(s) assigned to this role would be responsible for loading and bringing down the print server. The user(s) assigned to this Organizational Role object would have to be added to the Print Server Operator property of the print server to which they have been given print server operator responsibilities.
- **Print Queue Operator** (for queue-based printing). The person(s) assigned to this role would be responsible for changing the status of the print queue, and managing print jobs within the print queue. The user(s) assigned to this Organizational Role object would have to be added to the Print Queue Operator property of the print queue to which they have been given print queue operator responsibilities.
- **Print Job Operator** (for NDPS-based printing). The person(s) assigned to this role would be responsible for all aspects of managing print jobs, including deleting, modifying, copying, and otherwise manipulating them. The user(s) assigned to this Organizational Role object would

have to be added to the NDPS Job Configurations property of the NDPS printer to which they have been given print job operator responsibilities.

When assigning roles and responsibilities, consider assigning all rights (not just [S] and [I]) if it is appropriate to do so. This ensures the administrator still has needed rights if an IRF is implemented to block the [S] right. Also, so that the Admin user is not blocked out of parts of the tree by an IRF which blocks the [S] right, grant the Admin user object an exclusive trustee assignment to containers with the Supervisor object right. In addition, be sure to give container administrators the [S] right to the Server object within their container if they are to also manage the file system on that server. If not, implement an IRF to block the [S] right to the Server object after ensuring that someone has explicit [S] rights to that Server object.

Securing the File Server

The NetWare 5 network revolves around NDS, but is implemented by NetWare 5 file servers. Both physical and logical security of the NetWare 5 server is important to ensure that only authorized users access the network, and access only what they are authorized to access. NetWare servers and their resources are logically protected through password and other security methods. You must still provide physical security to NetWare 5 file servers, however.

Physical Security

Physical security can take more than one route. For example, you provide physical security by putting NetWare servers into a locked room or area, sometimes referred to as the server room. Mainframe computers have successfully taken advantage of this type of physical security for many years, so there is no reason why NetWare's client/server file servers should not do the same.

If you cannot provide a locked area for your NetWare servers, you can purchase a physical lock specifically for the keyboard. While this will prevent anyone from accessing the server from the console keyboard, it doesn't protect from deliberate or accidental problems such as:

- Powering off the server while it is in regular operation
- Disconnecting the power cord from the server or outlet
- Shutting off the UPS (Uninterruptible Power Supply)

While a keyboard lock is better than no physical protection, you can see that it certainly isn't the most ideal. However, there also are some other ways of providing physical security for NetWare servers, including:

- Use of the Secure Console command
- Use of a password for Remote Console Access

SECURE CONSOLE COMMAND

One way you can protect your NetWare server is by preventing anyone from loading unauthorized NLMs on the server from outside of the **Sys:System** or **C:\Nwserver** directories. NetWare is designed to let other companies write and run NLMs which access and obtain information from NDS. It is part of what makes NetWare so versatile. But there are people who take pleasure in writing programs which are designed to disrupt, destroy, or steal vital information. Viruses are a perfect example. You don't want any of these types of NLMs to find their way onto your NetWare server if someone gains physical access to it. To provide further protection, you can use NetWare's Secure Console command.

You enter the Secure Console command at the file server prompt. By doing so, users cannot load any NLMs which are not already stored in the **Sys:System** or **C:\Nwserver** directory. Therefore, even if an individual gains access to the server console, they cannot run any NLMs which you or NetWare have not already placed in the **Sys:System** directory.

In addition, Secure Console prevents a user who might gain access to the server console from changing either the date or time on a server. Even though at first glance the thought of changing the server's date or time seems innocent enough, it can have serious consequences for NDS. For example, replication takes place based at least in part on time and dates associated with the network. An incorrect server date or time could cause small problems in NDS which might eventually become big problems and lead to corruption of NDS. Thus, Secure Console helps protect the NetWare server in more ways than one.

To load Secure Console on a NetWare server, type **Secure Console** at the server prompt, then press **Enter**. Disabling Secure Console requires that you first bring down the server and then reboot it, a task you don't generally want to do unless you have to. Determine whether using Secure Console is more beneficial in your environment than not before deciding to use it.

REMOTE CONSOLE PASSWORD

Secure Console helps keep people from causing trouble by accessing the console directly, but NetWare lets authorized individuals access the console from a workstation as well through a utility known as remote console. To use remote console and keep it secure, you load two NLMs at the server, both of which require a password for access:

- **Rconag6.nlm**
- **Remote.nlm**

KEY CONCEPT

The remote console agent uses encrypted passwords to prevent someone from breaking in and reading the password. The encryption process takes a password that you supply, and converts it to a string of characters that otherwise make no sense and do not display themselves as being the password. Then, when you enter the password into the console, it is translated to the same string of characters, and the two are matched. If they are exactly the same, access to the console is granted.

To use remote console with a password you must first cause the computer to generate an encrypted password, then load the remote console agent using that password. To generate an encrypted password, complete the following steps:

1. Type **Rconag6.nlm** encrypt at the server console and press **Enter**.
2. When prompted, provide a password, a TCP port number, and an SPX port number.
3. Specify whether you want the encrypted password used and placed into the appropriate ncf file, then choose **Yes**. The encryption will be used and the command placed into the **Sys:System\Ldrconfag.ncf** file.
4. Use the encrypted password by typing **Rconag6 -E password TCPport SPXport** at the server console, and pressing **Enter**. Replace *password* with the encrypted password, and *TCPport* and *SPXport* with the TCP and SPX port information you provided when generating the encrypted password.

To load remote console using the encrypted password, type **Remote password** at the file server console, then press **Enter**. Replace *password* with the encrypted password. Otherwise, you can simply type **Remote** and press **Enter**. You are prompted for the password.

You can also have **Remote.nlm** create an encrypted password by typing **Remote ENCRYPT** at the file server console, then pressing **Enter**. (ENCRYPT is case sensitive and must be entered in all upper-case letters). Once created, you can use the password when you run Remote Console by typing **Remote -E password** (replacing *password* with the encrypted password), and then pressing **Enter**.

Screen Saver and Password Security

In addition to using the Secure Console command and a remote control password, you can also use NetWare's screen saver and password security option at the NetWare console. Earlier versions of NetWare relied on the Monitor utility to provide a screen saver at the server console. This screen saver could be set to require a password to release the screen saver and let you access the console, if you chose to use this feature. That meant that in order to have a password-protected screen saver you had to load the Monitor utility. With all of Monitor's capabilities besides the screen saver, Monitor takes up valuable memory space. With NetWare 5, the screen saver is no longer part of the Monitor utility, so you do not have to have Monitor running for the sole purpose of providing a screen saver on the server. Now, you load the much smaller **Scrsaver.nlm** to add a screen saver with password to the server console.

To stop the screen saver and unlock the console, press any key to get its attention, then provide the password and authenticate to NDS. To use **Scrsaver.nlm**, load it from the server prompt. Figure 3-6 shows you some of the different parameters you can use with **Scrsaver.nlm**. To see the equivalent of Figure 3-6 on your own NetWare 5 file server, type **Scrsaver Help** and press **Enter**.

Using Sbackup After the Upgrade

Besides using Sbackup to back up and restore the bindery, NDS, and file systems before completing an upgrade, you can use Sbackup on a regular basis to ensure you will always have a fairly recent copy of your NDS

```
SSSCO: Scrsaver help
SCRSAVER HELP
The following SCRSAVER commands are available:
          ACTIVATE
          AUTO CLEAR DELAY
          DELAY
          DISABLE
          DISABLE AUTO CLEAR
          ENABLE
          ENABLE AUTO CLEAR
          ENABLE LOCK
          NO PASSWORD
          HELP
          STATUS


Multiple commands, separated by semicolons, may be entered on the same line.
Example: SCRSAVER ENABLE; DELAY=2; DISABLE LOCK
Type SCRSAVER HELP [command] to obtain help on a specific command.
```

FIGURE 3-6 The Scrsaver help file displaying parameters you can run with this NLM.

and file system. NetWare 5 ships with the Enhanced Sbackup utility, but if you prefer, you can use backup and restore products by other manufacturers. The important thing is that you decide what you will back up and what backup strategy and frequency you will follow. No matter what product you choose to use, you should adopt a regular routine for backing up your network's NDS and file system.

Using Enhanced Sbackup

If you choose to use Enhanced Sbackup, you can back up and restore any of the following:

- NetWare server file system
- DOS partition on a NetWare server
- NDS database
- Windows 95 and Windows NT workstation file systems
- GroupWise databases

Backup Strategies

What you back up and the backup strategy you choose depends on your needs. There are three defined types of backup strategies:

- Full
- Incremental
- Differential

The *full backup* involves backing up all data on your network on a routine basis. Implementing this strategy means that you do not care whether or not the data was backed up last time you completed a backup, or whether it has changed since its last backup. You use a full backup with every backup session, so you need only restore the most recent backup session to ensure you restore all of the most recent data.

The *incremental backup* involves backing up only those files which have been added or modified since the last full or incremental backup. For example, if you back up files on Monday using a full backup, then you run an incremental backup on Tuesday, you will back up on Tuesday only those files which were added or changed since Monday's full backup.

 The network helps you track which files have been backed up by setting a flag on each file called an *archive bit*. When a file is backed up using either the full or incremental back up, the archive bit is cleared (effectively set to off). When the file is first created, and

NOTE

each time it is modified, the archive bit is set to not cleared (effectively set to on).

The *differential backup* involves backing up all files that have been added or changed since the last full backup was performed. Unlike the incremental backup, which will back up only files which have been added or changed since the last full or the last incremental backup, the differential backup doesn't care if a differential backup has already backed up files since the last full backup. It backs up those added or changed files every time until another full backup has been completed.

NOTE

When establishing and following a backup strategy, combine the full backup only with a differential or an incremental backup. Do not combine a differential and incremental backup strategy, or changes that have been made since the last full backup will not be backed up when the differential backup is run.

KEY CONCEPT

Each type of backup has its own benefits and limitations. The time it takes to perform the backup can be either a benefit or a limitation. A full backup takes the longest to perform, but only the one group of backup tapes has to be restored in order to ensure all data is restored. The incremental backup takes the least amount of time because only new or changed files since the last incremental backup are backed up. However, the incremental backup means you may have to locate and restore multiple tapes, including those for the latest full backup, to ensure you restore all of the data. The differential backup takes less time than a full backup to complete, but more time than an incremental backup. With each differential backup, the backup time takes a little longer as the list of new and modified files continues to grow until a new full backup is done. When it is time to restore a differential backup, however, you have to restore the full backup as well as the differential tapes, but there may be fewer total tapes to restore.

Deciding which backup strategy to follow can be determined in part by how much time you have to dedicate to doing backups of your network. It is also determined by how large your network is. On a small network, a full backup is the easiest to do, and may require such a small amount of time that the length of time is insignificant compared to the effort needed to perform one of the other two types. You can use the full backup in combination with one of the other strategies on a small network, however.

Assigning Backup Rights and Responsibilities

As a network administrator you can also reduce the time you spend doing backups by assigning the responsibility to someone else. If you do so, however, you will have to make sure that individual has the proper rights. Logging in to the network as the Admin user automatically gives you all the rights you need to do the backup, but you probably don't want to give the person doing backups the full administrative rights.

The rights needed to perform a backup are:

- **For backing up NetWare server files:** Read and File Scan
- **For backing up NDS:** Browse object and Read property (for the entire tree)

To restore backed up data, the user must also have Create rights. In addition, the user needs to know the passwords for the servers being backed up (targets), and the servers from which the backup is run (hosts). The user also needs to know the password to any workstation that they will be backing up.

Whether you do the backup yourself, or assign it to someone else, keep the following in mind before beginning a backup:

- To avoid compromising security, the host server must have an attached backup device, and its media must have sufficient space to complete the backup if you will not be around to swap in additional media if prompted
- At least 1 MB of space on volume **Sys** of the host server must be available for temporary files created during the backup
- Restrict access to the Enhanced Sbackup NLMs
- Do not mount or dismount volumes or unload drivers during the backup session

Use Enhanced Sbackup

The Enhanced Sbackup software that ships with NetWare 5 consists of several NLMs you load on the file server and a workstation-based utility. The workstation-based utility launches when you run the **Nwback32.exe** file. You use this utility to configure and submit backup and restore jobs to Enhanced Sbackup running on a host NetWare file server. The NLMs on the host server then:

- Process the job request
- Create a session
- Establish communication with the target
- Run the backup or restoration process

In order for the job request to be processed and a session created, a Target Service Agent (TSA) must be loaded on the target device (server or workstation). The TSA is responsible for processing the data as it moves between the target and Enhanced Sbackup software. The TSA that is loaded depends on what you want to back up. For example, to back up a Windows 95 workstation, the W95TSA must be installed and configured on the Windows 95 workstation (it is part of the Novell Client modules installed during the installation of the client). To back up a Windows NT workstation, both the **TSAmain.exe** and **TSAPrefs.exe** files must be run and configured.

Using Enhanced Sbackup, you can back up both a NetWare 5 server and Windows NT or Windows 95 workstations. You should back up a NetWare 5 server before using it to perform an across-the-wire migration; Chapter 1, *Planning a NetWare 5 Network*, explains the process to follow. For details on backing up a workstation, refer to Novell's online documentation.

Chapter Summary

Once you upgrade your network to NetWare 5, there are still some post-upgrade tasks you should perform. While most are optional, they are generally recommended. For example, you don't have to upgrade your existing queue-based printing to NetWare 5's NDPS print services, but you will find it beneficial to do so. This chapter discussed post-upgrade tasks which are recommended, including:

- Customizing configuration files
- Setting up NDS security
- Securing the file system
- Using Enhanced Sbackup (or other backup software)

Configuration files let you control the NetWare server just as DOS configuration files let you control a computer. **Autoexec.bat** and **Config.sys** are the configuration files used by an IBM or compatible PC. **Startup.ncf** and **Autoexec.ncf** are the startup files used by the NetWare file server. When created initially, server configuration files are stored either on the DOS partition in the **C:\Nwserver** boot directory (**Startup.ncf**), or in the server's **Sys:System** directory (**Autoexec.ncf**). The **Startup.ncf** file contains commands such as those needed to load disk drivers, while the **Autoexec.ncf** file contains commands such as those needed to identify the name and internal network number of the NetWare server. If you make changes to the server, such as adding another hard disk requiring the use of a different disk driver, you can modify the configuration file to accommodate the change.

You use the Edit NLM to create or modify server script files just as you use Edit NLM to create or modify server configuration files. The important thing to remember is that the server cannot run a server script file unless it recognizes it as a configuration file. In order for the server to run the script file you create, you must store the file where it can find it by default, such as in **Sys:system**, and the file must have a .ncf filename extension.

NDS security was also discussed in this chapter. A review of basic terms such as *trustee* and *rights* was provided. In addition, tables containing information about default rights assignments were included, as were the following guidelines for implementing NDS security, beginning with starting with the basics which all users need. For example, all users should be able to view the directory tree structure and have access to shared files and applications on the network. Other basic NDS security guidelines include:

1. Avoid using the All Properties option for assigning rights.
2. Assign specific rights using Selected Properties to avoid security problems.
3. Be cautious when assigning the Write property right to the object's Trustee or the Supervisor object right to a Supervisor object.
4. When assigning the Supervisor object right, consider its implications.
5. Be aware that the Supervisor object right can be filtered out.

In addition to the basic guidelines for implementing NDS, you should also consider following several guidelines for administering NDS security:

- Provide users with access to resources in multiple contexts by creating Directory Map objects.
- Create Profile objects and create a login script for them.
- Assign each individual object right and all property rights to all users who are to be administrators of the network.
- Rename the Admin user object.
- Avoid using the security-equivalent option to provide administrative rights.
- Configure the Administrator's (and other user's) passwords to require frequent password changes.

This chapter also discussed how you could delegate network administration when the network was too large or too geographically dispersed for a single administrator to handle. The main suggestion included creating other roles and assignments you might choose to make, such as:

- Password Manager
- Print Server Operator (for queue-based printing)
- Print Queue Operator (for queue-based printing)
- Print Job Operator (for NDPS-based printing)

The final topic of this chapter was security—including physical security, such as locking up the file server, and dealing with potential data loss. NetWare 5's Enhanced Sbackup software was discussed along with a plan for creating regular network backups which included the use of full, incremental, or differential backups.

Practice Test Questions

1. As a post-upgrade task, you must:
   a. Add new directories to the file system
   b. Upgrade network clients
   c. Rename the Sys directory
   d. None of the above

2. The two configuration files used to configure the server are:
   a. **Startup.ncf**
   b. **Nwserver.ncf**
   c. **Autoexec.bat**
   d. **Autoexec.ncf**

3. The configuration file which must be run while Server.exe is loading is:
   a. **Startup.ncf**
   b. **Nwserver.ncf**
   c. **Autoexec.bat**
   d. **Autoexec.ncf**

4. The configuration file which loads LAN drivers is:
   a. **Startup.ncf**
   b. **Nwserver.ncf**
   c. **Autoexec.bat**
   d. **Autoexec.ncf**

5. To create or modify a text file on either a DOS or NetWare partition, you can use which NLM?
   a. Nwconfig
   b. Config
   c. Edit
   d. Startup

6. You can create what to perform tasks or procedures you would manually do from the server console?
   a. Edit NLM
   b. Server script file
   c. System file
   d. **Startup.ncf** file

7. Which of the following is not a command you might typically use in a server script file?
   a. CLS
   b. STARTUP
   c. SPEED
   d. VOLUME

8. Although NetWare server settings are initially established to optimize the NetWare 5 server, you may want to modify which three settings?
   a. Video
   b. Keyboard
   c. System
   d. Background

9. You should create a login script and what else to assist in providing users with access to resources in multiple contexts?
   a. A Profile object
   b. The **Edit.nlm** file
   c. A server script file
   d. None of the above

10. Which of the following tasks is generally better performed by multiple network administrators instead of by a single central network administrator?
    a. Creating or renaming the NDS tree
    b. Managing partioning
    c. Managing user passwords
    d. Assigning distributed network administration responsibilities

11. Which of the following is not a task you might perform in order to set up distributed network management?
    a. Create exclusive container administrators
    b. Assign explicit NDS rights to the container for the exclusive container administrator
    c. Create an organizational role object
    d. Implement an IRM

12. A network administration role you can create in order to ensure someone handles password problems for users would be:
    a. Print Server Operator
    b. Password Manager
    c. Administration Manager
    d. None of the above

13. So that the Admin user is not blocked out of parts of the tree by an IRF which blocks the [S] right,
    a. Grant the Admin user object an exclusive trustee assignment to containers with Supervisor object right.
    b. Implement an IRF at the Server object
    c. Create a Password Manager
    d. Establish physical security for the NetWare server

14. Two methods of providing physical security for NetWare servers are:
    a. Change the Admin user's password
    b. Secure console command
    c. Set a Remote Control Access password
    d. Rename the Admin user

15. The backup strategy which backs up only those files that have been added or modified since the last full or incremental backup is:
    a. Full
    b. Incremental
    c. Differential
    d. All of the above

Answers to Practice Test Questions

1. b	6. b	11. d
2. a, d	7. b	12. b
3. a	8. a, b, d	13. a
4. d	9. a	14. b, c
5. c	10. c	15. b

CHAPTER 4

Working with the NetWare 5 Console

W orking with the NetWare 5 console involves four main tasks, each of which are discussed in this chapter:

- Understanding and Customizing ConsoleOne
- Setting Up Remote Access to the Console
- Accessing the Console from a Workstation
- Using the Monitor NLM at the Server

Understanding and Customizing ConsoleOne

ConsoleOne is a GUI (Graphical User Interface) utility that runs at the NetWare Server console. Using ConsoleOne, you can perform several basic administrative tasks. Before you can use ConsoleOne, you will have to load it (if it is not already loaded). ConsoleOne is Java based, so you can either load it from the NetWare GUI menu, or you can run **C1start.ncf** at the console prompt.

ConsoleOne's Main Window

The ConsoleOne utility's main window is divided into two window panes (see Figure 4-1). The left window pane lets you browse the

Directory tree. You can use standard browse methods, collapsing and expanding containers within the Directory tree as needed.

The **My World** object displays in the left window. By default, it contains three objects:

- My Server
- The Network
- Shortcuts

You expand the **My Server** object to perform most of the network administration tasks for which you will use ConsoleOne. Expanding the **My Server** object displays:

- **Volume objects.** Using Volume objects, you can navigate the network and perform several file system tasks.
- **Tools object.** Using the Tools object, you can manage local and remote server console access.
- **Configuration Files object.** Using the Configuration Files object, you can edit server configuration files.

You expand **The Network** object to view the network, and the **Shortcuts** object to view any existing shortcuts (text files that define a Novell or third-party file, folder, or Java applet that can be snapped into Console One to expand its functionality).

The right window pane displays the contents of the selected container object, such as the contents of a file system folder or of a server or NDS container object. For example, when you expand the **Configuration Files** object, a list of common server configuration files opens in the right

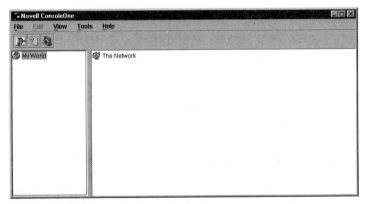

FIGURE 4-1 The ConsoleOne main window.

window pane. From that list of common server configuration files, you can choose a configuration or other text-based file to edit. In addition, you can perform other basic tasks associated with files.

If you have difficulty seeing both sides of the ConsoleOne main window, you can use the mouse to grab and drag the window's edge to change its size.

NOTE

Working with Files Using ConsoleOne

Using ConsoleOne, you can edit server configuration files as well as regular text files. In addition, you can:

- Rename files
- Copy files
- Delete files

Editing server configuration files using ConsoleOne is relatively easy. In the right window pane, double-click the configuration file you want to edit. The Edit graphical utility automatically launches and opens the configuration file. Alternatively, you can right-click the configuration file, then choose **Edit** from the menu that appears, to launch the graphical editor and open the configuration file for editing.

KEY
CONCEPT

You can also edit regular text files using ConsoleOne by following these steps:

1. Click the **My Server** object in the left window pane to expand it.
2. Expand the **Volumes** object, then expand a server volume.
3. Expand the directories in a server volume until you locate the file you want to edit.
4. In the right window pane, click to select the file you want to edit.
5. Click **File**, then click **Edit**.

In addition, you can rename, copy, or delete files using ConsoleOne by following these steps:

1. Click the **My Server** object in the left window pane to expand it.
2. Expand the **Volumes** object, then expand a server volume.
3. Expand the directories in a server volume until you locate the file you want to rename, copy, or delete.
4. In the right window pane, click to select the file you want to copy, rename, or delete.

5. Click **File**, then click either **Copy**, **Rename**, or **Delete**, and follow the prompts. For example, if you choose to delete a file, you are prompted to verify the delete process before it proceeds.

Performing Network Management Tasks Using ConsoleOne

In addition to using ConsoleOne to view the network and to edit and manage configuration or other files, you can also perform the following network management tasks using ConsoleOne:

- Access this server's text-based console screens
- Access other servers' consoles
- Administer NDS from the server console

ACCESSING THIS SERVER'S TEXT-BASED CONSOLE SCREENS

NetWare 5 has two tools with which you can access a NetWare server from a remote location such as a workstation or the console:

- RconsoleJ
- Console Manager

To gain access to servers using either of these utilities, the server to which you want to gain access must have the **Rconag6.nlm** loaded on it. During installation, the command to load this NLM is added to the server's **Autoexec.ncf** file, but it is not activated. The command itself is inserted with a semicolon (;) in front of it, which identifies the information that follows on this line as being a remark instead of a command. To change the line so that the server will load this NLM, you must edit the **Autoexec.ncf** file and remove the semicolon. From then on, each time the file server is started, the **Rconag6.nlm** line in the **Autoexec.ncf** file will be treated as a command line instead of a remark, and this NLM will be loaded. To load it once:

1. Type **Rconag6** at the server console prompt, and press **Enter**.
2. When prompted, type the TCP port number to be used then press **Enter**, or simply press **Enter** to accept the default value provided.
3. When prompted, type the SPX port number to be used then press **Enter**, or simply press **Enter** to accept the default value provided.
4. When prompted, type a password and press **Enter**.

Once the server you want to access through a remote console session has **Rconag6.nlm** loaded (that includes the current server on which Console Manager is to be run), you can use either Console Manager or RconsoleJ to view the server's system console or loaded NLMs on this or other servers.

To run Console Manager on a server, load **Rconag6.nlm** (if it is not already loaded), then use the current server's ConsoleOne utility.

1. With ConsoleOne on the screen, click the **My Server** icon, then click the **Tools** folder. Console Manager and RconsoleJ both display in the left window pane.
2. Click **Console Manager**.
3. Change the port number for the local server (this server) if you did not accept the default port number when you loaded **Rconag6.nlm** on this server.
4. Type in the password you set for this server when you loaded **Rconag6.nlm**.
5. Click **Connect**. You will see the different consoles available on this server. For example, you will see **System Console** and **ConsoleOne** at a minimum, as every server has a server console running as long as the server is up. Since you run Console Manager through ConsoleOne, it also has to be loaded.

ACCESSING OTHER SERVERS' CONSOLES

You can also access the console of other NetWare 5 servers either from the console of a NetWare 5 server or from a workstation. To access the console of one NetWare 5 server (remote server) from another NetWare 5 server (local host), make sure that **Rconag6.nlm** has first been loaded on the remote server, then complete the following steps:

1. With ConsoleOne on the local host's screen, click the **My Server** icon, then click the **Tools** folder. Console Manager and RconsoleJ both display in the left window pane.
2. Click **RConsoleJ**. The right window pane displays the remote server connection window.
3. Type in the server's IPX address (such as 123.45.678.910), and password (set when you loaded **Rconag6.nlm** on the remote server), then click **Connect**. The current server console displayed on the remote server is now displayed in the RConsoleJ right window pane of the local host server's console.
4. Click **Connect**.

ADMINISTERING NDS FROM THE SERVER CONSOLE

You can also use ConsoleOne to administer NDS without having to leave the server and go to a workstation. You use the Network container object to access NDS objects. Just as you can from a workstation, you can expand the NDS tree to view and administer NDS objects. You can also create four types of NDS objects using ConsoleOne:

- Group
- Organization
- Organizational Unit
- User

To create, view, or administer NDS objects using ConsoleOne, follow these steps:

1. Click **The Network** in the left window pane of ConsoleOne to expand it.
2. Locate the tree you want to work with, then expand it. If you are not already authenticated to that tree, the Login window opens.
3. If the Login window opens, provide the context for the administrator's User ID, then provide the administrator's Username and Password and click **OK**.
4. Continue to expand the Directory tree until you locate the container where you want to create, view, or administer the NDS object (see Figure 4-2), then click to select (highlight) either the container where you want to create an object, or the object itself that you want to administer.

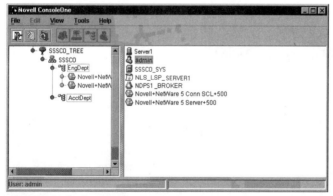

FIGURE 4-2 The ConsoleOne expanded tree view.

If you are creating an object in NDS, complete the following steps once you have completed the steps above:

1. Click the **Create** icon for the type of NDS object you want to create, or click **File** in the menu bar, then click **New**, and click the class of object you want to create (Group, Organization, Organizational Unit, or User). The related create dialog box opens. For example, if creating a new User object, click the **User** icon. The New User dialog opens.

2. Provide the required information depending on the type of NDS object you are creating. For example, if creating a User object, provide a Login Name and the user's Last Name in the provided fields. Then, click either **Define Additional Properties** (click this one unless you are creating multiple User objects) or **Create Another User** (see Figure 4-3).

3. Click **Create**. Additional windows may open prompting you for more information depending on the type of object you are creating. For example, if you are creating a User object, a dialog opens prompting you to provide a password for this new User object (see Figure 4-4).

4. Provide any additional information if prompted (see Figure 4-5 for information you may want to provide when creating a User object), then click **OK**.

KEY
CONCEPT

You can also view information about any given object using ConsoleOne. For example, you can view trustee information associated with the new User object you created by right-clicking the object in the right window pane and choosing to view the trustees. A window similar to that shown in Figure 4-6 opens.

New User	
Login Name:	**Create**
DLee	Cancel
Last name:	Help
Lee	
☑ Define Additional Properties	
☐ Create Another User	

FIGURE 4-3 The Create User dialog that opens when creating a new User object from ConsoleOne.

FIGURE 4-4 The Create Authentication Secrets dialog, into which you provide a password for the new User object you are creating through ConsoleOne.

Customizing ConsoleOne's Interface

To make the most of any tool, including software utilities, it is helpful if you can customize the tool to your specific needs. One way you can improve ConsoleOne's functionality for you is by customizing its interface. You use Shortcuts and ConsoleOne snap-ins to customize ConsoleOne's functionality.

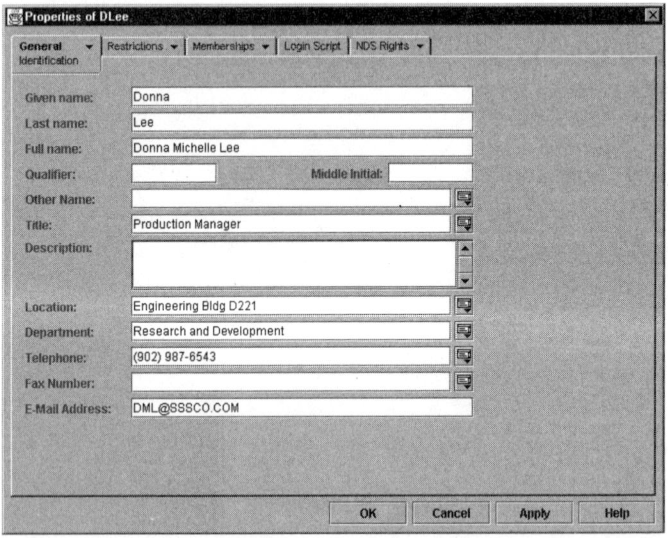

FIGURE 4-5 Properties page for the new User object created using ConsoleOne.

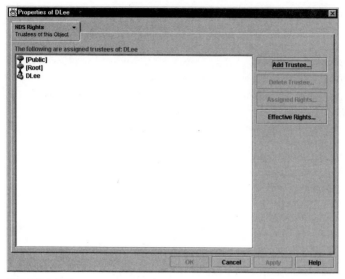

FIGURE 4-6 The trustees view for a User object as seen in ConsoleOne.

As noted earlier, Shortcuts can be files, folders, or applets you use to make it easier to navigate to other objects, such as ConsoleOne snap-ins or the server configuration files for which NetWare includes shortcuts. You can add a shortcut to a text file by completing the following steps:

1. Using any editor which allows you to create a text-based configuration file, create such a file and put into it only the path and filename of another text file that you want to have run when this configuration file is launched.

2. Save the configuration file with the name you want to have displayed by ConsoleOne as the Shortcut name. For example, name a Shortcut to a server configuration file something like **Server_Config**. (Don't add a filename extension unless you want the extension to display in ConsoleOne.)

3. Put the file that your configuration file calls into the **Sys:Public/ Mgmt/Console1/Configfiles** directory (or a subdirectory in this path you have created).

4. Click **View**, then click **Refresh**.

You can also create Shortcuts to directories (folders) and to applets. To do so, you still create a text file that either contains only the path to the folder or the configuration information for the applet, depending on which type of Shortcut you are creating (folder or applet). Then, complete these steps:

1. Save the configuration file with the name you want to have displayed by ConsoleOne as the Shortcut name.
2. Put the file that your Folders shortcut configuration file calls into the **Sys:Public/Mgmt/Console1/Shortcuts/Folders** directory or if you created an Applets shortcut configuration file, put the file it calls into the **Sys:Public/Mgmt/Console1/Shortcuts/Tools** (or **Applets**) directory, depending on where you want it to display.
3. Click **View**, then click **Refresh**.

Setting Up Remote Access to the Console

You may want to perform server or network management tasks which must be done from the file server console without having to be at the console. Using remote access, you can make your workstation look as though you were sitting at the file server console, with the same result. Before you can access the file server console from a remote workstation, however, you must set up the server to accept remote console access.

 To access a NetWare 5 server's console across an IP connection, you must run the RConsole agent at the NetWare 5 server. To run the RConsole agent, either enable the command in the **Autoexec.ncf** file which loads it automatically when you start the server (**Rconag6.nlm**) then restart the server, or type **Rconag6** at the server's console prompt, and provide a password, TCP port number, and SPX port number. Now, you will be able to access the NetWare 5 file server's console from a workstation.

KEY
CONCEPT

Accessing the Console from a Workstation

NetWare 5 provides two utilities which you run from NetWare Administrator at your workstation in order to access and take control of a NetWare 5 server console:

- RconsoleJ
- Remote Console

To use RConsoleJ to establish a remote connection to a server, log in to the network, then complete the following steps:

1. Click **Start**, then click **Run** (on a Windows 95/98 workstation, or the equivalent on a Windows NT workstation)
2. Click **Browse**, locate the **Sys:Public** directory on the server, then click **RconJ.exe**.

3. Click **OK**. Wait while RConJ.exe loads and opens the RConsoleJ window (see Figure 4-7). It may take a few seconds, depending on how heavy the network traffic is at the time.

4. Provide the IP address of the server whose console you want to access remotely. For example, type an IP number similar to the following, depending on the server's actual IP number: 123.45.678.910.

NOTE

To find the server's IP number, go to the server console, type **Config** at the console prompt, and press **Enter**. Configuration information for this server is displayed, and should contain the server's IP number (in a format similar to the previous example). You can also use ConsoleOne to view the number in the **Autoexec.ncf** file.

5. Type in the password used when the **Rconag6.nlm** was loaded, then click **Connect**.

The system makes the remote connection to the server and identifies that it is "Waiting for reply." Once the connection is made, the RConsoleJ window displays the system console window for the server to which you connected. You can now enter console commands for this server directly at your workstation, within the RConsoleJ window.

You can also view and work with other console views, including any NLM that has been loaded on the server. You can also load any NLM you want to load using RConsoleJ. Simply load the NLM the same way you would if you were standing at the console itself, by typing the name of the NLM at the console prompt, then pressing **Enter**.

To change the RConsoleJ view to a different view (such as to an NLM that has already been loaded):

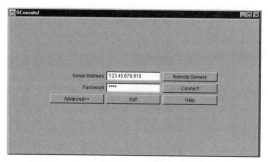

FIGURE 4-7 The RConsoleJ window displaying the login screen by which you identify the exact NetWare 5 server whose console you want to access remotely.

1. Click the **down arrow** next to the Server Screens field. A list of available screens opens.
2. Click the name of the screen you want to see. The display changes to that screen.
3. If the view does not appear to be responding, click the **Activate** button, as some views initially display as only a current snapshot.

You can also access the server console remotely when using an asynchronous modem. The server must be running the following NLMs:

- **Remote.nlm**
- **Aio.nlm**
- **Rspx.nlm**
- **Rs232.nlm**

You can also access the server just from a workstation on the local network. Either way, the PC must be running **Rconsole.exe**.

To run ConsoleOne from a workstation, map a drive to **Sys:public\ mgmt**, and launch **Console1.exe**.

KEY
CONCEPT

Using the Monitor NLM at the Server

The Monitor utility, like many utilities run at the server console, is brought up by loading its associated NLM (**Monitor.nlm**) at the server console prompt. When you load monitor, it brings up an initial view (see Figure 4-8) which provides several different statistics related to this server. In addition to viewing these statistics to get general information about the server and its performance, you can also use Monitor to:

- Set read and write caching parameters
- Review and set communications-related parameters

View General Statistics Using Monitor

General statistics provided by the Monitor utility make it possible for you to check on the server's performance. The statistics you will be most interested are already grouped to display in the main Monitor screen (General Information). This view opens automatically when you start Monitor. The view can be expanded or contracted by pressing the **Tab** key at the server console when Monitor is displayed.

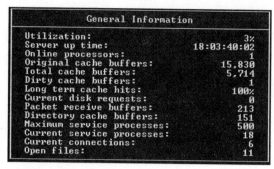

```
                    General Information
 Utilization:                              3%
 Server up time:                  18:03:40:02
 Online processors:                          1
 Original cache buffers:              15,830
 Total cache buffers:                  5,714
 Dirty cache buffers:                      1
 Long term cache hits:                  100%
 Current disk requests:                    0
 Packet receive buffers:                 213
 Directory cache buffers:               151
 Maximum service processes:             500
 Current service processes:             18
 Current connections:                     6
 Open files:                             11
```

FIGURE 4-8 The Monitor NLM's General Information area.

In addition to the name of the server, the version of NetWare running on this server, and the name of this NLM, the following statistics are provided on Monitor's initial screen in the General Information area:

- **Utilization.** Tells what percentage of the processor's capacity is currently being used.
- **Server up time.** Specifies how long the server software has been running since the last time it was started.
- **Online processors.** Identifies how many processors this file server has.
- **Original cache buffers.** Shows how many blocks of memory were set aside to be used for file caching (temporary storage of files in server memory until they can be processed or permanently stored on the hard disk) when the server was first started.
- **Total cache buffers.** Indicates how many buffers are currently available for file caching.
- **Dirty cache buffers.** Specifies how many buffers are currently being used to hold data that has not yet been stored on the hard disk.
- **Long term cache hits.** Shows how many times the system was able to find requested data already in RAM instead of having to access the hard disk to retrieve it.
- **Current disk requests.** Shows how many requests for access to the hard disk are waiting to be processed.
- **Packet receive buffers.** Number of buffers available for holding requests received from clients until the processor is ready for them.
- **Directory cache buffers.** Indicates how many buffers are currently available for directory caching.
- **Maximum service processes.** Specifies how many task handlers have been set aside to handle processing requests from workstations.
- **Current service processes.** Specifies how many workstation requests currently exist.

- **Current connections.** Lists the current number of server connections (licensed and unlicensed).
- **Open files.** Shows how many files are currently open for use by the server and workstations combined.

KEY CONCEPT

These statistics can be valuable in assessing the current state of your NetWare file server. For example, determining the maximum number of current service processes used then comparing that to the maximum number of service processes defined helps you determine whether the maximum number of service processes is sufficient, or excessive. As each defined service process captures a certain amount of memory and holds it in reserve even if it is never used, setting the maximum number of service processes unnecessarily high uses up valuable memory. If the peak number of current service processes never comes close to the maximum number of service processes defined, you may want to change the maximum number of service processes, particularly if the server seems to run low on memory.

Caching and communications management are also important statistics you want to be familiar with. In addition, you can modify the default caching and communication settings to improve the efficiency of your network.

Setting Read and Write Caching Parameters

A *cache* is a temporary area in server RAM where information can be stored for quick access. Accessing data from RAM is much quicker than accessing it from the hard disk each time it is needed. Therefore, response and processing time are quicker when the needed information can be found in RAM.

NLMs and other services that are loaded into RAM take up space that could otherwise be used for caching. However, if the server has too much caching space set aside, services and NLMs may not have enough space to run. The trick is then to balance caching space with service and NLM space for maximum performance. With the appropriate balance, the percentage of cache hits (times the server found the data in RAM and thus didn't have to access the hard disk) will be higher. Ideally, the long term cache hits should be 90% or higher. To see the long term cache hits:

1. Load the Monitor NLM, if it is not already loaded.
2. Choose **Disk Cache Utilization** from the Monitor Available Options menu. The Cache Utilization Statistics window opens.

You will also notice that other cache statistics are displayed in this window. For example, you can also view long term cache dirty hits, as well as short term cache hits. Figure 4-9 shows the Cache Utilization Statistics window.

To improve server performance when users make lots of small write requests, consider changing the following parameters using either Monitor or the **SET** command (put into **Autoexec.ncf** to make the changes permanent):

- Dirty Disk Cache Delay Time
- Dirty Directory Cache Delay Time
- Maximum Concurrent Disk Cache Writes
- Maximum Concurrent Directory Cache Writes

NOTE

Use Monitor to view the current read and write cache settings for your server, and use Monitor's Help to see the default settings for each of these parameters.

To improve server response to requests for disk reads, consider changing the following parameters using Monitor or the **SET** command (put into **Autoexec.ncf** to make the changes permanent):

- Maximum Concurrent Directory Cache Writes
- Maximum Concurrent Directory Cache Writes
- Directory Cache Buffer NonReferenced Delay

KEY
CONCEPT

Processor utilization and memory utilization are also critical factors in network performance. Processor utilization which occasionally reaches 100%, is not only acceptable, but an indication that a particular service or NLM is efficiently using the CPU. For example, file compression will cause processor utilization to run at 100%, but

```
         Cache Utilization Statistics
Short term cache hits:                    100%
Short term cache dirty hits:              100%
Long term cache hits:                      99%
Long term cache dirty hits:                93%
LRU sitting time:               13:15:31:45.2
Allocate block count:                  116,509
Allocated from AVAIL:                  116,509
Allocated from LRU:                          0
Allocate wait:                               0
Allocate still waiting:                      0
Too many dirty blocks:                       0
Cache ReCheckBlock count:                    0
```

FIGURE 4-9 The Cache Utilization Statistics window in Monitor NLM.

shouldn't do so for more than a couple of minutes at a time. However, if processor utilization frequently remains at 100% , you should consider whether you need to upgrade your server to one with greater processing capacity.

The efficient design of NLMs and the ability to load and unload them as needed also helps make memory utilization more efficient. Before loading NLMs on the server, consider that they require not only the amount of memory that the NLM itself requires, but also any memory that prerequisite NLMs (NLMs which must be loaded before this NLM) require memory space as well. Also, consider that some NLMs are capable of allocating additional memory while they are running, if they need it. Thus, if you are unsure about an NLM's memory usage, check the System Resource Information window in Monitor to view memory information both before and after loading the NLM. A simple math calculation will then tell you the effective amount of memory required to load and run that particular NLM.

Reviewing and Setting Communications-Related Parameters

Communications across the network effect server and network performance. Thus they are also important to consider when assessing the status of a NetWare server.

PACKETS AND BUFFERS

There are two communications-related terms you need to become familiar with if you are to understand how settings assigned to various communications-related parameters effect the network:

- **Packet.** A packet is a unit of information.
- **Buffer.** A buffer is a storage area in memory where, in this case, packets which cannot be immediately serviced or sent out are temporarily stored.

All data, requests for service, and messages are sent across the network in the form of packets. It is similar to sending a letter the old-fashioned way—through the United States Postal Service in a stamped, addressed envelope. On the network, the data, request for service, etc., is effectively enclosed in special identification codes (an envelope), and together with its contents, it becomes a packet. Just as the postal service defines what size envelopes can be used to send mail, the NetWare server and workstation determine what size (in bytes) the packet can be. For a packet to be successfully sent and received, the server and workstation must agree upon the packet's size.

KEY CONCEPT

A workstation can handle packets that range in size from 576 bytes to 6500 bytes. The packet size a workstation can handle is determined by the LAN driver. However, you can use Monitor to change the Maximum Physical Receive Packet Size parameter. You should set this parameter (in the **Startup.ncf** file, not using the **SET** command at the console) to identify the maximum size packet that any LAN driver (workstation) on the network can send. If this is set to smaller than the largest possible packet size, your network may experience problems when packets larger than the set acceptable size are sent.

A *packet receive buffer* is an area in server memory that has been set aside to hold packets, making memory space otherwise unavailable for server use. Therefore, it is important to network processing that you do not set buffer parameters to a size that is either too large or too small.

Closely related to packet receive buffers are service processes. A *service process* is what handles and processes the packets containing requests for data, programs, and other service requests sent from network clients. To optimize the server's use of memory and its ability to handle service requests, you should monitor and modify the following communications parameters if needed:

- **Minimum Packet Receive Buffers.** Default setting is 128. This parameter must be set in **Startup.ncf**.
- **Maximum Packet Receive Buffers.** Default setting is 500. A busy server does better with a setting between 700 and 1,000.
- **Minimum Service Processes.** The allowed range is 10 to 500 (requests to be handled in a single group).
- **Maximum Service Processes.** The allowed range is 5 to 1,000.

To view these parameters, complete the following steps:

1. Load Monitor, if it is not already running.
2. Choose **Server Parameters** from the Monitor Available Options menu.
3. Choose **Communications**.
4. Scroll the window down until you find these specific parameters (see Figure 4-10).

FIGURE 4-10 Communications screen showing the Packet Receive Buffer and
Service Processes statistics.

NETWORK BOARDS, DISK DRIVERS, AND CONTROLLERS

There are two other communications-related issues which can effect network performance, and with which you should be familiar:

■ Network boards
■ Disk Drivers and Controllers

The network board is responsible for handling packet transmission between the workstation and the server. Through Monitor, the network board drivers provide statistics related to the network board. When monitored regularly, changes in these statistics can help you pinpoint potential communication problems.

Several network board statistics can be viewed using Monitor. For example, you can view the "Receive discarded, no available buffers" statistic. This statistic tells you how many packets were simply ignored (dropped) because there was no available buffer space where they could wait their turn to be processed. When a packet is dropped due to lack of buffer space, the workstation that sent the packet must resend the packet and hope that it either gets processed immediately, or that there is now some available buffer space in which it can wait to be processed. (The resend is handled automatically; the user does not have to actually resend the request themselves.)

If this statistic is very high (greater then than two percent of total packets received), you should consider:

■ Increasing the number of packet receive buffers;
■ Upgrading the server for greater processing capabilities; or
■ Both

Disk drivers (the software which ensures that the disk controller or host bus adapter can communicate with the hard disk) and controllers can also affect network performance. Access to the hard disk can only occur as quickly as the disk driver and controller can handle it. To maximize performance in this area, consider using high-end disk drivers and controllers. For example, consider using advanced disk controllers capable of using bus-mastering and 32-bit technology if your server is not already using them.

Chapter Summary

Working with the NetWare 5 console involves four main tasks, each of which were discussed in this chapter:

- Understanding and Customizing ConsoleOne
- Setting up Remote Access to the Console
- Accessing the Console from a Workstation
- Using the Monitor NLM at the Server

ConsoleOne is a GUI (Graphical User Interface) utility that runs at the NetWare Server console. It has two main window panes. From the left window pane you choose the view, and from the right window pane you choose the file or object with which you want to work.

To run ConsoleOne from a workstation, map a drive to **Sys:public\ mgmt**, and launch **Console1.exe**. Then, using ConsoleOne, you can perform several basic administrative tasks, including:

- Editing server configuration or regular text files
- Renaming files
- Copying files
- Deleting files

In addition to using ConsoleOne to view the network and to edit and manage configuration or other files, you can also use it to perform the following network management tasks:

- Access this server's text-based console screens
- Access other servers' consoles
- Administer NDS from the server console

You can also set up remote access to the console to make your workstation look as though you were sitting at the file server console, with the same result. Before you can access the file server console from a remote workstation, however, you must set up the server to accept remote console access. This requires that you load the **Rconag6.nlm** file on the file server whose console you want to remotely access. Then you can run the **Sys\public\Rconj.exe** file from a workstation to access the file server's console.

Using **Rconj.exe** requires that you know the address of the server to which you want to connect, as well as the remote console password that was set for this server when you loaded the **Rconag6.nlm** into that server's RAM.

You can also access the server console remotely when running across an Asynchronous modem. The server must be running:

- **Remote.nlm**
- **Aio.nlm**
- **Rspx.nlm**
- **Rs232.nlm**

You can also access the server just from a workstation on the local network. Either way, the PC must be running **Rconsole.exe**. Once you access the server, either remotely or from the server's console, you can then use utilities such as Monitor to view several different statistics related to this server. These statistics provide you with general information about the server and its performance. If needed, you can then use Monitor as well as SET commands in **Autoexec.ncf** or **Startup.ncf** to set read and write caching parameters, as well as to review and set various communications-related parameters.

Monitor's general statistics which make it possible for you to check on the server's performance can be viewed both on the main Monitor screen (General Information), as well as on other screens which you access through the different options found on Monitor's main menu.

In addition to the name of the server, the version of NetWare running on this server, and the name of this NLM, the following statistics are provided on Monitor's initial screen (in the General Information area):

- **Utilization.** Tells what percentage of the processor's capacity is currently being used.
- **Server up time.** Specifies how long the server software has been running since the last time it was started.
- **Online processors.** Identifies how many processors this file server has.
- **Original cache buffers.** Shows how many blocks of memory were set aside to be used for file caching (temporary storage of files in server memory until they can be processed or permanently stored on the hard disk) when the server was first started.
- **Total cache buffers.** Indicates how many buffers are currently available for file caching.
- **Dirty cache buffers.** Specifies how many buffers are currently being used to hold data that has not yet been stored on the hard disk.
- **Long term cache hits.** Shows how many times the system was able to find requested data already in RAM instead of having to access the hard disk to retrieve it.

- **Current disk requests.** Shows how many requests for access to the hard disk are waiting to be processed.
- **Packet receive buffers.** Number of buffers available for holding requests received from clients until the processor is ready for them.
- **Directory cache buffers.** Indicates how many buffers are currently available for directory caching.
- **Maximum service processes.** Specifies how many task handlers have been set aside to handle processing requests from workstations.
- **Current service processes.** Specifies how many workstation requests currently exist.
- **Current connections.** Lists the current number of server connections (licensed and unlicensed).
- **Open files.** Shows how many files are currently open for use by the server and workstations combined.

Two other important uses for the Monitor NLM include setting read and write caching parameters, and reviewing and setting communications-related parameters. You can set several parameters. For example, to improve server performance when users make lots of small write requests, consider changing the following parameters using either Monitor or the SET command (put into **Autoexec.ncf** to make the changes permanent):

- Dirty Disk Cache Delay Time
- Dirty Directory Cache Delay Time
- Maximum Concurrent Disk Cache Writes
- Maximum Concurrent Directory Cache Writes

You can also view statistics for and set parameters associated with network boards as well as disk drivers and controllers. Network board statistics are important because the network board is responsible for handling packet transmission between the workstation and the server. When statistics are monitored regularly, changes in these statistics can help you pinpoint potential communication problems. Modifying the following network board related parameters can help maintain the health of your network:

- Increasing the number of packet receive buffers;
- Upgrading the server for greater processing capabilities; or
- Both

Disk drivers (the software which ensures that the disk controller or host bus adapter can communicate with the hard disk) and controllers can also affect network performance. Access to the hard disk can only occur as quickly as the disk driver and controller can handle it. To maximize performance in this area, consider using high-end disk drivers and controllers. For example, consider using advanced disk controllers capable of using bus-mastering and 32-bit technology if your server is not already using them.

Practice Test Questions

1. Expanding the My Server object in ConsoleOne allows you to see all of the following except:
   a. Volume objects
   b. Tools object
   c. Configuration files
   d. Deleted files

2. Which utility allows you to edit or rename files from the server console?
   a. ConsoleOne
   b. Remote Console
   c. Monitor
   d. None of the above

3. Of the following, which is *not* a network management task you can perform using ConsoleOne?
   a. Access the server's text-based console screens
   b. Access other server's console
   c. Backup a user's workstation
   d. Administer NDS

4. The two tools with which you can access a NetWare server from a remote location are:
   a. RconsoleJ
   b. ConsoleServer
   c. Remote Console
   d. Console Manager

5. The NLM you must load at the server in order to access it from a remote location is:
   a. Remote
   b. Rconag6
   c. Monitor
   d. ConMan

6. To access other server's consoles, you must:
   a. Ensure Monitor is loaded on each of the other servers
   b. Run Monitor from your workstation
   c. Load **Rconag6.nlm** on each of the other servers
   d. Load **Rconag6.nlm** only on the server from which you are accessing the other server's consoles

7. Which of the following NDS objects cannot be created using ConsoleOne at a server?
   a. Group
   b. Organization
   c. Organizational Unit
   d. Alias

8. Which two can you use to customize ConsoleOne's interface?
   a. Folders
   b. Shortcuts
   c. Snap-ins
   d. Java files

9. Two utilities you run from NetWare Administrator in order to access and take control of a NetWare 5 server console are:
   a. RconsoleJ
   b. Remote Console
   c. ConsoleOne
   d. Monitor

10. To establish an IP connection and remotely control a server's console, which two items of information do you need to supply?
    a. IP address
    b. Server's name
    c. Password
    d. Configuration information

11. Which is *not* required when remotely accessing a server from an asynchronous modem?
    a. RconJ.exe
    b. Remote.nlm
    c. Aio.nlm
    d. Rspx.nlm

12. To run ConsoleOne from a workstation you must:
    a. Load **RconJ.exe** on the server
    b. Map a drive to **sys:public\mgmt** and run **Console1.exe**
    c. Load **Startup.ncf** on the server
    d. None of the above

13. You can use _____ to view caching parameters.
    a. Monitor
    b. RconJ
    c. ConsoleOne
    d. Rconsole

14. The parameter which identifies how many blocks of memory were set aside to be used for temporary storage of files in server RAM is:
    a. Utilization
    b. Long term hits
    c. Original cache buffers
    d. Packet receive buffers

15. The parameter which identifies how many times the system found the requested data in server RAM is:
    a. Utilization
    b. Long term hits
    c. Original cache buffers
    d. Packet receive buffers

Answers to Practice Test Questions

1. d	9. a, b
2. a	10. a, c
3. c	11. a
4. a, d	12. b
5. b	13. a
6. e	14. c
7. d	15. b
8. b, c	

CHAPTER 5

Understanding and Establishing Network Printing

NetWare 5 supports NDPS (Novell Distributed Print Services) as well as the original queue-based printing services which shipped with earlier versions of NetWare. In this book's companion, the *Accelerated NetWare 5 CNA Study Guide*, NDPS printing is discussed. This chapter provides you with an understanding of queue-based printing, and how to set it up and manage it.

This chapter discusses how to set up a network printing environment using Print Queue, Printer, and Print Server objects. It also discusses printing hardware set up, how to regulate print services, and how to manage print jobs.

Understanding Network Printing

This chapter covers queue-based printing. Queue-based printing is centered around the idea that print jobs are submitted to a print queue (a storage area on a NetWare server) where they wait until they are sent to the specified printer to be printed. To take advantage of queue-based printing, your network needs to have its related components set up and made accessible to users.

Components of queue-based printing include:

■ Printing objects

- Print servers
- Printers

Figure 5-1 shows how the components of queue-based printing function to provide network print services.

As with several aspects of NetWare, you must set up and enable queue-based printing before your network users can take advantage of it. Then, you must continue to manage your network's printing services and work with print jobs as needed.

Setting Up Network Printing

Setting up queue-based network printing requires that you perform three basic tasks:

- connecting printers to the network
- creating and configuring printing objects
- activating printers

Connecting Printers to the Network

Before users can access network printers, the printers themselves must be physically (as well as logically) connected to the network. Physical connection requires that a cable be attached to each printer, and that the printer's cable then be attached to the network in one of the following ways:

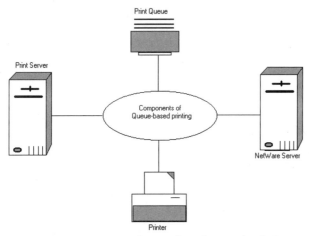

FIGURE 5-1 Components of queue-based network printing.

- to a Windows 95 workstation attached to the network
- to a NetWare server attached to the network
- to a print server attached to the network
- directly connected to the network

The physical connection, however, is not enough to make a printer accessible to network users. The printer must also have a logical connection, which means that appropriate software must be set up, configured, and running so that a logical connection to the printer is established.

The type of software that must be running and configured depends on how the printer is connected to the network. For example, if the printer is connected to a Windows 95 workstation which is itself connected to the network, then the workstation must have the **Nptwin95.exe** software running on it.

KEY CONCEPT

Logical printer connections are established by loading the appropriate software on the related device. For a printer attached to a print server or to any NetWare server to have a logical connection, the print server or NetWare server must have **Nprinter.nlm** loaded and configured. A printer attached to a Windows 95 workstation requires that **Nptwin95.exe** be running on the workstation. A printer connected directly to the network requires that its own print server software be running.

Before establishing the logical connection, the printer must be physically attached to the network in one of the four ways mentioned. Then, a printer object must be created in NDS. Once those two tasks are accomplished, you can establish the logical connection by activating the print server software and running Nprinter as needed. This section discusses how to connect and configure the four types of printer connections (two of which share the same procedure—printers connected to print servers and printers connected to NetWare servers). The section titled "Creating and Configuring Printing Objects" explains how to create a printer object in NDS.

CONNECTING AND CONFIGURING A PRINTER ATTACHED TO A WINDOWS 95 WORKSTATION

To connect a printer to a Windows 95 workstation, you physically attach the printer's cable to the workstation's parallel printing port. You then configure the printer to make it available to the network by completing the following steps:

1. Create a Printer object in NDS, and configure it as Manual Load (also called Remote). See the section titled "Creating and Configuring Printing Objects" for instructions on how to complete this step.

2. Load the print server software on the print server that will supply this printer with jobs to be printed.

3. Run **Nptwin95.exe** on the workstation. Nprinter for Windows 95 runs, and the NetWare Nprinter Manager opens.

4. In the Add Network Printer window, select either the Printer object that you created in Step 1, or an alternative Printer object. That identifies this printer as being one to which the selected Printer object can send print jobs.

5. (Optional) To ensure this configuration is permanent and will be reestablished each time this workstation is restarted, click the **Activate printer when Nprinter Manager loads** check box.

CONNECTING AND CONFIGURING A PRINTER ATTACHED TO A NETWARE SERVER

To connect and configure a printer attached to a NetWare server that is not a print server, you physically attach the printer's cable to a printing port on the NetWare server. You then configure the printer to make it available to the network as follows:

1. Create a Printer object in NDS, and configure it as Manual Load (also called Remote). See the section titled "Creating and Configuring Printing Objects" for instructions on how to complete this step.

2. Load the print server software on the print server.

3. Load the network printer software on this NetWare server by typing **Nprinter ps_name printer_name**, replacing **ps_name** with the name of the print server, and **printer_name** with the name of the Printer object.

4. (Optional) To ensure that the network printer software is loaded on this NetWare server each time the server is restarted, put the `Nprinter ps_name printer_name` command in the NetWare server's **Autoexec.ncf** file.

CONNECTING AND CONFIGURING A PRINTER ATTACHED TO A PRINT SERVER

To connect and configure a printer attached to a print server, you physically attach the printer's cable to a printing port on the print server. You then configure the printer to make it available to the network by following these steps:

1. Create a Printer object in NDS, and configure it as Auto Load (also called Local). See the section titled "Creating and Configuring Printing Objects" for instructions on how to complete this step.

2. Load the print server software (**Pserver.nlm**) on the NetWare print server. **Nprinter.nlm** will then automatically load for any printer with the Location property set to Auto Load.

CONNECTING AND CONFIGURING A PRINTER ATTACHED DIRECTLY TO THE NETWORK CABLE

You use the printer's software to configure a printer which can be directly connected to the network cable. Thus, how you configure its software depends on the printer. Follow the instructions provided by the printer's manufacturer.

Creating and Configuring Printing Objects

There are two types of printing objects you must create in order to set up non-NDPS printing on your network:

- Print Queue
- Printer

The Print Queue object is one of the two types of printing objects you must create in order to set up non-NDPS printing on your network. (You must also sometimes create one or more Print Server objects, depending on how you configure your network printing, and whether you use the QuickStart utility to set up printing. The QuickStart utility is discussed later in this chapter.)

The function of the Print Queue object is to logically represent in NDS the print queue (storage location on a NetWare server where print jobs reside until they are sent to a physical printer). Figure 5-2 shows the relationship of Print Queue objects in NDS to other printing objects including Printer objects and Print Server objects.

Although there is only one type of NDS Printer object see (Figure 5-3), Printer objects can be configured in two different ways. The two resulting types of Printer objects are:

- Remote (manual load)
- Local (auto load)

A *remote printer* is one that is attached to either a Windows 95 workstation, or to a NetWare server that is not a print server. A *local printer* is one that is attached to a print server (a NetWare server with **Pserver.nlm** running on it). Thus, you create a Printer object configured for remote printing when the printer is attached to a NetWare file server or a Windows 95 workstation, and you create a Printer object configured for local printing when the printer is attached to a print server.

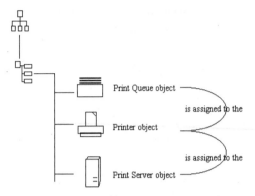

Print Queue object ⎤
                    ⎥ is assigned to the
Printer object   ⎥
                    ⎥ is assigned to the
Print Server object ⎦

FIGURE 5-2 The three non-NDPS printing objects in the Directory tree and how they relate to each other.

You must create and configure at least one Printer object when setting up non-NDPS printing services. You may need to create both types of printing objects, however, depending on how your printers are connected to the network.

CREATE A PRINT QUEUE OBJECT

When a network user requests that a document, graphic, etc., be printed, that print job request is sent to a print queue. From the print queue, the job is then sent to a printer. For the print queue to know where to send this particular print job request the print queue needs to know which printers it is allowed to print to. In addition, each Printer object

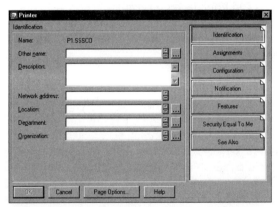

FIGURE 5-3 The Identification dialog for the Printer object P1.SSSCO.

you create needs to have at least one Print Queue from which it receives print jobs.

Just as with other objects in NDS, including Printer objects, you can create Print Queue objects using NetWare Administrator. To do this, run NetWare Administrator then complete the following steps:

1. Right-click the container object into which you want to place the Print Queue object when it is created.
2. Click **Create**. A list of classes of objects you can create is displayed.
3. Scroll through the list until you find the Print Queue object, then select it.
4. Click **OK**. The Print Queue object information screen opens.
5. Provide a name for the Print Queue and identify which volume the Print Queue is to use to store print jobs when it receives them.
6. Click the check box next to **Define Additional Properties** to enable this option, then click **Create**. The Print Queue object's Identification page displays.
7. Provide any additional information about this Print Queue object that you want to provide on this Identification page. For example, you might want to identify whether new print servers can attach to this print queue in order to service available print job requests.
8. (Optional) Click any of the other associated page tabs (Assignments, Operator, Users, etc.) and provide related information. For example, click the **Users'** page tab to identify which users can submit jobs to this print queue.
9. Click **OK** to close this Print Queue's properties pages and create the Print Queue object in the Directory tree.

To see the Print Queue object you just created in the Directory tree, you must collapse and then expand the container in which you created this Print Queue object.

When creating a Print Queue object, there are two properties considered to be critical (required before the Print Queue object can be created): the Print Queue object's name, and the volume on which the print queue directory will reside.

KEY
CONCEPT

CREATE AND CONFIGURE A REMOTE PRINTER OBJECT

If you have network printers that are attached either to a Windows 95 workstation or to a NetWare server that is not a print server, you must create and configure a remote Printer object. To create and configure a remote Printer object, open the NetWare Administrator utility, then complete the following steps:

1. Right-click the container object where you want this Printer object to reside. A limited menu of options opens (see Figure 5-4).
2. Click **Create**. A list of classes of objects you can create is displayed.
3. Scroll through the list until you find the Printer (non NDPS) object, then select it.
4. Click **OK**. The Printer object information screen opens.
5. In the Printer Name field, type a name for this new Printer object.
6. Click the check box next to **Define Additional Properties** to enable this option, then click **Create**. The Printer object's Identification page displays.
7. Click **Configuration**. The Configuration page opens.
8. Provide the needed information for this Printer object, specifically identifying the Printer Type (Parallel, Serial, etc.).
9. Click the **Communication** button on the configuration page. The Communication dialog opens.
10. In the fields provided, identify the Port and Interrupts being used by this printer.
11. Set the Connection type to **Manual Load (Remote from Print Server)**, then click **OK**.
12. Click the **Assignments** page tab. The Assignments page opens.
13. Click **Add**, then double-click the Print Queue object you created to assign that print queue to this Printer object.
14. Click any other page tabs to open the associated page, configure or modify any current settings, then click **OK** when you have configured the Printer object to meet your network's needs. The Printer object is created.

To see the remote Printer object you just created in the Directory tree, you must collapse then expand the container in which you created this Printer object.

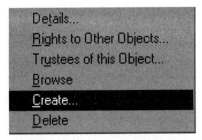

FIGURE 5-4 The menu from which you choose to create an object after right-clicking the container into which the new object is to be placed.

KEY
CONCEPT

Whether you create a remote or local Printer object, there are several items of information which are considered to be critical properties of the Printer object. Those critical properties are: Printer Type (Parallel, Serial, etc.), Printer Port (LPT or COM), Interrupts, and Connection Type (Auto Load or Manual Load).

CREATE AND CONFIGURE A LOCAL PRINTER OBJECT

If you have printers on your network that are attached to a print server (a NetWare server with **Pserver.nlm** running on it), you must create and configure one or more Local printing objects. To create and configure a Local printer object, Open the NetWare Administrator utility, then complete the following steps:

1. Right-click the container object where you want this Printer object to reside. A limited menu of options opens.
2. Click **Create**. A list of classes of objects you can create is displayed.
3. Scroll through the list until you find the Printer (non NDPS) object, then click to select it.
4. Click **OK**. The Printer object information window opens.
5. In the Printer Name field, type a name for this new Printer object.
6. Click the check box next to **Define Additional Properties** to enable this option, then click **Create**. The Identification page for this Printer object displays.
7. Click **Configuration**. The Configuration page opens (see Figure 5-5).
8. Provide the needed information for this Printer object, specifically identifying the Printer Type.
9. Click the **Communication** button on the configuration page. The Communication dialog opens.
10. In the fields provided, identify the Port and Interrupts being used by this printer.
11. Set the Connection type to **Auto Load (attached to the Print Server)**, then click **OK**.
12. Click the **Assignments** page tab. The Assignments page opens.
13. Click **Add**, then double-click the Print Queue object you created to assign that print queue to this Printer object.
14. Click any other page tabs to open the associated page, configure or modify any current settings, then click **OK** when you have configured the Printer object to meet your network's needs. The Printer object is created.

To see the local Printer object you just created in the Directory tree, you must collapse then expand the container in which you created this Printer object.

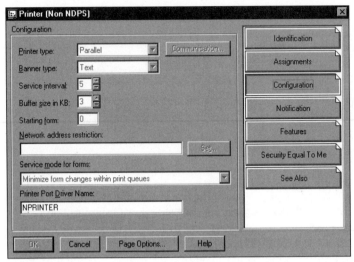

FIGURE 5-5 Sample Configuration property page for a Non-NDPS Printer object.

Activating Print Servers

A print server's primary function is to take print jobs that have been placed into print queues and send them to the network printer for which they are destined. The print server's primary benefit is that it lets you physically locate printers anywhere on the network, so that printer access is convenient for the network users rather than for the server containing the print queue.

Before you can take advantage of print servers, they must be activated. Activating print servers simply requires that you load and configure the print server software on a NetWare file server. To activate a print server, load the **Pserver.nlm** into RAM on the NetWare server you want to have as the print server.

In addition to creating Printer and Print Queue objects in the Directory tree, you also create Print Server objects. To create a print server object, complete the following steps:

1. With NetWare Administrator running, right-click the Organization or Organizational unit where you want to create the Print Server object, then click **Create**. The New Object dialog opens displaying a list of objects you can create.
2. Scroll the list until you find Print Server, then double-click it. The Create Print Server dialog opens.

3. Type a name (47 characters or less, all upper case) for this Print Server object into the Print Server Name field.

4. Click the **Define Additional Properties** box, then click **Create**. The Print Server Identification property page opens.

5. Click **Assignments** to add printers to the print server, click **Add**, then select the Printer object you want to add, and click **OK**.

6. Provide the needed information in the Print Server Identification and other property pages, then click **OK**. The Print Server object is created.

To view the Print Server object you just created in the Directory tree, collapse and then expand the container into which you created the Print Server object.

KEY CONCEPT

There are two critical Print Server properties, information for which you must provide before the Print Server object can be created: the Print Server object's name, and the names of the Printer objects it manages.

Enabling Network Printing

Setting up network printing requires that you create Print Queue, Print Server, and Printer objects, and that you load and configure the appropriate files on servers or workstations, depending on where your network's printers are connected. NetWare 5 also provides a quick method by which you can enable basic network printing: the Print Services Quick Setup option in NetWare Administrator.

When you run the Print Services Quick Setup option in NetWare Administrator, it creates the NDS print services objects you need on your network, and configures the basic properties associated with these objects as needed for setting up a function printing environment on your network. When run, Quick Setup:

- creates each printing services object the network needs for a simple, basic network set up (Print Queue, Printer, and Print Server)
- provides a default name for each printing services object it creates
- adds the Print Queue object it creates to the list of print queues for the Printer object it creates
- adds the Printer object it creates to the list of printers in the Print Server object it creates
- provides default information for the Printer object's printer type, connection type, interrupt, and port.

Setting up printing services using the Quick Setup is functional if you have a small network with only one printer. However, you still may have to change some of the properties that the Quick Setup program implements by default. For example, you may need to identify different interrupt and port numbers for the Printer object if the default does not match the actual printer's defined properties. In addition, if you want to use more than one print server, printer, or print queue, you will still have to create additional printing services objects. You may also need to rename the printing services objects that Quick Setup created.

To quickly enable printing on your network using the Print Services Quick Setup option in NetWare Administrator, complete the following steps:

1. Click the container into which you want all printing services objects created, then click **Tools** on the menu bar. The Tools menu opens (see Figure 5-6).
2. Click **Print Services Quick Setup (Non-NDPS)**.
3. In the fields provided, type in names for the Print Server and Printer objects.
4. Select a printer type, then provide additional printer information when prompted.
5. Provide a name for the Print Queue object, and then specify on which volume the print queue will reside.
6. Click **Create**. The associated printing services objects are created in the current container, and the printer is associated with the print server.

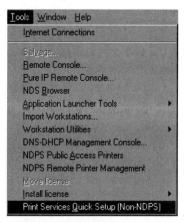

FIGURE 5-6 The Tools menu, showing the option you choose to run QuickSetup.

**KEY
CONCEPT**

Quick Setup creates, configures, and names the first Print Server object as **PS_containername** (replacing *containername* with the name of the container into which the Print Server object is placed when it is created). It names the Printer object it creates **P1**, and the Print Queue object it creates **Q1**. When it creates the Print Queue object, it uses the first volume in the current container it finds as the volume on which the print queue is to reside. Also, if a Print Server object already exists in the current container when you run Quick Setup, it adds the Printer object it creates to the same context as the existing print server. In addition, if you have run Quick Setup before and a Printer object already exists, it names the second Printer object it creates as **P2**, the third as **P3**, and so on.

The major drawback associated with using Quick Setup, besides the fact that default object names are not very descriptive, is that some objects created by Quick Setup cannot be edited at all. In addition, of those objects which can be edited, some object properties of those objects cannot be edited.

Setting Up Printing Service Assignments

Whether you use Quick Setup or the traditional method to set up your network printing, one thing you must consider is which users will have what rights and related printing services assignments. There are six basic printing services assignments you can give to users:

- Container Administrator
- Print Queue Operator
- Print Queue User
- Member of Printer Notify List
- Print Server Operator
- Print Server User

Each of these printing services assignments have certain rights and responsibilities associated with them. For example, if you want a user to be able to create, delete, or otherwise manage a Printer, Print Queue, or Print Server object, or to modify print queue or print server user and operator lists, they must be assigned as a container administrator. Other assignments and associated responsibilities are:

- **Print Queue Operator.** Can modify print queue assignments, operator flags, and print jobs in the print queue.

- **Print Queue User.** Can only use the print queue to which they are assigned, and modify their own print jobs once they have sent them to the print queue.
- **Member of the Printer Notify List.** Can receive printer error messages.
- **Print Server Operator.** Can modify the printer's Notify list and printer status, and can bring down the print server.
- **Print Server User.** Can receiver printer error messages and monitor the print server, but cannot make any modifications to the print server.

KEY CONCEPT

By default, when a Print Queue object is created, the user who created it is given the assignment of Print Queue Operator and Print Queue User. In addition, they are a user of the Print Queue's parent container. Also by default, when a Print Server object is created, the user who created it is given the assignment of Print Server Operator, and becomes a user of the Print Server's parent container.

Managing Network Printing

To manage printing on your network requires that you manage these three major areas:

- Print queues
- Print servers
- Printers

When you manage print queues, you manage work flow, print jobs in each print queue, and access to the print queue. When you manage print servers, you manage the print server's status, who has rights to use and control each print server, and you unload the print server software to bring down the print server when needed. When you manage printers, you manage the status of the printer as well as any error messages and the correction of the associated problem.

Managing Print Queues

Managing Print Queues means that you are responsible for three major tasks, each of which require you to perform one or more associated tasks. The three major tasks of print queue management are:

- managing work flow
- managing print jobs
- managing print queue access

MANAGING WORK FLOW

Work flow refers to the print jobs which enter the print queue and are eventually sent to a printer for servicing, unless something interferes with that process while a print job is in the print queue. You can affect a print queue's work flow by:

- stopping print jobs from entering the print queue
- preventing new print servers from using the print queue
- managing a print job once it is in the print queue

Stopping print jobs from entering the print queue and preventing new print servers from using the print queue are both done by setting Operator flags associated with the print queue. To prevent jobs from being submitted to the print queue, click the box next to the Allow users to submit print jobs operator flag. To prevent new print servers from using the print queue, click the box next to the Allow new print servers to attach operator flag. You can also prevent print jobs from being sent to printers by clicking the box next to the Allow service by current print servers operator flag. In addition, you can control who is allowed to send print jobs to the queue, as well as who is allowed to manage print jobs in the print queue.

MANAGING PRINT QUEUE ACCESS

Part of managing print queues is managing who accesses which print queues. Accessing print queues can mean either submitting or managing a user's own print jobs, or having another authorized user act as the print queue operator with the right to manage all jobs in the print queue.

To control who is allowed to send print jobs to the queue, complete the following steps:

1. Start the NetWare Administrator utility, then locate the Print Queue object for the print queue whose access you want to manage.
2. Double-click the **Print Queue** object. The Print Queue object's Identification page opens.
3. Click **Users**. The Print Queue object's Users page opens.
4. For those users who you want to allow to add print jobs to this print queue, add their User objects to the list of users, then click **OK**.

You may want users other than just yourself to help manage printing on your network. You can assign users as operators to manage print jobs in print queues. To assign users as print queue operators (manage who can control the print queue), complete the following steps:

1. Start the NetWare Administrator utility.

2. Locate the Print Queue object for the print queue whose access you want to manage.
3. Double-click the **Print Queue** object. The Print Queue object's Identification page opens.
4. Click **Operators**. The Print Queue object's Operators page opens.
5. For those users who you want to allow to manage print jobs in this print queue, add their User objects to the list of Operators, then click **OK**.

Managing Print Jobs

In addition to controlling who can send print jobs to a print queue and who can manipulate and manage print jobs in the print queue, you can also manage the print jobs themselves. Once a print job has been sent to a print queue, you can:

- change its print sequence (order within the print queue)
- delete it from the print queue
- put it on hold so that it does not print until you allow it to
- modify the print job's attributes

To perform any of these management tasks, you begin by:

1. Starting the NetWare Administrator utility, then locating the Print Queue object for the print queue whose print jobs you want to manage.
2. Double-clicking the **Print Queue** object. The Print Queue object's Identification page opens.
3. Clicking the **Job List** properties page button. The Job List properties page opens.

You then perform different steps depending on the type of management task you want to perform. If you want to change the print sequence of a job within the print queue, click and drag the job whose sequence you want to change from its current location in the list of print jobs to the location (order in the sequence) in which you want it to be placed.

If you want to delete a print job from the print queue:

1. Select the job you want to delete.
2. Click **Delete**.
3. Confirm the deletion of the print job.

If you want to put a print job on hold so that it does not print until you remove the hold:

1. Click to select the job you want to place on hold.
2. Click **Hold Job**.
3. View information about the job you placed on hold by clicking **Job Details**. The Print Job Detail dialog opens, and a check exists in the Operator hold check box.

To remove the hold, click the box next to Operator hold. The job will then be printed as soon as it becomes the first print job in the print queue.

A print job's attributes are those items of information associated with the print job when it was submitted to the print queue. For example, a print job's attributes can include the size of the file, a description of the print job, the name of the client (usually a user's name) who submitted the print job, whether a banner (page identifying the print job and its client) is to be printed before the print job, and a variety of other information. Although you may not be able to modify all attributes of a print job, if you want to modify one or more of a print job's attributes, choose the attribute you want to modify, then make the appropriate changes.

For example, to make sure the user is notified when the print job has finished printing, click the **Notify Print Job Owner** box on the Print Job Notification property page (see Figure 5-7).

You can also simply view details about any print job by selecting the print job in the Job List page for the print queue, then clicking **Job Details** to open its associated Print Job properties pages.

Managing Print Servers

Managing print servers also means that you are responsible for handling three major tasks, each of which may require you to perform one or

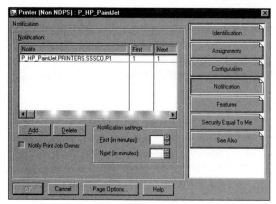

FIGURE 5-7 The Printer object's Notification property page.

more associated tasks. The three major tasks of print server management are:

- controlling print server status
- bringing down the print server
- managing print server user and operator assignments

CONTROLLING PRINT SERVER STATUS

There are several items of information related to the print server that you can view in order to determine the status of the print server. For example, you can see what version of the print server software the print server is using, whether the print server is currently running or if it is down, how many printers it supports, and what name the print server has been assigned.

To view this information, use NetWare Administrator as follows:

1. Locate the container where the Print Server object exists.
2. Double-click the **Print Server** object. The Identification property page for the Print Server object opens.
3. View the information about this Print Server object that you want to view, then click **OK** or **Cancel** to close the Print Server object's details.

BRINGING DOWN THE PRINT SERVER

Bringing down the print server means that you unload the print server software. There are two ways to bring down the print server: from the NetWare server console or by using NetWare Administrator.

To bring down the print server from the NetWare server console, at the server console prompt type **Unload Pserver**, then press **Enter**. To restart the print server, type **Pserver** at the console prompt, followed by the name of the print server, including its context. The syntax is: **Pserver [.CN= printservername. OU=container.O= container]**.

To bring down the print server using NetWare Administrator, follow these steps:

1. Locate the container where the Print Server object exists.
2. Double-click the **Print Server** object. The Identification property page for the Print Server object opens.
3. Click the **Unload** button and follow the prompts. The Print Server object is unloaded, and the print server is brought down.

Managing Print Server User and Operator Assignments

As with print queues, you can manage which users can access the print server, and which users can manage the print server. To specify which users can use the print server, complete the following steps:

1. Start the NetWare Administrator utility.
2. Locate the Print Server object for the print server whose access you want to manage.
3. Double-click the **Print Server** object. The Print Server object's Identification page opens.
4. Click **Users**. The Print Server object's Users property page opens.
5. For those users to whom you want to grant access to this print server, add their User objects to the list of users, then click **OK**.

You can also assign users as operators to manage print servers. To assign users as print server operators (users who can manage the print server), complete the following steps:

1. Start the NetWare Administrator utility.
2. Locate the Print Server object to which you want to assign users as operators.
3. Double-click the **Print Server** object. The Print Server object's Identification page opens.
4. Click **Operators**. The Print Server object's Operators page opens.
5. Determine the users who you want to allow to manage this print server, add their User objects to the list of Operators, then click **OK**.

Managing Printers

Managing printers has only two major tasks associated with it:

- controlling printer status
- managing printer error messages

Controlling Printer Status

Controlling printer status means that you review important information about the printer to ensure it is up and running and correctly processing print jobs. The Printer Status window lets you view the printer information. In addition to being able to see whether the printer is active, you can also verify whether the printer is connected, and if it is out of paper. You can also make printer status changes to an active printer.

For example, you can mount specific forms such as payroll checks, or change the service mode for forms. You can also:

- choose whether to use form feed
- choose whether to mark the top of the form
- stop, pause, or restart the printer
- abort a print job that is currently running

Managing Printer Error Messages

When the printer experiences a problem such as being out of paper, needing the toner cartridge replaced, or having a paper jam, it sends out an error message. For the printer to know who it should send the error message to, you have to configure the Printer object's notify list.

You assign users to the Printer object's notify list using NetWare Administrator as follows:

1. Start the NetWare Administrator utility.
2. Locate the Printer object to which you want to assign users to be notified when a problem occurs.
3. Double-click the **Print Server** object. The Print Server object's Identification page opens.
4. Click the **Notify List** property page button. The Notify List page opens.
5. Add users to the list of users to notify in the event of a printer error, then click **OK**.

Chapter Summary

NetWare 5 supports NDPS (Novell Distributed Print Services) as well as the original queue-based printing services that shipped with earlier versions of NetWare. This chapter discussed how to set up a non-NDPS network printing environment using Print Queue, Printer, and Print Server objects. It also discussed printing hardware set up, how to regulate print services, and how to manage print jobs. (In this book's companion, the *Accelerated NetWare 5 CNA Study Guide*, NDPS printing is discussed.)

Before users can access network printers, the printers themselves must be physically as well as logically connected to the network. Physical connection requires that a cable be attached to each printer, and that the printer's cable then be attached to the network in one of the following ways:

- to a Windows 95 workstation attached to the network
- to a NetWare server attached to the network
- to a print server attached to the network
- directly connected to the network

Logical printer connections are established by loading the appropriate software on the related device. For a printer attached to a print server or to any NetWare server to have a logical connection, the print server or NetWare server must have **Nprinter.nlm** loaded and configured. A printer attached to a Windows 95 workstation requires that **Nptwin95.exe** be running on the workstation. A printer connected directly to the network requires that its own print server software be running.

There are two types of printing objects you must create in order to set up non-NDPS printing on your network:

- Print Queue
- Printer

In addition, you may also have to create a Print Server object. Whether creating a Print Queue, Printer, or Print Server object, you can create these objects using NetWare Administrator. You create these objects the same way you create any other objects in NDS, by completing the following steps:

1. Right-click the container into which you want to place the object, then click **Create**.
2. From the Class of new objects list displayed in the window that opens, click the class of object you want to create (**Print Queue**, **Printer**, or **Print Server**), then click **Create**.
3. Follow the prompts and provide the needed information, then click **OK** to create the object and place it into the NDS tree.
4. Update the view of the NDS tree to show the new object by collapsing and then expanding the container into which you put the object.

Some items of information associated with each of the three types of printing objects is considered to be critical information. Unless you provide the critical information, the object cannot be created.

When creating a Print Queue object, there are two properties considered to be critical: the Print Queue object's name, and the volume on which the print queue directory will reside. Whether you create a remote or local Printer object, there are several items of information which are considered to be critical properties of the Printer object. Those critical properties are: Printer Type (Parallel, Serial, etc.), Printer Port (LPT or COM), Interrupts, and Connection Type (Auto Load or Manual Load). There are two critical Print Server properties: the Print Server object's name, and the names of the Printer objects it manages.

Practice Test Questions

1. Which of the following is *not* a component of queue-based printing?
   a. Printers
   b. Print Servers
   c. Print Queues
   d. NDPS Printers

2. Which three tasks are part of setting up queue-based network printing?
   a. Connecting printers to the network
   b. Creating an NDPS Printer object
   c. Creating and configuring printing objects such as Print Queues
   d. Activating printers

3. Printers can be connected to all of the following except which one if they are to be accessed by users on the network?
   a. Windows 95 workstation
   b. NetWare server
   c. Stand-alone Windows 95 computer
   d. Print Server

4. To access a printer attached to a Windows 95 workstation, which file must you run at the workstation?
   a. **Nptwin95.exe**
   b. **Win95npt.exe**
   c. **Pserver.nlm**
   d. None of the above

5. To connect and configure a printer attached to a NetWare server that is not a print server, you must create a Printer object in NDS and configure it as:
   a. Manual load
   b. Auto load
   c. Local
   d. None of the above

6. The print server software you load on a print server is:
   a. **Nprinter.nlm**
   b. **Nprinter.exe**
   c. **Pserver.nlm**
   d. **Pserver.exe**

7. A remote printer is defined as:
   a. Attached to a print server
   b. Attached to a workstation
   c. Attached to a NetWare server not acting as a print server
   d. Both A and B
   e. Both B and C

8. A local printer is defined as:
   a. Attached to a print server
   b. Attached to a workstation
   c. Attached to a NetWare server not acting as a print server
   d. Both B and C
   e. Both B and C

9. On which property page do you identify which users are allowed to submit jobs to a print queue?
   a. Operators
   b. Identification
   c. Users
   d. Associations

10. Which two are considered critical when creating a Print Queue object?
    a. Name
    b. Volume
    c. Users
    d. Operators

11. Which is *not* considered a critical Printer object property?
    a. Printer port
    b. Printer Type
    c. Interrupts
    d. Volume

12. What is a print server's primary function?
    a. To collect print jobs to be sent directly to the printer
    b. To send print jobs from the queue to the printer
    c. To activate network printing
    d. To order print jobs for processing

13. Which two are considered to be critical properties of the Print Server object?
    a. Printer's physical location
    b. Print Server object's Name
    c. Printer objects it manages
    d. Print Queue objects it manages

14. Which of the following is *not* a true statement regarding Print Services Quick Setup?
    a. It is run from NetWare Administrator
    b. All printers are named P# (with # being replaced by a numeric)
    c. It cannot be used if more than one printer exists on the network
    d. Some of the properties of the objects it creates cannot be modified

15. By default, when a Print Queue object is created, the user who created it is given the assignment of:
    a. Print Queue User
    b. Print Queue Operator
    c. Print Queue Manager
    d. Only A and B
    e. Only B and C

Answers to Practice Test Questions

1. d
2. a, c, d
3. c
4. a
5. a
6. c
7. e
8. a

9. c
10. a, b
11. d
12. b
13. b, c
14. c
15. d

CHAPTER 6

Enabling Remote Network Access

N etWare 5 provides two remote access options: Novell Internet Access Server (NIAS) and Remote Authentication Dial In User Service (RADIUS). Using NIAS or RADIUS, remote users can access the network and the services it provides.

Before a remote user can access the network through a NIAS or RADIUS server, however, the network administrator must have completed several remote access design and configuration tasks. Before designing and configuring NIAS or RADIUS, you may find a basic understanding of these remote access protocols to be useful. Therefore, this chapter provides you with information to help you understand what NIAS and RADIUS are, as well as to help you properly set up and configure your network for remote access using NIAS and RADIUS.

Understanding NIAS

NIAS is a remote access protocol you install and configure on a NetWare 5 server. With NIAS, you can have multiple modems connected to a server which then provides remote users with all the network services they need across a secure connection. NIAS runs on a NetWare 5 server and requires only 5 MB of server memory to run.

Once loaded and configured, NIAS makes it possible for remote users to have access to virtually all of the same network services they would be able to access if they were working from a local workstation instead of from a remote computer configured for NIAS access. Remote access is slower than direct connection to the network of course, because voice lines were not designed to carry data. The connection also isn't as secure as direct connection either, and it can be much more costly. However, properly configuring NIAS can help to reduce some of the drawbacks of remote access versus direct connection.

Understanding RADIUS

RADIUS (Remote Authentication Dial-In User Service) is a remote-access protocol that lets users access a NetWare network through an Internet Service Provider (ISP). It requires that a RADIUS host (proxy) server and a RADIUS accounting server exist.

A RADIUS proxy server is a server that runs the RADIUS protocol, and which stores and retrieves the dial-in user and authentication information from a central database. Through their ISP, users connect to the RADIUS proxy server, which then makes it possible for them to ultimately connect and remotely authenticate to the NDS tree on their company's network.

A RADIUS accounting server verifies that the remote user attempting to access the network through the RADIUS proxy server at an ISP is a valid user with rights to remotely access the network. Once the validity of the user is established, the RADIUS accounting server then logs user connection information and grants the remote connection. The RADIUS accounting not only logs information about the user's dial-in connection, but stores it so that it can be made available when needed for statistical analysis, troubleshooting, and billing purposes.

With RADIUS, you do not have to have modems attached to a NetWare server. You can outsource all of the dial-in hardware to an Internet Service Provider (ISP). Users then access the network from a remote location using the ISP they have contracted for Internet access services.

With RADIUS, you only have to provide a host server to run the RADIUS protocol so that information about remote user's dial-in connections can be logged. The ISP provides a RADIUS proxy which intercepts requests by remote users for network access, and forwards that request to the RADIUS server on your network.

RADIUS provides other benefits besides those discussed above, including:

■ Speedy and reliable access to network resources, and with NetWare 5, more flexibility for users in how they access the network.

- Security, authorization, and accounting services that allows for authentication as well as configuration information detailing the type of service to deliver to the user (SLIP, PPP, Telnet, rlogin, etc.).
- Centralized point of authentication (verifying user name and password) and authorization to access or administer network resources.
- Fewer management tasks since the RADIUS server relies on NDS to authenticate users, there is one less directory to manage, one less point of failure, and one less directory and user account to manage.

Whether you choose to implement remote access using NIAS, RADIUS, or both, you must first prepare to enable remote access to your company's network. As the Novell NetWare 5 Advanced Administration course concentrates more on NIAS than on RADIUS, so too does this chapter.

Preparing to Enable Remote Network Access

Just as you would not simply walk into a dealership, lay down your hard earned cash for a car, and drive it off the lot before determining your own automotive needs, you should not contract for or install and configure remote access to your network without first determining the needs of your remote-access users. Determining your remote-access user's needs is part of assessing the current network environment, and an integral part of the process of establishing remote access on your network.

To successfully prepare for remote-access implementation, there are three design tasks the network administrator must perform before configuring the network for remote access:

- Assessing the current environment
- Choosing a data transmission medium
- Designing security for remote access

Assessing the Current Environment

Before you configure your network and workstation, you must determine where to locate the NIAS remote access server (if you will be using NIAS), or the RADIUS accounting server (if you will be using RADIUS). Part of determining where to locate the server should be decided by the needs of the network's remote users. Thus, you must also determine the remote user's needs for network access and services.

You must also check to ensure the server on which you plan to load NIAS or RADIUS has sufficient space for the NIAS software, and that it has sufficient routing and WAN links to handle the increased network traffic. In addition, because NIAS and RADIUS software can be loaded on existing NetWare 5 servers, you should consider which server is most strategically located to minimize the expenses associated with having users remotely connect to the server.

When using NIAS, you need to know where to locate the server modems to provide the best remote access capability. You will also need to know how many remote users to support, as the number of modems required will be effected by that information. In addition, you need to know how many simultaneous accesses the NIAS server will have to handle, whether there is an anticipated increase in the number of users expected to access the server, and which users and groups will need remote access.

Choosing a Data Transmission Medium

How users obtain access to the remote server is another important pre-installation decision you need to make. There are three common data transmission options from which to choose:

- **ISDN (Integrated Services Digital Network).** ISDN replaces analog telephone service. You can purchase either the more common Basic Rate Interface (BRI) or the Primary Rate Interface (PRI) format. You can achieve a maximum rate of 128 KB with the BRI format. Using ISDN requires that you support a TA (Terminal Adapter) and a NT1 (Network Termination 1) device on the server and each workstation. Choose ISDN when fast access by remote clients is your primary concern.

- **POTS (Plain Old Telephone Services).** POTS are traditional voice lines, a good data transmission choice when keeping costs low is more important than speedy access, or when no other realistic telecom service is available. POTS can provide transmission speeds of up to 56 KB, although 33.6 KB is realistically the best speed at which communications will usually occur.

- **xDSL (Digital Subscriber Line).** The xDSL data transmission is a high-speed, more recent technology which works simultaneously with the existing copper twisted-pair telephone wire currently found in most homes and businesses. Unfortunately, the xDSL is not yet widely available, but where it is available, xDSL communications are normally dedicated point-to-point lines requiring no set up or dialing. There are three variations of xDSL communications: ADSL, HDSL, and "Splitterless" DSL. The first two offer a maximum of 8.192 Mbps and 1.544 Mbps transfer speed respectively, but require special hardware to utilize. The "Splitterless" DSL communication requires no special hardware, but offers a maximum transfer rate of 1 Mbps.

Before choosing a data transmission medium, also consider:

- which telecom (telephone) carrier (Local Exchange Carrier—LEC) is available
- whether the telecom provider can support remote access
- the cost of access
- what services (speed, bandwidth, etc.) the LEC will be able to provide

You should also consider the features of each of the commonly available data transmission options, and the most common situation you can expect to have to deal with when providing remote access to users.

Designing Security for Remote Access

Remote access is typically a less secure method of network access than is direct connection. This is primarily true because much of the remote access today is accomplished using POTS as the transmission media. This type of media is relatively easy to tap, and thus relatively unsecure. Remote access security can be improved, however, particularly if you consider the security risks associated with remote access at the time you design your network's remote access plan.

When designing remote access, consider that users want their access to be as quick and easy as possible. That is one of the reasons why the default security for NIAS is so minimal: any user on any properly-configured client can access any server from any valid port. You can plan and implement three aspects of security that will help make communications and data more secure on your network, while continuing to make remote access relatively painless for its users:

- Remote access security policies
- Secure network configurations
- Isolation and physical security of remote access servers

Both remote access security policies and secure network configurations can be developed by first gathering a variety of related information. You need to decide whether user access should be restricted or unrestricted, and if restricted, how restricted that access should be. For example, you need to decide whether you will restrict the locations from which remote users can access the server, limit the time of day and day of week within which remote users can access the server, and whether your password restrictions will be simple or complex (required encryption, required minimum length and number of days after which the password must be changed, and so on).

In addition, you may want to consider the data itself that will be moving across the communications media when a remote access session occurs. For example, you may choose to prevent certain files or programs on the server from ever being accessed from a remote client.

You may also want to use routing restrictions to limit access to the servers from remote users. But you will probably also want to consider limiting physical access to the network's remote servers as well. To limit physical access to remote servers, you need to find a location where the remote servers can be locked up. (This is a generally recommended security approach, even when the server is not running remote access software.)

If an unauthorized user does gain a connection to the remote server, the result does not have to be completely disastrous. If you design your remote access server security so as to prevent an unauthorized user from being able to access the entire network, or at least the critical components of it, you have provided another measure of network security.

You accomplish this by providing a screening router. A *screening router* filters remote access traffic, and either accepts the remote access traffic or rejects it based on security criteria that you establish. If the screening router rejects the remote access traffic, the traffic can get no further into your network than to the screening router. This is because the screening router sits between the remote access server and the rest of your network (see Figure 6-1).

NOTE

This philosophy of remote access security is known as creating a "demilitarized zone" security design.

Configuring Remote Network Access

Once you have gathered the needed information and planned how to implement remote access for your network, you can begin configuring remote network access. To configure remote access on your network you must complete the following tasks:

- Configure the NIAS server and Windows clients
- Maximize remote access performance

Configuring the NIAS Server and Windows Clients

You must enable both the NIAS server and the Novell Client for Windows 95 (or Windows NT) in order for users to be able to access the network from a remote location using NIAS.

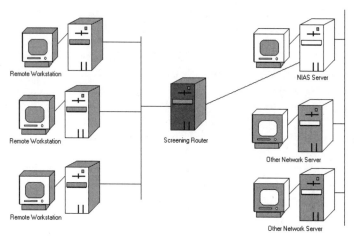

FIGURE 6-1 Diagram of how a screening router fits in with a security design for remote access.

ENABLE THE NIAS SERVER FOR REMOTE ACCESS

To enable the NIAS server to support remote access, you must:

- Install the communications hardware
- Configure the NIAS server software

KEY CONCEPT

Installing the NIAS server communications hardware requires that you attach communication devices such as modems to the server that will be running the NIAS server software, and that you connect those modems to allow them to access the communications media you chose. As the server communication hardware for RADIUS is the responsibility of the ISP, you do not have to install any separate server hardware for the server running the RADIUS software.

Configuring the NIAS server software requires that you:

- Load and define an Asynchronous Input and Output (AIO) port
- Identify the communication device attached to the server
- Choose the remote services to run on the server
- (optional) Configure IP and IPX parameters
- Configure NIAS according to your network design

To load the NIAS software on the server, define the AIO port and set other NIAS configuration settings, and configure it to run according to the security design you chose. If necessary, bring down and power off the NIAS server, then connect and power on the modems, and restart the server. Then, complete the following steps at the NIAS server console:

1. Type **Niascfg.nlm** at the server console, then press **Enter** to load it.
2. When prompted, press **Enter** to transfer driver commands, then press **Enter** again.
3. Bring down and then restart the server.
4. Type **Niascfg.nlm** at the server console, then press **Enter** to load it.
5. Choose **Configure NIAS**, then choose **Remote Access**.
6. When prompted, authenticate to the NDS tree.
7. When prompted, choose **Yes** to read an overview of the configuration process, or **No** to skip reading the overview. If you choose **Yes**, you will have to press **Esc** to exit the overview information before you can continue.
8. Press **Enter** twice to begin the setup process.
9. When prompted with "Do You Have Any Synchronous Adapters?" choose **No** if configuring only asynchronous modems for remote client access. Otherwise, choose **Yes** and follow the prompts.
10. Press **Enter** to load the AIO port and define it.
11. Choose the Serial Port to which the modem is connected (Com#), then press **Enter**.
12. Follow the additional prompts to continue after the driver is loaded, and skip loading any additional AIO drivers.
13. When prompted to auto-detect the modem, press **Enter**. If your modem cannot be auto-detected, follow the prompts to manually configure the modem type.
14. Follow the prompts, providing information and pressing **Enter** as needed. In particular, choose **PPPRNS**, then choose **IP** and provide the following information, or make the appropriate selection when prompted:
    - A valid IP address and subnet mask
    - Enable Header compression
    - A client range for dynamic IP addressing, if your network uses dynamic IP addressing within a specified range
15. If necessary, press **Esc** then choose **Yes** to save IP address changes.
16. Choose **IPX**, provide a unique IPX address, and press **Enter**.
17. Press **Esc** then **Enter** to save the changes you made. A warning message is displayed indicating that the current configuration will be activated and all active connections lost.
18. When prompted, press **Enter**, then choose **Yes** to start this service now.
19. When prompted, choose **RAMA**, then choose **Yes** if you want to be able to manage this NIAS server using an SNMP-based utility.

20. Press **Esc**, read any information if provided, the press **Enter** to continue.

21. Choose **Configure Security**, then choose **Set User Remote Client Password Restrictions**.

22. Set those parameters you decided on when you determined what security you would implement on the NIAS server. The security parameters you can set are:

- **Enable Long Passwords.** Allows passwords up to 16 bytes to be used.

- **Maximum Invalid Login Attempts.** Specifies how many times a user can try to log in within a set period of time if they are using either an invalid User name, password, or combination.

- **Set User Remote Client Password.** Sets a password for users to use when they access the NIAS server. If you implement this password, each individual user does not have to use their password set up in NDS.

23. When you have set the security parameters you want to set, press **Esc** then choose **Yes** to save your security settings.

24. Set any other security parameters you want to set, then press **Esc** and **Yes** to save your settings.

Completing this setup configures the NIAS server to allow users to dial in and access the network from a remote location. The security parameters you set will be implemented to ensure the desired level of remote access security. Now that the server is prepared for remote access by clients, you need to set up the clients for remote access as well.

ENABLE THE WINDOWS CLIENT FOR REMOTE ACCESS

You can use Windows 95 and Windows NT workstations to remotely access the network and its services using NIAS. The Novell client software you load on these two types of workstations can interact with Windows Dial-up feature, making it possible for you to set the Novell client so that it uses Windows Dial-up to connect to the network. If this feature is available, the Windows Dial-up tab displays when you click the Advanced button on the login window (see Figure 6-2).

Setting up a Windows 95 and Windows NT client for remote access is very similar. The following steps show only how to set up a Windows 95 client.

1. Double-click the **My Computer** icon on the desktop, and open Control Panel.

2. Double-click **Add/Remove Programs**, then click **Windows Setup**.

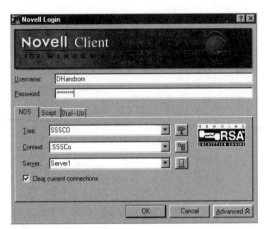

FIGURE 6-2 The Novell Client for Windows 95 login dialog showing the Dial-Up tab.

3. Double-click **Communications**, then click the check box for **Dial-Up Networking**, and click **OK**.
4. Click **OK** again. Windows copies the needed files to their appropriate location. (If prompted, insert the Windows 95 CD-ROM, then click **OK**.)
5. When Windows has finished copying files (close the Windows CD-ROM window if you had to insert the Windows 95 CD-ROM), locate and double-click **Dial-Up Networking** found in **Start > Programs > Accessories**, or close then reopen the My Computer window, then double-click **Dial-Up Networking**.
6. At the welcome screen, click **Next**.
7. Follow the prompts to have Windows auto-detect your modem and communications port, and finish setting up your modem, then click **Next**. (If auto-detect cannot locate your modem, you can configure it manually.)
8. When prompted, provide the telephone number of the NIAS server's modem, the name of the server you will be dialing in to, and other information as needed, clicking **Next** to move to other dialogs as needed.
9. Click **Finish**. A Dial-up server icon is created in the Dial-Up Networking folder. If you choose, you can move it to your desktop.
10. Right-click the **Dial-up server** icon, then click **Properties**.
11. Click **Server Type**. The Type of Dial-Up Server dialog opens.
12. Verify that the settings in the this dialog are as follows (see Figure 6-3), changing any settings if needed:

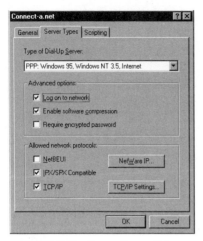

FIGURE 6-3 The Server Types dialog.

- **Type of Dial-up Server:** PPP: Windows 95, Windows NT 3.5, Internet
- **Advanced options:** Check those options you want to use
- **Allowed network protocols:** Check IPX/SPX Compatible and TCP/IP

13. Click the **TCP/IP Settings** button. The TCP/IP Settings dialog opens (see Figure 6-4).

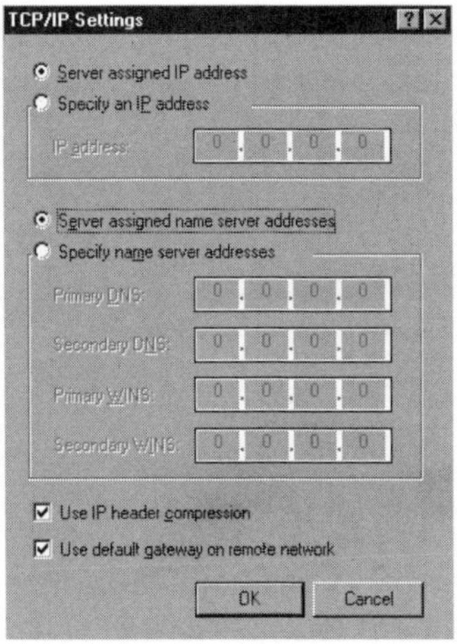

FIGURE 6-4 The TCP/IP Settings dialog.

14. Verify that both the **Use IP header compression** and **Use default gateway** boxes have a check in them, then click **OK**.

15. Click **OK** repeatedly until returned to the Dial-Up Networking window, then close it.

After performing these set up tasks, the Windows 95 workstation should now be able to establish a remote connection to your company's NIAS server.

Maximizing Remote Access Performance

Secure remote access is very important, especially for companies with sensitive data on their network. Of course, most companies have some sensitive data—payroll and employee records, for example—but other companies and government agencies may have data on their network that is so sensitive, letting even a small amount of it get into unauthorized hands can be extremely dangerous, even life-threatening. However, for those companies whose absolute top concern does not have to be extremely tight security, issues such as performance and cost of administration can be considered as well.

Maximizing performance can be done at both the client (workstation) and the server. Security is often less of an issue at the client, but performance frequently becomes an important issue.

MAXIMIZING REMOTE ACCESS PERFORMANCE AT THE WORKSTATION

Speed of access and data retrieval and storage are big issues for users who access the network from a remote location. By its very nature, remote access to the network is already substantially slower than access through a direct connection. The communications media and the modems themselves contribute heavily to the increased access time. Therefore, if you can maximize performance, your remote access users will be happier.

Typical remote access client performance issues (complaints) include:

- Slow login to the network once initial access is established
- Slow execution of applications, particularly ones such as databases which require heavy data transfer
- Slow file transfers
- Slow display of graphics, large data files, NDS information, and so on

To help ensure that the workstation's remote connections and the user's access to the network occur as quickly as possible, consider implementing the following suggestions for user's workstations:

- Reduce as much as possible the content of configuration files which must run when the user establishes a connection and requests access to the network. For example, make sure only those commands that absolutely must be run appear in the login script.

- Install applications directly to workstations when possible to reduce the number of applications the remote user has to run across the transmission media. For example, if remote users commonly access their email from their remote workstation, consider putting the email software on the workstation so that only the messages themselves have to be sent across the transmission media.

- Create Windows shortcuts at the remote user's workstation for commonly used remote servers and files on the network. Also, take as much advantage of the capabilities of Windows on each remote user's workstation as possible, reducing transfers across the communications media.

- Upgrade the hardware used to access the network including the modem, so that speed is as fast as possible. Where possible, also consider upgrading the communications media itself, even though you may have to find a different LEC.

- Copy frequently-used user files to the remote access user's workstation whenever possible. The user may want to have a docking notebook so that files can easily be taken from location to location.

- Teach users to expect slower performance and not jump ahead of the system. Sometimes in our impatience, users click, double-click, and click several more times, all the time adding to the slowness of the transmission, when all they really needed to do was to sit patiently and wait.

MAXIMIZING REMOTE ACCESS PERFORMANCE AT THE SERVER

To maximize remote access performance at the server, you can work to optimize both the server's hardware and the server's software (management). To maximize the server's hardware, consider implementing the following suggestions:

- Upgrade the server's memory and remote access device drivers to ensure that at least the minimum amount of memory and the most current drivers are available for each remote access server.

- Upgrade the server's CPU, or replace the remote access server with hardware which has greater CPU capacity.

- Upgrade the network's available bandwidth to ensure it successfully handles the maximum number of concurrent connections you anticipate on your network. (Pre-planning is very useful here.)

Proper administration of your remote access configuration can also help to optimize remote access performance. Administration falls into the following categories:

- **NDS.** Because NIAS supports NDS, you can use NDS and Novell's NetWare Administrator utility to manage remote users and groups through NDS. NIAS supports RAMA (Remote Access Management Agent), thus ensuring that any SNMP-based utility, such as ManageWise, can be used to monitor and manage NIAS servers.
- **Security.** You can place heavy restrictions on users and groups to increase remote-access security, or limit the restrictions you place on users and groups to reduce remote-access security. With NIAS, the default is limited security. If you choose to do so, however, you can add day, time, dial-in port, and protocol security restrictions.
- **IP or IPX.** Remote IP workstations need an IP address (valid at least until the remote access connection is broken, and supporting Dynamic Host Configuration Protocol), DNS service, and access to a gateway router, all of which are provided by the NIAS remote access server. If you prefer not to accept the configuration of these parameters that the NIAS remote access server can provide, you can manually configure each of these three parameters. IPX workstations require no special settings as addressing and routing are handled automatically.

Establishing a Remote Connection

When a user attempts to remotely access the user's company network using RADIUS, the following process occurs (see Figure 6-5 for a graphical representation of this process):

1. The remote user dials in to their ISP, providing their ISP User name and Password. (Companies with their own server capable of directly accessing the Internet can also act as their own ISP for their company's remote access users.)
2. Once connected to their ISP, the remote user provides their network User name and password.
3. The RADIUS proxy server on the ISP's network then sends the user's request for access to the RADIUS accounting server on the company's network.
4. The RADIUS accounting server verifies that this is a valid user with rights to remotely access the network, then grants the remote connection.

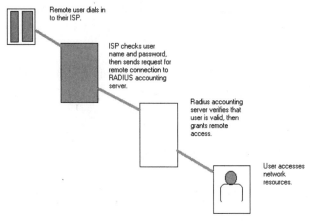

Remote user dials in
to their ISP.

ISP checks user
name and password,
then sends request for
remote connection to
RADIUS accounting
server.

Radius accounting
server verifies that
user is valid, then
grants remote
access.

User accesses
network
resources.

FIGURE 6-5 The remote access process that occurs when a user makes a remote connection to their network using RADIUS.

When the user attempts to access the network remotely using NIAS, the following process occurs:

1. The user at the remote workstation launches the dial-up software.
2. The dial-up software initiates the workstation's modem, obtains a dial tone on the outgoing line, then dials the number to the modem on the server.
3. The modem on the server answers the call (dial-in request), and requests authentication information from the workstation.
4. The dial-up software on the workstation provides the user name and password to the server.
5. The server verifies the user name and password, and authenticates the user to NDS.
6. Access to the network is granted, and the user can access any network data, programs, or services to which they have authorized access.

Chapter Summary

NetWare 5 provides two remote access options: Novell Internet Access Server (NIAS) and Remote Authentication Dial In User Service (RADIUS). Using NIAS or RADIUS, remote users can access the network and the services it provides.

NIAS is a remote access protocol you install and configure on a NetWare 5 server. With NIAS, you can have multiple modems connected to a server which then provides remote users with all the network services they need, across a secure connection. NIAS runs on a NetWare 5 server and requires only 5 MB of server memory to run.

RADIUS (Remote Authentication Dial In User Service) is a remote-access protocol that lets users access a NetWare network through an Internet Service Provider (ISP). It requires a RADIUS host (proxy) server and a RADIUS accounting server.

A RADIUS proxy server is a server that runs the RADIUS protocol. It stores and retrieves the dial-in user and authentication information from a central database. Through their ISP, users connect to the RADIUS proxy server, which then makes it possible for them to ultimately connect and remotely authenticate to the NDS tree on their company's network.

A RADIUS accounting server is a server that verifies the remote user attempting to access the network through the RADIUS proxy server at an ISP as a valid user with rights to remotely access the network. Once the validity of the user is established, the RADIUS accounting server then logs user connection information and grants the remote connection. The RADIUS accounting not only logs information about the user's dial-in connection, but stores it so that it can be made available when needed for statistical analysis, troubleshooting, and billing purposes.

To successfully prepare for remote-access implementation, there are three design tasks the network administrator must perform before configuring the network for remote-access:

- Assessing the current environment
- Choosing a data transmission medium
- Designing security for remote access

Assessing the current environment requires that you determine:

- where to locate the NIAS remote access server (if you will be using NIAS), or the RADIUS accounting server (if you will be using RADIUS)
- the needs of the network's remote users
- whether each server on which you plan to load NIAS or RADIUS has sufficient space for the NIAS software, as well as sufficient routing and WAN links to handle the increased network traffic
- which server is most strategically located so as to minimize the expenses associated with having users remotely connect to the server
- where to locate the server modems so as to provide the best remote access capability
- how many remote users you will have to support
- how many simultaneous accesses the NIAS server will have to handle

- whether there is an anticipated increase in the number of users expected to access the server
- which users and groups will need to have remote access

There are three common data transmission options from which to choose:

- **ISDN (Integrated Services Digital Network).** Integrated Services Digital Network replaces analog telephone service. You can purchase either the more common Basic Rate Interface (BRI), or the Primary Rate Interface (PRI) format. You can achieve a maximum rate of 128 KB with the BRI format.
- **POTS (Plain Old Telephone Services).** POTS are traditional voice lines, a good data transmission choice when keeping costs low is more important than speedy access, or when no other realistic telecom service is available. POTS can provide transmission speeds of up to 56 KB, although 33.6 KB is realistically the best speed at which communications will usually occur.
- **xDSL (Digital Subscriber Line).** The xDSL data transmission is a high-speed, more recent technology which works simultaneously with the existing copper twisted-pair telephone wire currently found in most homes and businesses.

Designing security for remote access involves planning and implementing three aspects of security to help make communications and data more secure:

- Remote access security policies define such issues as whether users will be restricted or unrestricted in the network access, whether some data or program files should be prevented from being transmitted across the data communications media, and whether to use routing restrictions to limit remote access to the server.
- Secure network configurations involves determining such issues as whether to establish a demilitarized zone for your network.
- Isolation and physical security of remote access servers includes determining and then implementing physical isolation of remote access servers to prevent unauthorized physical access.

Configuring remote access must be done once all the decisions are made and the necessary information gathered. Remote access configuration requires that you:

- Configure the NIAS server and Windows clients using **Niascfg.nlm** at the server and Dial-up networking at the client.

■ Maximize remote access performance can be accomplished at both the server and workstation. At the server, maximize remote access performance by upgrading the hardware most utilized by remote access: RAM, CPU, and bandwidth. At each workstation, you maximize performance by limited the number of commands in all login scripts that run for remote users, configure the workstation with shortcuts and locally installed applications whenever possible, copy data files locally to workstations, upgrade the workstation's hardware and the communications media it uses, and teach users to expect slower performance.

Once all planning, configuration, and performance improvements are made, users can then access the network from a remote location using RADIUS or NIAS, depending on the remote access setup implemented on your network.

Practice Test Questions

1. If your primary concern is speed of communication, which remote access data transmission medium is likely to be your best choice?
   a. ISDN
   b. POTS
   c. xDSL
   d. Either A or C
   e. Either B or C

2. Of the following, which is *not* an important consideration when designing remote access to your network?
   a. Assessing the current environment
   b. Choosing a data transmission medium
   c. Designing security for remote access
   d. Maximizing remote access performance
   e. The number of DOS workstations needing remote access

3. The data transmission medium readily available, rarely requiring special equipment, and reasonably affordable is:
   a. ISDN
   b. POTS
   c. xDSL
   d. Both A and C
   e. Both B and C

4. A filter designed to prevent unauthorized access to the rest of the network through a remote access server is called:

a. Specialty security

b. Remote access security server

c. Screening router

d. Screening server

5. Which three can you implement to help provide faster performance for remote users?

a. Minimal login scripts

b. Faster modems

c. More copies of frequently-used applications on the server

d. Copies of frequently-used files stored on user's workstations

6. Of the following, which is not a typical remote access client performance complaint?

a. Slow login to the network once initial access is established

b. Slow execution of applications

c. Slow file transfers

d. Short login scripts

7. Which of the following is not an aspect of security that can help make communications and data more secure on your network?

a. Remote access security policies

b. Secure network configurations

c. Isolation and physical security of remote access servers

d. Upgraded server CPU

8. Because NIAS supports NDS, you can use NDS to:

a. Manage remote users and groups through NDS

b. Implement IPX configuration manually

c. Create shortcuts on user's workstations

d. None of the above

9. To limit access to the servers from remote users, you can:

a. Accept the default security restrictions set by NIAS

b. Use routing restrictions

c. Use RADIUS instead of NIAS for remote access

d. Require an ISP user name and password when using NIAS

10. Which of the following is the optional NIAS server software configuration step?
    a. Load and define an Asynchronous Input and Output (AIO) port
    b. Configure NIAS according to your network design
    c. Configure IP and IPX parameters
    d. Choose the remote services to run on the server

11. Proper administration of your remote access configuration involves each of the following categories except:
    a. SNMP
    b. NDS
    c. Security
    d. IP or IPX

12. Which three of the following are found on the Server Types dialog used to set up a Windows 95 client for remote access?
    a. Advanced options
    b. Allowed network protocols
    c. Server name
    d. Log on to network

13. Which of the following security parameters is *not* set during the NIAS server configuration?
    a. Enable Long Passwords
    b. Maximum Invalid Login Attempts
    c. Type of Dial-Up Server
    d. Set User Remote Client Password

14. If you want to be able to manage the NIAS server using an SNMP-based utility, which option must you choose during NIAS server configuration?
    a. TCP/IP
    b. RAMA
    c. PPP
    d. Internet

15. The remote access security approach that ensures traffic can get no further into your network than to the screening router is known as:
    a. Demilitarized zone
    b. Buffer zone
    c. Screening zone
    d. Security zone

Answers to Practice Test Questions

1. d	9. b
2. e	10. b
3. b	11. a
4. c	12. a, b, d
5. a, b, d	13. c
6. d	14. b
7. d	15. a
8. a	

CHAPTER 7

Understanding and Using DNS and DHCP Services

A dministering TCP/IP can be quite time-consuming. DNS and DHCP are services provided by Novell to simplify administration of the TCP/IP protocol on a NetWare 5 network. Both of these services function to make TCP/IP administration easier for network administrators.

While installation and configuration of DNS and DHCP are covered in separate sections of this chapter, the discussion of these two services is combined as their purpose and much of their functionality is similar. Therefore, the first section of this chapter provides an understanding of DNS and DHCP, comparing and contrasting the two services.

Understanding DNS and DHCP

DNS (Domain Name System) and DHCP (Dynamic Host Configuration Protocol) have been integrated into NetWare 5's NDS to provide centralized and enterprise-wide management of IP (Internet Protocol) network addresses and host names. You use DNS to meet IP's requirement that every machine on the network have its own unique IP address, and yet still meet the user's need for a simple way to locate computers—by name instead of IP address (referred to as *hostname-to-IP address mapping*).

While DNS uses a database system to provide hostname-to-IP address mapping, DHCP uses the client-server model and provides the needed configuration parameters so that a successful connection can be made to Internet hosts. You use DHCP to simplify the process of providing the needed name and address information for each network computer so that locating other machines (hosts—clients or servers) on the network is automatic. Through DHCP, initialization parameters that assist in establishing the host- to-host connection are provided (see Figure 7-1).

How DNS/DHCP Works

When you access a Web site on the Internet, you either go through your company's server with an Internet connection, or through an ISP (Internet Service Provider). The connection you make when you request access to a Web site is to a server referred to as a *master name server* (also called a *primary name server*). The master name server can be one of your company's Web servers, or the ISP's Web server.

The master name server is responsible for taking a user's name-based (host name) request for a Web site (such as **www.novell.com**), and translating that name into the corresponding IP (Internet Protocol) address for the server (such as **123.45.678.910**). The master name server can accomplish this task because it stores configuration information in a file using a special format known as BIND (Berkeley Internet Name Domain).

 Host names have been a part of the Internet since its earliest days. For years the only way Internet computers could locate each other was by looking up the computer's host name in a database that had to be regularly downloaded from the Network Information Center.

NOTE

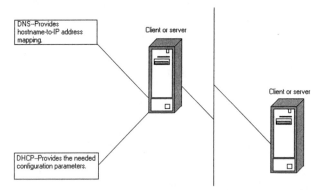

FIGURE 7-1 Diagram of how DNS and DHCP help simplify and centralize the administration and management of IP network addresses and hostnames.

As the number of computers on the Internet grew, this flat-file host-name database became cumbersome, time-consuming, and quite difficult to replicate across the Internet. DNS and its Internet hierarchical naming scheme was developed in an attempt to solve these and other related problems.

While ISPs have master name servers so they can ensure that users have access to the Web sites they are seeking, your NetWare 5 server running DNS/DHCP can also be a master name server. When a NetWare 5 DNS/DHCP server functions as a master name server, it stores and updates the related configuration information in NDS. For a NetWare 5 server to be able to store and update DNS data in the Directory tree (in NDS), the NetWare 5 server must be a designated domain name server.

A domain name server is a NetWare 5 server that is assigned to service a DNS Zone object. A *DNS Zone object* is a container object in NDS that holds all of the data for a single DNS zone. A DNS zone is a *domain*—a hierarchy of Internet sites as identified by their Web site name, the highest level (top-level domain) of which is identified by the end of their Web site name such as .com, .edu, .org, and so on. Below the top-level domains are the subdomains represented by individual organizations (see Figure 7-2). A host's domain name is simply a list of all domains in the path from the host back to the root. For example, in the domain host name of **support.novell.com.**, the top-level domain is **com**, its immediate subdomain is **novell**, and novell's immediate subdomain name is **support**.

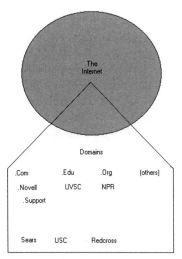

FIGURE 7-2 Graphical representation of domain naming.

As stated earlier, the master name server uses the BIND file to resolve domain names into IP addresses so that users can access the Web sites they requested: that BIND file is stored on a master name server. Therefore, without access to a master name server, your network users could not resolve host names, and thus could not access Internet Web sites.

Your network can have its own master name server, or it can depend on the master name server provided by an ISP. When your network does not have its own master name server and the master name server resides instead at the ISP's site, resolving host name addresses can be quite slow and subject to a greater number of errors. If your company does not have its own master name server but does have DNS/DHCP, your company can instead use a NetWare server with DNS/DHCP on it as a secondary name server. Even if your company does have its own master name server, it can also take advantage of having one or more secondary name servers on its network.

KEY CONCEPT

Having a secondary name server lets you take advantage of the speed and accuracy of access to a primary name server, even when the primary name server is not physically located close to your network users (or even on your company's network). The secondary name server's responsibility is to provide the same name-to-IP address resolution as the primary name server. You can have multiple secondary name servers on your network. Doing so ensures you always have at least one name server available to users for host-name-to-IP resolution. In addition, multiple secondary name servers placed at strategic physical locations on your network can greatly reduce the time it takes to resolve host names, prevent users from having to cross WAN links to accomplish hostname-to-IP resolution, and reduce the work load on any one NetWare server.

The secondary name server is responsible for contacting the master name server, retrieving updated database (BIND file) information, and in turn providing that updated database information to the copy (replica) of that database in the secondary DNS Zone object stored in your company's Directory tree. This design provides several important benefits:

- It ensures simple and quick access to Web sites by all of your network users as hostname-to-IP address resolution is done on a local server.
- It provides fault tolerance: if one server containing the hostname-to-IP address resolution information is unavailable, another server containing a replica of that information can provide it.
- It makes a current copy of the hostname-to-IP address always readily available as *zone transfers* (configuration updates to the replica of the

database on secondary name servers from primary name servers) are initiated each time a change in the database is detected. This occurs when the SOA—Start of Authority—serial number of the BIND master file is higher than that of the BIND file's replica.

- It provides load balancing for NDS, as multiple servers can simultaneously provide a current copy of the database for hostname-to-IP address resolution for multiple users.
- It applies all of the benefits of NetWare's NDS, as the information is part of NDS objects in the Directory tree.

To simplify the initial process of obtaining the BIND file information, you can import an existing BIND file using the **Import DNS Database** button in the DNS/DHCP Management Console.

KEY CONCEPT

As stated earlier, a designated server is a NetWare server that is assigned to service a DNS Zone object. Designated servers can be of two types: primary and secondary. If a NetWare server is designated to service a primary DNS Zone object, it is responsible for:

- Querying NDS to resolve host names into IP addresses
- Adding and deleting Resource Records
- Updating the zone serial number

If a NetWare server is designated to service a secondary DNS Zone object, it is responsible for:

- Receiving zone transfers from a master name server
- Storing the updated information it received in NDS

NDS then replicates the updated information throughout the network, thus ensuring that all users have access to the most current information.

DNS and DHCP Components

DNS consists of two specific components:

- The **hierarchy**, which identifies the structure, naming conventions, and delegation of authority used in the DNS service.
- The **name service**, which provides the mechanism for hostname-to-IP address mapping.

DNS's name service is the component that actually maps the host name to the IP address so computers can locate each other on a network. The name service uses a client-and-server setup in which client programs (resolvers) query one or more name servers for host address information. When a name server can't resolve a name because it does not have the needed domain information, the name server relays the request to other name servers up or down the domain hierarchy until it receives an authoritative answer to the client's query.

A group of domains and subdomains for which an organization has authority is called a *zone*. In traditional DNS, the one name server that maintains an authoritative database for an entire zone is called the *primary name server*, and the domain administrator updates it with host names and addresses as changes occur. *Secondary name servers* contain read-only copies of the primary name server's DNS database. Periodically, they receive a new copy of the primary's DNS database through a zone transfer.

DNS databases contain numerous blocks of data called resource records (RRs), some of which are:

- **Address (A).** Provides the IP address for the zone.
- **Name Server (NS).** Binds a domain name with a host name for a specific name server.
- **Start of Authority (SOA).** Specifies a server's zone of authority.
- **Canonical Name (CNAME).** Identifies the primary name of the owner.
- **Pointer (PTR).** Points to other records for looking up a domain name when the IP address is known.

DHCP also consists of two components:

- The protocol by which specific configuration parameters are sent from the DHCP server to a host (either client or server).
- The protocol by which network addresses are assigned to hosts. The protocol provides for three types of assignments: *Automatic Allocation* (the protocol assigns a permanent IP address to the host), *Dynamic Allocation* (the protocol assigns a temporary IP address which lasts as long as the host needs it), and *Manual Allocation* (the protocol delivers whatever IP address the network administrator manually assigns).

DNS and DHCP NDS Objects

You manage DNS/DHCP objects using the NetWare Administrator utility. You can do so because installing and configuring these services extends the NDS schema and adds the appropriate snap-in files and objects. When the NDS schema is extended during the installation of DNS/DHCP, five DHCP objects and four DNS objects become available in NDS:

■ Available DHCP objects

 DHCP Server

 Subnet

 Subnet Address Range

 IP Address

 Subnet Pool

■ Available DNS objects

 DNS Name Server

 DNS Zone

 Resource Record Set

 Resource Record

 In addition, three objects (DNSDHCP-GROUP, DNS-DHCP locator, and RootServerInfo zone) are automatically added to the Directory tree for you. Only one of each of these three types of objects can exist in any one NDS tree.

KEY
CONCEPT

The three objects automatically added to the Directory tree during the installation of DNS/DHCP and their purpose are:

 DNSDHCP-GROUP. This object works the same as other NDS Group objects (see Figure 7-3). You assign users as members of the DNSDHCP-GROUP object, any NetWare servers running

DNS and DHCP are automatically made members of this Group object, and this GROUP object is automatically made a trustee of each DNS or DCHP object that is created.

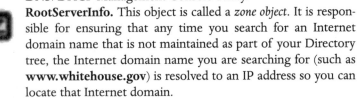

DNS-DHCP. This object is called a *locator object*. It contains global configuration information, DHCP options, and a list of all DHCP and DNS servers, subnets, and zones in the NDS tree. The DNS/DHCP Management Console uses this object to locate other DNS/DHCP objects in the Directory tree. Because this object cannot be configured, it does not display in the DNS/DHCP Management Console utility.

RootServerInfo. This object is called a *zone object*. It is responsible for ensuring that any time you search for an Internet domain name that is not maintained as part of your Directory tree, the Internet domain name you are searching for (such as **www.whitehouse.gov**) is resolved to an IP address so you can locate that Internet domain.

KEY CONCEPT

Once DNS/DHCP is installed, you can create, view, and manage DNS/DHCP objects in NDS using NetWare Administrator. However, management of these objects using NetWare Administrator is limited to performing such tasks as moving and deleting DNS/DHCP services objects. To configure those objects, you use a different utility called the *DNS/DHCP Management Console*. This utility is installed when you install DNS/DHCP, and can be launched as a separate utility on a workstation with at least 48 MB of RAM (64 is recommended) that has the Novell Client installed, or from within NetWare Administrator.

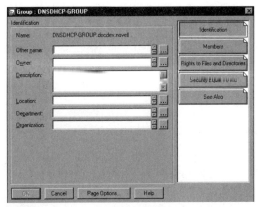

FIGURE 7-3 The DNSDHCP-GROUP Group Object's Identification page in NDS.

Installing DNS and DHCP

By default, all of the files you need to run DNS/DHCP are copied to either the **Sys:System** or **Sys:System\Public\DNSDHCP** directory on the NetWare 5 server when you install NetWare 5. Therefore, installing DNS/DHCP services means that you only have to run the server installation for it the same way you would for any other product being added, so that the NDS schema can be extended to allow for DNS and DHCP objects in the Directory tree. You must then also install the software needed to manage DNS/DHCP to a workstation.

Installing Server Software

There are three ways you can install DNS/DHCP services software on a NetWare 5 server. When you install the NetWare 5 server itself, you can click to check the **Novell DNS/DHCP Services** box in the Additional Products window. The NetWare 5 server installation will then also install Novell's DNS/DHCP Services. Alternately, you can install the DNS/DHCP software after the NetWare 5 server has been installed and is running using either the Install menu option in ConsoleOne, or by running a server utility called **Dnipinst.nlm**.

To install the DNS/DHCP server software using the Install menu option in ConsoleOne, complete the following steps from the console of the NetWare 5 server on which you want to run DNS/DHCP services:

1. In ConsoleOne, click **Novell**, then click **Install**. The Install utility loads, and a list of products already installed on this server is displayed.
2. Click **New Product**, provide the path to the INSTALL directory on this NetWare 5 server, then click **OK**. The Additional Products and Services window displays. (You can also complete this installation from another server on the network by browsing to the path for the files on the other server.)
3. Click the checkbox next to Novell DNS/DHCP Services, then click **Next**.
4. When prompted to authenticate to NDS, provide the user name and password for user Admin or for another user who has Supervisor object rights to the [Root] of the Directory tree, then click **OK**.
5. When prompted, provide the context within the Directory tree into which you want the Novell DNS/DHCP Services installation process to create the three default objects (DNSDHCP-GROUP, DNS-DHCP locator, and RootServerInfo zone), then click **Next**.

6. When the Summary window is displayed, review it, click **Finish**, then click **Yes** to reboot the server and implement DNS/DHCP.

To install the DNS/DHCP server software using **Dnipinst.nlm**, complete the following steps from the server console of the NetWare 5 server on which you want to run DNS/DHCP services:

1. Change the console display to the server console prompt (if a different screen is currently displayed), then type **Dnipinst** and press **Enter**. The Dnipinst.nlm loads.
2. When prompted to authenticate to NDS (see Figure 7-4), provide the fully distinguished user name and password for user Admin (or for another user who has Supervisor object rights to the [Root] of the Directory tree), then follow the prompts to login to NDS. For example, when the Admin User object resides at the SSSCO (highest) organization level in the SSSCO tree, you would type **.Admin.SSSCO** as the fully distinguished user name.
3. When prompted (see Figure 7-5), provide the context within the Directory tree into which you want the Novell DNS/DHCP Services installation process to create the three default objects (DNSDHCP-GROUP, DNS-DHCP locator, and RootServerInfo zone), then follow the prompts to create the objects.
4. When prompted, press **Enter** to close Dnipinst.nlm.

Installing Workstation Software

To run the DNS/DHCP Management Console, you must first ensure the workstation meets the minimum requirements for RAM (48 MB),

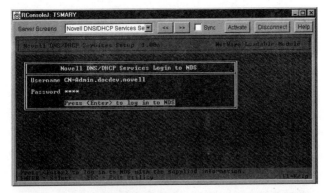

FIGURE 7-4 The Novell DNS/DHCP Services Login to NDS dialog.

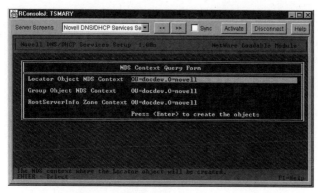

FIGURE 7-5 The NDS Context Query Form, into which you enter the fully distinguished name for each of the three objects this DNS/DHCP install creates.

and then you must install the required software: the NetWare 5 or later release of the Novell Client software and the DNS/DHCP Management Console software. Instructions for installing the Novell Client software come with the Novell Client. To install the DNS/DHCP Management Console software on a workstation, complete the following steps:

1. Log into your NetWare server as user Admin, and if one does not already exist, map a drive to the **Sys:\Public** directory on the NetWare server (right-click **Network Neighborhood**, then click **Novell Map Network Drive**).

2. Using My Computer, Explore, or Run on the Start menu, locate and run **Sys:\Public\Dnsdhcp\setup.exe**.

3. Install the DNS/DHCP Management Console to your workstation's hard disk.

4. Install the NetWare Administrator snap-in files to the same directory as the NetWare Administrator files (**Sys:\Public\Win32** is the default directory for the NetWare 5 NetWare Administrator files).

5. When all files have been installed, the DNSDHCP icon is added to the desktop.

6. If you want, double-click the **DNSDHCP** icon to verify that it opens the Launch Novell DNS/DHCP Management Console dialog. If you have any problems opening this dialog, reboot the workstation and try again.

Both the NetWare server and at least one workstation on the network are now capable of taking advantage of DNS/DHCP services, and managing related NDS objects.

Setting Up and Running DNS

To set up and run DNS requires that you first configure DNS. Next, start the DNS server. Once you have started the DNS server, you can then configure workstations to use DNS.

Configuring DNS

One of the important keys to successfully implementing DNS on your network is its proper configuration. Configuring DNS means that you:

- Create and configure a DNS Server object (to designate which server can respond to queries about the DNS zone)
- Create and configure a DNS Zone object (to create a container object in NDS to hold all of the data for a single DNS domain)
- Create and configure a Resource Record object (to store information about a single resource record)

Once you have completed these three DNS configuration tasks according to the instructions below, you must start the DNS server and configure workstations to use DNS.

CREATE AND CONFIGURE A DNS SERVER OBJECT

The purpose of creating and configuring a DNS Server object is to specify which server will respond to queries about the DNS zone. You create a DNS server object using the DNS/DHCP Management Console. Start this utility, then complete the following steps:

1. With the DNS/DHCP Management Console DNS Service tab open, click the **Create** button (see Figure 7-6). The Create New DNS Record dialog opens.
2. With DNS Server highlighted, click **OK**. The Create DNS Server dialog opens.
3. Browse to locate the server object you want to designate as the DNS server, then provide a Host Name (the DNS server's name) and a Domain name (the name of domain in which the DNS server will reside). Click **Define Additional Properties**, then click **Create**. Several related tabs open in the right window pane. The DNS Server you just created displays in the Zones tab under: **DNS Server Domain Name**.

You cannot take advantage of this DNS Server object's availability, however, until you start the DNS server (discussed later in this chapter under "Starting the DNS Server"). In the meantime, you need to create and configure a DNS Zone object and a Resource Record object.

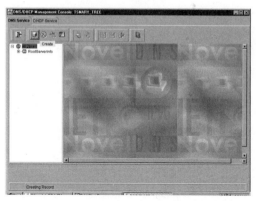

FIGURE 7-6 The DNS Service tab in the DNS/DHCP Management Console with the pop-up name of the Create button displayed.

CREATE AND CONFIGURE A DNS ZONE OBJECT

To create and configure a DNS Zone object, follow these steps:

1. With the DNS Service tab of the DNS/DHCP Management Console utility open, click the **All Zones** object in the left of the window pane. (If you just finished creating a DNS Server object before starting this procedure, the tabs that were displaying in the right window pane now close.)

2. Click the **Create** button. The Create New DNS Record dialog opens.

3. Click **Zone**, then click **OK**. The Create Zone dialog opens.

4. Choose the type of Zone you want to create: a standard DNS zone (choose **Create New Zone**), an IN-ADDR.ARPA zone, or an IP6.INT zone (only one of which can exist in the tree).

5. Modify the NDS context into which the Zone is to be placed if you do not want to put it into the context currently displayed.

6. Provide a name for the Zone and identify the zone as either a Primary or Secondary zone. If you choose Secondary zone type, the Zone name you provide must match the Zone name of the primary zone, and you must provide the IP address for the name server (primary zone) it will use for zone transfers.

7. Assign a server (existing DNS server or a new one to be defined) to service the zone so that the DNS zone object can be created. If assigning a DNS server that has not yet been created, it will be created. However, you must also provide the Host Name and Domain for the DNS server to be created.

8. Click **Define Additional Properties**, then click **Create** to create and configure this DNS Zone object.

9. You are notified that the DNS Zone object has been created, and prompted to create the resource record. Click **OK**. Two tabbed pages open in the right window pane of the DNS/DHCP Management Console.

CREATE AND CONFIGURE A RESOURCE RECORD OBJECT

To create and configure a Resource Record object when you have just finished creating and configuring a DNS Zone object, complete the following steps:

1. With the DNS Zone object you just created highlighted, click the **Create** button. The Create New DNS Record dialog opens.
2. Click **Resource Record**, then click **OK**. The Create Resource Record dialog opens.
3. Provide a name for this Resource Record in the Host Name field, choose the resource record type (**A**, **CNAME**, or **Others**), then fill in any other needed information and click **Create**.

Some of the more commonly available Resource Record objects from which you can choose are:

- **A.** This Resource Record maps names to IP addresses.
- **CNAME.** This Resource Record maps alias names to DNS names.
- **MX (mail eXchange).** This Resource Record maps SMTP mail addresses to domain names.
- **NS.** This Resource Record maps domain names to host names.
- **PTR.** This Resource Record maps IP addresses to host names within an IN-ADR.ARPA zone.

Resource Records cannot be modified. If you need to change configuration information in a Resource Record, you must delete the existing Resource Record and create a new one with the changed configuration.

KEY
CONCEPT

Starting the DNS Server

Now that you have created and configured the DNS Zone object and a Resource Record object, you can start the DNS Server. Once the DNS server is started, the DNS object at the bottom of the DNS/DHCP Management Console window no longer displays with a line through it.

To start the DNS server, type **Named** at the server console. Before you can configure workstations to use DNS, you must start the DNS server.

KEY
CONCEPT

Configuring Workstations to Use DNS

To configure a Windows 95 workstation to use your network's DNS server for name resolution, complete the following steps:

1. Right-click **Network Neighborhood**, then click **Properties**.
2. Click **TCP/IP**, then click **Properties**.
3. Click the **DNS Configuration** tab.
4. Click **Enable DNS**.
5. Type the name of your workstation into the Host field.
6. Type the domain name you configured in NDS into the Domain field.
7. Type your DNS server's IP address in to the DNS Server Search Order field.
8. Click **OK** to close the TCP/IP Properties dialog, then click **OK** to close the Network dialog.

To configure a Windows NT workstation to use your network's DNS server for name resolution, follow these steps:

1. Right-click **Network Neighborhood**, then click **Properties**.
2. Click the **Protocols** tab.
3. Click **TCP/IP protocol**, then click **Properties**.
4. Click the **DNS** tab.
5. Type the name of your workstation into the Host Name field.
6. Type the domain name you configured in NDS into the Domain field.
7. Click **Add**, then follow the prompts to add your DNS server's IP address to the DNS Server Search Order field.
8. Click **OK** to close the Microsoft TCP/IP Properties dialog, then click **OK** to close the Network dialog.

Setting Up and Running DHCP

To use DHCP services on your network, you must set up and run DHCP just as with DNS. The configuration setup to run DHCP is done using the DNS/DHCP Management Console. You used this same utility to set up DNS services on your network. The setup and configuration for DNS that was discussed earlier in this chapter had you launch the DNS/DHCP Management Console from the DNSDHCP desktop icon. However, the DNS/DHCP Management Console utility can also be launched from within the NetWare Administrator utility. Start the DNS/DHCP Management Console utility from NetWare Administrator, as follows:

1. Start the NetWare Administrator utility by running **NWAdmn32.exe** from the file server's **Sys:\system\public\win32 directory**.
2. Click **Tools** on the menu bar. The Tools menu opens.
3. Click the **DNS-DHCP Management Console** option on the Tools menu (see Figure 7-7). The DNS/DHCP Management Console utility starts.
4. Click the **Launch** button to open the main window for the DNS/DHCP Management Console utility.

Configuring DHCP

To configure DHCP, you create DHCP objects, open their associated configuration pages, then set the configuration as needed. To actually create and configure these objects, you use the DNS/DHCP Management Console utility. Before launching the utility and creating the objects, it is helpful to have a basic understanding of the DHCP configuration options available to you. This section discusses the configuration options first, then provides the procedure for you to follow in order to create and configure the needed DHCP objects.

DHCP CONFIGURATION OPTIONS

Configuring DHCP lets you set up two types of DHCP options: those that configure administration features (such as whether the DHCP server should ping an IP address to ensure it is not in use before it assigns the IP address), and those that deliver configuration information (such as a Preferred Server name and NDS context) to network workstations.

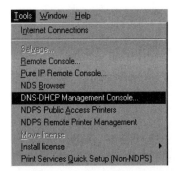

FIGURE 7-7 The Tools menu in NetWare Administrator showing the DNS-DHCP Management Console option, from which you can launch the DNS/DHCP Management Console utility.

Administrative options you can set (configure) on the DHCP Server object in the Options tab are:

- **Simple Network Management Protocol (SNMP) traps.** These options determine what types of DHCP server information can be monitored by management software.
- **Audit Trails and Alerts.** These options control the level of event and audit logging generated by the DHCP server.
- **Mobile Users.** These options let you configure how a workstation is dealt with if it is moved from one subnet to another.
- **Ping Enabled.** This option lets the server ping an IP address before it assigns it to ensure it does not assign a duplicate IP address and cause a conflict on the network.

Options you can set at the Subnet level are:

- **IP address preferences (from the Subnet Options tab).** This option lets you set the length of time a workstation can lease an IP address. The default is three days. If the subnet lease needs to be longer, you can lengthen this time, or make the assignment permanent.
- **BOOTP protocol (from the Subnet Options tab).** This option lets you configure DHCP to provide a *BOOTP workstation* (a workstation without a hard disk which must boot from a boot image file stored on a network server) with the server name, server address, and boot image filename the workstation can access to obtain a boot image.
- **Other DHCP options (from the Other DHCP Options tab).** Additional parameters are available for you to configure on the Other DHCP Options tab.

Configurations can be set to be either global (affecting all DHCP configurations in the NDS tree), or limited to a specified subnet.

KEY CONCEPT

Using the DNS/DHCP Management console, you can configure DHCP services. If your network already has version 2.0 of DHCP Services running on it, and you are upgrading to DHCP Services 3.0, you do not have to manually configure DHCP services. Instead, you can import the existing DHCP Services 2.0 configuration information into DHCP Services 3.0 by clicking the **Import DHCP Database** button in the DNS/DHCP Management Console utility, and providing the necessary information, including the location and name of the MAC address configuration file to be imported.

CREATE AND CONFIGURE DHCP OBJECTS

To configure DHCP using the DNS/DHCP Management Console, you create DHCP objects and configure them as needed. The objects you create and configure are:

- DHCP Server object
- Subnet object
- Domain Name Server
- Subnet Address Range

Because you create and configure these objects one after another inside the DNS/DHCP Management Console utility, the following procedure explains how to create and configure all the needed DHCP objects.

1. Start the DNS/DHCP Management Console utility if you have not already done so, then click the **HCP Service** tab to open the associated view.
2. Click the **Create** button, select **DHCP Server**, then click **OK**. The Create DHCP Server dialog opens.
3. Browse the directory tree to the container where the DNS/DHCP server object is located, select the server object, then click **OK**.
4. Click the **Define Additional Properties** check box on the Create DHCP Server dialog, then click **Create**. The DHCP Server object is created, and a page showing two tabs (Server and Options) opens.
5. Click the **Options** tab to open its associated page. Make changes to the options you want to configure. For example, under the Set SNMP Traps Option, click the **Major Events** radio button to capture relevant information when a major event occurs. When you have finished setting DHCP Server object options, continue with the next step.
6. Click the **Create** button, select **Subnet**, then click **OK**. The Create Subnet dialog opens.
7. Provide a name for this Subnet object, verify that the NDS context is correct (change it if it is not), provide the subnet address and subnet mask information for your server, change the Default DHCP Server if needed, click **Define Additional Properties**, then click **Create**. The Subnet object is created and an associated page with three tabs displays. The Subnet Options tab page is open by default.
8. Click to choose whether the Lease Type is to be Permanent or Timed. If Timed with a Lease Time of 3 days is sufficient for your network, leave the setting at its default.
9. Click any of the other two tabs (Addressing or Other DHCP Options), then set the configuration as needed for your network. For example, you can click **Other DHCP Options**, then click **Modify** to

open the Modify DHCP Options dialog. From there you can click **Router** and add an IP address for a Router, click **Domain Name Server** and configure a Domain Name Server address to be delivered to the workstations on the subnet, or click one of the other Available DHCP Options and configure it. When you have finished setting Subnet object options, click **OK** and choose **Yes** to save your changes.

You can change many more configuration options than the ones discussed here. If you want more information about configuring DNS/DHCP services on your network, use the **Help** button in any of the DNS/DHCP Management Console windows.

Starting the DHCP Server

Starting the DHCP server is as easy as starting the DNS server; the command is just different. To start the DHCP server, enter **DHCPSRVR** at the server's console prompt.

Configuring Workstations to Use DHCP

You can configure Windows 95 and Windows NT workstations to obtain an IP address from a DHCP server. To configure a Windows 95 workstation to obtain an IP address from a DHCP server, complete the following steps:

1. Right-click **Network Neighborhood**, then click **Properties**.
2. Click **TCP/IP**, then click **Properties**.
3. Click **Obtain an IP address automatically**.
4. If prompted to enable DHCP using an IP address that was already configure manually, click **Yes**.
5. Click **OK** to close the TCP/IP Properties dialog, then click **OK** to close the Network dialog.
6. Reboot the workstation.

To verify that the Windows NT workstation successfully obtains its IP address configuration information from a DHCP server, look for the IP address in the Winipcfg file. (To open the Winipcfg file, click **Run** on the Start menu, then type **Winipcfg** into the Open field, and click **OK**. Then click **More Info** in the IP Configuration window.)

To configure a Windows NT workstation to use your network's DNS server for name resolution, complete the following steps:

1. Right-click **Network Neighborhood**, then click **Properties**.

2. Click the **Protocols** tab.
3. Click **TCP/IP protocol**, then click **Properties**.
4. Click **Obtain an IP address from a DHCP server**.
5. If prompted to enable DHCP using an IP address that was already configure manually, click **Yes**.
6. Click **OK** to close the Microsoft TCP/IP Properties dialog, then click **OK** to close the Network dialog.
7. Reboot the workstation.

To verify that the Windows NT workstation successfully obtains its IP address configuration information from a DHCP server, look for the IP address in the Winipcfg file. (To open the Winipcfg file, click **Programs** on the Start menu, click **Command Prompt**, then type **Ipconfig /all** and press **Enter**. The IP Address should display.)

Chapter Summary

DNS and DHCP are services provided by Novell to simplify administration of the TCP/IP protocol on a NetWare 5 network. Both services function to make TCP/IP administration easier for network administrators.

DNS (Domain Name System) and DHCP (Dynamic Host Configuration Protocol) have been integrated into NetWare 5's NDS to provide centralized and enterprise-wide management of IP (Internet Protocol) network addresses and host names. You use DNS to meet IP's requirement that every machine on the network have its own unique IP address, and yet still meet the user's need for a simple way to locate computers—by name instead of IP address (referred to as *hostname-to-IP address mapping*).

When you access a Web site on the Internet, you go through your company's server with an Internet connection, or through an ISP (Internet Service Provider). The connection you make when you request access to a Web site is to a server referred to as a *master name server* (also called a primary name server). The master name server can be one of your company's Web servers, or the ISP's Web server.

The master name server is responsible for taking a user's name-based (host name) request for a Web site (such as **www.novell.com**), and translating that name into the corresponding IP (Internet Protocol) address for the server (such as **123.45.678.910**). The master name server can accomplish this task because it stores configuration information in a file using a special format known as *BIND* (Berkeley Internet Name Domain).

When a NetWare 5 DNS/DHCP server functions as a master name server, it stores and updates the related configuration information in

---

NDS. For a NetWare 5 server to be able to store and update DNS data in the Directory tree (in NDS), the NetWare 5 server must be a designated domain name server.

A domain name server is a NetWare 5 server that is assigned to service a DNS Zone object. A DNS Zone object is a container object in NDS which holds all of the data for a single DNS zone. A DNS zone is a domain—a hierarchy of Internet sites as identified by their Web site name, the highest level (top-level domain) of which is identified by the end of their Web site name such as .com, .edu, .org, and so on. Below the top-level domains are the subdomains represented by individual organizations. A host's domain name is simply a list of all domains in the path from the host back to the root. For example, in the domain host name of **support.novell.com.**, the top-level domain is **com**, its immediate subdomain is **novell**, and novell's immediate subdomain name is **support**.

Your network can have its own master name server, or it can depend on the master name server provided by an ISP. When the master name server resides at the ISP's site, resolving host name addresses can be quite slow and subject to a greater number of errors. If your company does not have its own master name server but does have DNS/DHCP, your company can instead use a NetWare server with DNS/DHCP on it as a secondary name server. Even if your company does have its own master name server, it can also take advantage of having one or more secondary name servers on its network.

Having a secondary name server lets you take advantage of the speed and accuracy of access to a primary name server, even when the primary name server is not physically located close to your network users or even on your company's network. The secondary name server's responsibility is to provide the same name-to-IP address resolution that the primary name server does. You can have multiple secondary name servers on your network. Doing so ensures you always have at least one name server available to users for hostname-to-IP resolution. In addition, multiple secondary name servers placed at strategic physical locations on your network can greatly reduce the time it takes to resolve host names, prevent users from having to cross WAN links to accomplish hostname-to-IP resolution, and reduce the work load on any one NetWare server.

Designated servers can be of two types: primary and secondary. If a NetWare server is designated to service a primary DNS Zone object, it is responsible for:

- Querying NDS to resolve host names into IP addresses
- Adding and deleting Resource Records
- Updating the zone serial number

If a NetWare server is designated to service a secondary DNS Zone object, it is responsible for:

- Receiving zone transfers from a master name server
- Storing the updated information it received in NDS

To take advantage of DNS/DHCP on your network, you must install the necessary server software and the necessary workstation software. Once DNS/DHCP is installed, you can create, view, and manage DNS/DHCP objects in NDS using NetWare Administrator. However, management of DNS/DHCP objects using NetWare Administrator is limited to performing such tasks as moving and deleting DNS/DHCP services objects. To configure those objects, you use a different utility called the DNS/DHCP Management Console. This utility is installed when you install DNS/DHCP, and can be launched as a separate utility on a workstation with at least 48 MB of RAM (64 is recommended) and which has the Novell Client installed, or from within NetWare Administrator.

By default, all of the files you need to run DNS/DHCP are copied to either the **Sys:System** or **Sys:System\Public\DNSDHCP** directory on the NetWare 5 server during the installation of NetWare 5. Therefore, installing DNS/DHCP services means that you only have to run the server installation for it the same way you would for any other product being added so that the NDS schema can be extended to allow for DNS and DHCP objects in the Directory tree.

There are three ways you can install DNS/DHCP services software on a NetWare 5 server. When you install the NetWare 5 server itself, you can click to check the **Novell DNS/DHCP Services** box in the Additional Products window. The NetWare 5 server installation will then also install Novell's DNS/DHCP Services. Alternately, you can install the DNS/DHCP software after the NetWare 5 server has been installed and is running using either the Install menu option in ConsoleOne, or by running a server utility called **Dnipinst.nlm**.

Regardless of the installation option you choose, you must create and configure the needed NDS objects to complete the installation. NDS objects which can be created are:

- DHCP Server
- Subnet
- Subnet Address Range
- IP Address
- Subnet Pool
- DNS Name Server
- DNS Zone

- Resource Record Set
- Resource Record

In addition, three objects (DNSDHCP-GROUP, DNS-DHCP locator, and RootServerInfo zone) are automatically added to the Directory tree for you, as only one of each of these three types of objects can exist in any one NDS tree.

All of the configuration you must do when installing DNS/DHCP services on your network is done through the DNS/DHCP Management Console utility. You can launch this utility through an icon on the desktop, or using the Tools menu in NetWare Administrator.

Once your configuration is complete, you must start the DNS or DHCP server, then configure user's workstations. To start the DNS server, type **Named** at the server console. To start the DHCP server, enter **DHCPSRVR** at the server's console prompt. To configure workstations, use Network Neighborhood on user's workstations.

Practice Test Questions

1. DNS and DHCP are services provided by Novell for what purpose?
   a. To make it possible for TCP/IP to exist on the network
   b. To allow an Internet connection from a NetWare 5 server
   c. To simplify TCP/IP protocol administration on a NetWare 5 network
   d. To make TCP/IP administration unnecessary

2. Which three objects are automatically created in NDS when you install DNS/DHCP services on the first server in the Directory tree?
   a. DNSDHCP-GROUP
   b. Start of Authority
   c. DNS-DHCP Locator
   d. RootServerInfo Zone

3. Which do you use to configure DNS/DHCP objects?
   a. DNS/DHCP Management Console
   b. DNS/DHCP Management Server
   c. ConsoleOne
   d. Both a and c
   e. Both b and c

4. To install DNS/DHCP, which right must you have?
   a. Supervisor object right to [Root]
   b. Supervisor object right to the DNS/DHCP Install object
   c. Supervisor property right to all properties in NDS
   d. Supervisor property right to the NDS Schema property

5. Which of the following methods *cannot* be used to install DNS/DHCP services on a NetWare 5 server?
   a. Dnipinst.nlm
   b. Dnipinst.exe
   c. ConsoleOne
   d. NetWare 5 server Install

6. Which server is responsible for translating a host name into a corresponding IP address?
   a. NetWare 5 server
   b. Master name server
   c. Domain server
   d. Zone server

7. What is another term for the highest-level domain on the Internet?
   a. Zone
   b. DNS
   c. Host
   d. Web site

8. For which three is the secondary name server responsible?
   a. Contacting the master name server
   b. Updating relicas of the hostname-to-IP address database
   c. Storing the original copy of the BIND file
   d. Retrieving the BIND file

9. What name is assigned to the blocks of records stored in a DNS database?
   a. Pointers
   b. Subnet Address Ranges
   c. Resource Records
   d. Subnet Pool

10. Which of the following is *not* one of the DNS objects made available when the NDS schema is extended during the installation of DNS?
   a. DNS Name Server
   b. Resource Record Set
   c. Resource Record
   d. IP Address

11. Which two are types of Resource Records?
   a. Zone
   b. A
   c. CNAME
   d. Subnet

12. To ensure DHCP does not duplicate an IP address when assigning it, which Administrative option can you set?
   a. SNMP Traps
   b. Mobile Users
   c. Ping Enabled
   d. Alerts

13. If you are importing a DHCP database from version 2.0 of DHCP to version 3.0, what type of file is it you will be importing?
   a. Subnet
   b. MAC
   c. DNS
   d. EXE

14. What is the minimum amount of memory a workstation requires in order to run the DNS/DHCP Management Console utility?
   a. 32 MB
   b. 48 MB
   c. 64 MB
   d. There is no minimum requirement

15. Which two of the following are designated server types?
   a. Zone Transfer
   b. BIND
   c. Primary
   d. Secondary

Answers to Practice Test Questions

1. c	6. b	11. b, c
2. a, c, d	7. a	12. c
3. a	8. a, b, d	13. b
4. a	9. c	14. b
5. b	10. d	15. c, d

CHAPTER 8

Installing and Configuring Netscape FastTrack and FTP Servers

I n Chapter 7, *Understanding and Using DNS and DHCP Services*, you were introduced to the Internet, and how it is structured into domains such as .com, .edu, and .gov, and subdomains. You also learned about the DNS/DHCP protocol, and how it makes it possible for you to locate Web sites by providing only their URL (Uniform Resource Locator)—the Web server's site name such as **www.novell.com**—and having it translated for you into an IP address that the Internet can use to locate the related Web server. (A Web server is software that runs on a computer which is physically connected to a TCP/IP-based network. The Internet is TCP/IP based.)

While DNS/DHCP is run on your own company's servers, it only provides the hostname-to-IP translation services. DNS/DHCP doesn't turn any of your NetWare 5 network servers into Web servers of their own, nor does it provide the ability to transfer files across the Internet. However, Netscape FastTrack Server for NetWare and Novell FTP Services for NetWare do provide these services, and both are discussed in this chapter.

Understanding the Internet, Netscape FastTrack Server, and FTP

Netscape FastTrack Server for Novell makes those documents and other files your company wants to publish on the Internet available to Internet users. Novell FTP Services for NetWare allows your company's users fast and easy access to published documents and other files on remote computers, across the Internet. Both of these services are Internet-centric. Therefore, if you don't already have a basic understanding of how the Internet works and of Internet terms such as HTTP, FTP, protocols, HTML, and others, you may find the section titled "Understanding the Internet" to be of some value. Otherwise, you may skip it (there are no specific questions on the NetWare 5 CNE exam about the Internet), and go on to the rest of this chapter. The rest of this first section in this chapter provides you with an understanding of Netscape FastTrack Server for Novell, and of Novell FTP Services for NetWare. This information will be helpful to know when you are ready to install, configure, and run them.

Understanding the Internet

You are probably no stranger to the term *Internet*. It refers to the worldwide connection ability of computers, and the capability of those computers to transfer files among and between themselves across this connection. Not just any individual PC can directly connect to the Internet, however. You probably realize by now that for a single computer to make an Internet connection, that computer must have access to another computer (a mainframe or more frequently a server) that is itself directly connected to the Internet and running special software which makes Internet communication possible. Individuals and many companies use an ISP (Internet Service Provider) to make that connection to the Internet, while some companies have their own servers capable of direct Internet connection.

Even if a single PC could connect directly to the Internet, it would be of little use if it weren't possible to exchange files and gather information. The World Wide Web (WWW) is the information retrieval initiative on the Internet that makes it possible for Internet users to have access to a seemingly infinite number of documents.

Those documents are available on the WWW because of servers (hosts) running software applications that publish HTML (HyperText Markup Language) and other types of documents to the Web. These Web servers accept and respond to requests for documents.

NOTE HTML is a special coding language used to create hypertext documents. (A *hypertext document* is any text document containing
links to other documents. Clicking on a link in a hypertext document opens the document to which it is linked.) In its simplest form,
HTML uses mostly ordinary English words and characters placed
inside angle brackets (< >) to identify those words and characters as
formatting codes instead of as document text. HTML provides formatting codes of varying types. For example if you use a starting
code such as <B>, then put text into the document after that starting code, and follow that text with the </B> ending code, all text
between the starting and ending codes will be bold when viewed
using an appropriate browser. (A *browser* is a software program
that you use to look at different kinds of Internet documents,
including hypertext documents, graphics, and others. There are several browsers available. Two of the most common ones are
Microsoft Internet Explorer and Netscape Navigator.)

Document requests must be in a format (protocol) the Web servers can
understand and translate, or communication and transfer of files across
the Web is not possible. Two common protocols used on the Internet are:

- **HTTP (HyperText Transfer Protocol).** A protocol used to transfer
  hypertext files across the Internet. To use HTTP, both the computer that
  requests the file (the client) and the computer responding to the request
  (the server) must have special HTTP server software on them. HTTP is
  one of the most important and commonly used protocols on the Web.
  When you enter a URL (Uniform Resource Locator)—Web site
  address—that begins with http:// (such as **http://www.novell.com**),
  you are specifying that the **www.novell.com** Web server is one which
  uses HTTP.
- **FTP (File Transfer Protocol).** This is another common protocol for
  transferring files across the Internet. FTP is a special way to log in to
  a Web site. Web sites that support this protocol may require that you
  have a special user account (user name) to log in with, but many FTP
  Web sites allow access to some of their files (public repositories) using
  an anonymous user name. These sites are called *anonymous FTP servers*.

Understanding Netscape FastTrack Server for NetWare

Netscape FastTrack Server for NetWare is software run on a NetWare file
server that gives that server Web server capabilities. When Netscape
FastTrack Server for NetWare is installed, configured, and running on a

NetWare server, it makes it possible for that server to publish HTML documents and other types of files on the Web. Other types of files this Netscape FastTrack Server for NetWare Web server can publish on the Web include:

- **Audio.** Files that carry voice (such as music, radio shows, and so on). These files usually end in an .AU or .WAV extension.
- **Compressed.** Files which have been specially processed (by software such as WinZip) to reduce their size as much as possible (compressing the files). Compressed file names end with the .ZIP extension.
- **Executable.** Files which run some type of software program. These files usually end with an .EXE extension.
- **Graphics.** Files of pictures, drawings, renderings, etc. Graphics files for use in hypertext documents on the Web most commonly end in a .GIF or .JPEG extension, but other extensions can be used as well.
- **Video.** Files containing animated sequences. These files commonly end with a .MOV or .AVI extension.

Understanding Novell FTP Services for NetWare

KEY
CONCEPT

Novell FTP Services for NetWare is software run on a NetWare file server that gives that NetWare server's users the ability to transfer (send or receive) files between a remote host computer, and the local (NetWare) computer across a TCP/IP network. The FTP server establishes the connection to a remote server on the user's behalf, then sends or receives files when the user requests them.

Once running, FTP provides the following functions:

- The ability to log in to a remote network
- The ability to view a list of directories and files on the remote network
- The ability to copy files to or from the remote network

Novell FTP Services for NetWare can handle up to 65 simultaneous active client sessions. It provides file transfer services through two modules:

- **Inetd.nlm.** The agent module responsible for accepting the connection and loading the Ftpserv.nlm to service the connection. The Inetd.nlm loads the Ftpserv.nlm when an FTP client (a network workstation with the needed files loaded and configured) initiates a session with the NetWare server running Novell FTP Services for NetWare software.
- **Ftpserv.nlm.** The server module responsible for enabling the connection and providing the requested services. This module only resides in server memory as long as there is at least one active session.

As with any software, you must install and configure Netscape FastTrack Server for NetWare and Novell FTP Services for NetWare before you can take advantage of the services they provide.

Installing and Configuring Netscape FastTrack Server for NetWare

Enabling Netscape FastTrack Server for NetWare on your network gives you a Web server of your own on which to publish documents and other files. To make your Web server available, you must:

- ensure the server meets minimum requirements
- install Netscape FastTrack
- understand how to use the Administrative Server and Server Manager
- configure, tune, and troubleshoot (if needed) your Netscape FastTrack Server

Minimum Requirements

The server on which you install Netscape FastTrack must be a NetWare 4.11 or higher server with its own unique IP address registered for Internet access. It must also have:

- 64 MB or more of RAM
- 100 MB or more of free space on the **Sys:** volume
- Long name space support on **Sys:** and other volumes that will hold Web server files
- DNS running if you will be using host names (not needed if you will just be using IP addresses)
- An attached workstation running Windows 95 or Windows NT, Netscape 3.x or higher, current Novell Client software, 100 MB of available hard disk space, and a CD-ROM drive if you will be installing Netscape FastTrack from CD

Installing Netscape FastTrack

Before starting the installation of Netscape FastTrack, be sure the server you will be installing it on *and* the workstation you will be installing it from meet the minimum requirements. In addition, be sure you are logged in to the network as the Admin user from a workstation that meets minimum requirements or as a user with Supervisor rights to the **Sys:** volume. You will also have to map a network drive to the root of

Sys: volume. Then, you can install Netscape FastTrack by completing the following steps:

1. With the CD containing the FastTrack files in the CD-ROM drive on the workstation, click **Start**, then click **Run**, and enter the CD-ROM's drive letter followed by the path and file name (**Products**\ **Webserv****Setup.exe**).

2. Click **OK** to open the Netscape FastTrack Server for NetWare welcome window, then click **Finish** to continue. The FastTrack files unpack (see Figure 8-1) and the setup Welcome screen opens.

3. Click **Next** to continue, then click **Yes** to agree to the software license.

4. Click the **Browse** button and locate the drive you mapped to the root of the server's **Sys:** volume, then click **Next**.

5. You are prompted to enter the IP address of the server to which you are installing Netscape FastTrack, and the host name of the NetWare server. If the IP address and host name (which may also be the IP address) do not display automatically, enter the information then click **Next**. The Server Configuration screen opens.

6. Provide the port number (the TCP port from which the Netscape FastTrack Server receives HTTP requests) for the FastTrack server in the Server Port field, and write down the port number it displays. (You will need it to access the Administration Server utility from which you configure the Netscape FastTrack Server.)

FIGURE 8-1 The welcome and files unpacking windows for the Netscape FastTrack Server installation program.

You can use any port number from 1 to 65535, but port 80 is the standard port number for an unsecured Web server, and 443 is the standard port number for a secured Web server. Using the standard port number makes user access much easier, as users only have to specify the port number when you use one different from the standard secured or unsecured port number.

7. Click **Next**. The Administration Server Port Configuration screen opens. A random port number is already provided. Write it down; you will need it later.

   Since the Admin Port number must be different from any other servers on the system, it is best to accept the randomly-generated port number, unless you know it conflicts with another Admin Port number on the network.

8. Click **Next** again to assign the Admin Port number, then click **OK** to close the Information window that opens to warn you to write down this port number. The Administration Server Authentication window opens.

9. Provide the Admin (or user with equivalent rights) username and password, then click **Next**.

   The username and password are entered into the FastTrack directory, and are case-sensitive. (This is separate from the NDS directory, but you can use the same username and password.)

10. Click **Next** when the Information window explaining how to use LDAP with FastTrack opens. The Autoexec.ncf options window opens.

11. Click the radio button next to the Change the Autoexec.ncf file option to enable the system to automatically load Netscape FastTrack Server each time the system is started (see Figure 8-2), then click **Next**. The Start Copying Files window opens.

12. Click **Next** to continue. The needed files are copied to the Novonyx Folder, and a progress bar is displayed along with information about the FastTrack Server for NetWare.

13. When the installation is complete and the Setup Complete screen displays, you are prompted to view the readme file or launch the Web server.

14. If you do not want to view the readme file or launch the Web server, click the **View the Read Me file** and **Launch Web server** boxes to uncheck them, then click **Finish**. The installation finishes.

    If you checked these boxes, the browser opens to the HTTP address of the Netscape FastTrack Server. Two windows (the readme file and the Web server boxes) open. Minimize or close one to see the other.

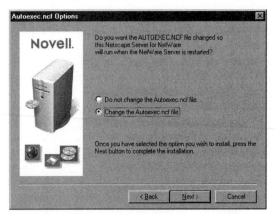

FIGURE 8-2 The Autoexec.ncf options window, from which you specify whether or not Netscape FastTrack Server is to autoload at server startup.

During the installation of Netscape FastTrack, several NLMs are copied to the Netscape FastTrack Server. These NLMs make various features and utilities available. When the FastTrack Server is started, the following NLMs are loaded into server memory:

- **Admserv.nlm.** Provides the Netscape Administration Server.
- **Btrieve.nlm.** Provides the client/server database.
- **Cron.nlm.** Provides the NetWare scheduler utility.
- **Cssysmsg.nlm.** Enables system messages on Netscape FastTrack.
- **Netdb.nlm.** Enables network database access.
- **Nshttpd.nlm.** Loads the Netscape FastTrack Server for NetWare.
- **Nslcgi.nlm.** Provides the LCGI support library.

The installation of Netscape FastTrack Server makes several modifications to your NetWare 5 server. First, two new files are created: **Nsweb.ncf** and **Nswebdn.ncf**. These two files contain the commands to load and unload the Netscape FastTrack Server respectively.

KEY CONCEPT

The NetWare server's **Autoexec.ncf** file is modified during installation. The line to run the **Nsweb.ncf** file is added to **Autoexec.ncf** so that the Netscape FastTrack server is automatically loaded each time the NetWare server starts. In addition, the command to run the Administration Server utility by which you can configure and manage the FastTrack Server is also added to this file, and run automatically whenever the NetWare server is started. (If you later choose to unload this utility, you can start it again manually by typing **Admserv** at the NetWare server console.)

Directories and files are also added to the server's directory structure. These directories and files are located under the main directory called **Novonyx**. One directory which affects users is the **Sys:Novonyx\ Suitespot\Docs** directory. The Netscape FastTrack Server uses this directory and its subdirectories to provide files to network users.

Use the Administrative Server and Server Manager

The Administrative Server utility is provided to make managing the Netscape FastTrack Server as easy as possible. To run the Administration Server, several NLMs must first be loaded. When you installed Netscape FastTrack Server, those NLMs were copied to the NetWare file server, and the command to automatically load those NLMs and start the Administration Server was added to the **Autoexec.ncf** file.

Unlike most server utilities, you do not use the Administration Server from the NetWare server console. You use the Administration Server from any standard Web browser such as Netscape or Internet Explorer. To access the Administration Server:

1. Load the browser on the workstation, then enter the URL as **http://server_hostname.admin_port_number**. (Remember that Admin port number you were prompted to write down when you installed the Netscape FastTrack Server software? That's the one you use here.)

2. When prompted, provide the username and password you assigned during the installation process (remember they are case sensitive), then click **OK**. You are then authenticated to the server, and the Administration Server home page displays (see Figure 8-3).

The Administrative Server's home page provides you with administrative access to all of your Netscape FastTrack Servers, whether there are several servers or only one. Each Netscape FastTrack Server is identified on the server home page by a button with the server's name on it. When you click the associated server button, the Server Manager becomes available for that server. You use Server Manager to configure and adjust the performance of the Netscape FastTrack Server.

NOTE

From the Administration Server's home page, you can stop and restart the FastTrack Server. Click the **Off** or **On** buttons under Netscape FastTrack Server to start or stop the server, then wait a few seconds for the server to shut down or start up. (The server's current state is identified by the "lit up" button.) You can also start and stop a Netscape FastTrack Server from within its associated Server Manager

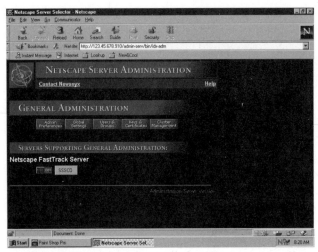

FIGURE 8-3 The Administration Server home page for the SSSCO Netscape
FastTrack Server.

page by clicking **Server Preferences**, then clicking **ON/OFF**, and
clicking either **Server On** or **Server Off**. When you have multiple
Netscape FastTrack Servers on your network, use this method to shut
down or restart a specific server, or enter the shut down command
(**nswebdn**) or the restart command (**nsweb**) at the server's console.

Configure and Adjust Netscape
FastTrack Server Performance

Server Manager is a collection of forms you use to configure parameters
and control what happens on your Netscape FastTrack Server. When
you click the associated server's named button, Server Manager launches and presents you with a page containing several tabs (see Figure 8-4).
Each time you click a tab, an associated list of links opens in the frame
on the left side of the window. Clicking one of these links opens its associated form, where you can change the server's configuration and adjust
parameters to improve its performance.

Some of the parameters you can modify using Server Manager are:

- The server's port number
- Which directories are to be document directories
- Access to Web server documents
- Performance parameters

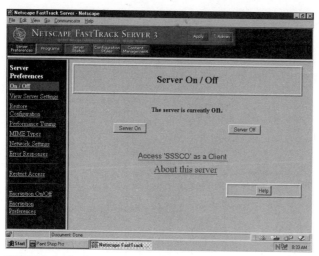

FIGURE 8-4 The Server Manager page that opens when you click the associated server's named button on the Netscape Server Administration page.

Modify the Server's Port Number

Before modifying the Netscape FastTrack Server's port number, consider that any time you use a port number other than the standard secured or unsecured number, users have to provide not only the URL needed to access this server, but also the port number. For example, if you set the port number to 300 and the server's URL is **www.novell.com**, users would have to enter **http://www.novell.com:300** to access it.

To modify the server's port number, launch Server Manager, then complete the following steps:

1. Click **Server Preferences**. The list of Server Preferences links displays in the left frame.
2. Click **Network Settings**. The Network Settings form opens.
3. Type the chosen port number into the Port field, then click **Apply** to save and apply the new settings.

You can return to the Administrative Server home page anytime from within Server Manager by clicking the **Admin** button.

NOTE

Set Primary and Additional Document Directories

By default, installation puts the Netscape FastTrack Server documents into **Sys:\Novonyx\Suitespot\docs**. Users who access the server are automatically sent to that initial (home) page directory, and the default home page HTML document (**info.html**) is launched. This occurs because a setting in the configuration files specifies that directory as the primary document directory. Should you prefer to use a different directory structure on your server for better organization, you will be able to do so and it will still be possible for users to automatically connect to the home page when they log in. To accomplish this, launch Server Manager then set the Primary Document Directory as follows:

1. Click **Content Management**. The list of Content Management links displays in the left frame.
2. Click **Primary Document Directory**. The Primary Document Directory form opens.
3. Type a different directory path into the Primary directory field, then click **Apply** to apply and save the change.

If you prefer not to keep all of your server's documents in the same directory, you can add directories to the network, then configure Server Manager to make them available. Each directory you choose to use must have the directory structure set up, then a different URL must be used to locate files in that directory. To configure additional document directories using Server Manager, follow these steps:

1. Click **Content Management**. The list of Content Management links displays in the left frame.
2. Click **Additional Document Directories**. The Additional Document Directories form opens.
3. Type the name of the directory to be part of the URL for this directory into the URL prefix: field. (For example, if the directory is called *Documents*, type **Documents** into this field. The URL will then include /**Documents** after the domain name (.com, edu, .gov, etc.).
4. Type the exact path to the additional directory in the **Map To Directory** field. For example, if the Documents directory is in the Public directory on volume Sys, then type **Sys:\Public\Documents**.
5. Click **Apply** to apply and save the changes.

Control User Access to Web Server Documents

There are several user access parameters you can set using Server Manager, including:

- What file the users see when they connect without specifying any particular file
- Whether users can view an index of subdirectories in the document directory, if subdirectories exist
- Which documents users can access on the server

To control what file the user sees when the file they requested does not exist, you specify an index filename. You can specify multiple index filenames if you want. The server will search for them in the order you specify, and present the first one it finds to the user. Two default index filenames exist: **index.html** and **home.html**.

If you want users to be able to see an index of the subdirectories in the document directory other than the one you provide in the **index.html** file, you can establish dynamic directory listing and configure how the index is to appear: Fancy directory indexing or Simple directory indexing. If you choose **Fancy directory indexing**, the index includes a graphic representing the file type, and information about the file such as its size and date last modified. If you choose **Simple directory indexing**, only the names of the files display.

Both the file the user sees and directory indexing are set using the Server Manager, as follows:

1. Click **Content Management**. The list of Content Management links displays in the left frame.
2. Click **Document Preferences**. The Document Preferences form opens (see Figure 8-5).
3. Type the name of the index file you want the users to see into the Index Filenames field.
4. Identify whether you want Fancy or Simple directory indexing, if applicable.
5. Identify which file you want users to see as the home page, if applicable.
6. Click **Apply** to apply and save the changes.

To control which documents users can see on the server, you must complete two major tasks: binding the Netscape FastTrack Server to NDS to take advantage of NDS security, and creating access restrictions. Establish user document access by completing the following steps:

1. Open the Administration Server (click **Admin** if you already are in a Server Manager page, or launch a browser and provide the URL to your Netscape FastTrack Server).
2. Click **Global Settings**.

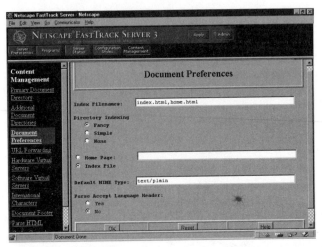

FIGURE 8-5 The Document Preferences form, where you can specify which file the user sees initially as well as directory indexing.

3. Click **Novell Directory Services** on the Obtain Directory Service From line.
4. When prompted that Netscape FastTrack Server is now in Directory Services mode, click **OK**.
5. Click **Insert Context**, and type an NDS context (without a leading period), then click **Save Changes**.
6. Click **OK** when prompted to shut down and restart the Administration Server and the FastTrack Server.
7. Type **Nswebdn** at the server console and press **Enter**.
8. Restart the Netscape FastTrack Server by typing **Nsweb** at the server console and pressing **Enter**.
9. Log in to the network as your Admin user, then created a directory for restricted files.
10. Start the NetWare Administrator utility, change to the container where the Netscape FastTrack Server is located (or another container where you want a Group object with rights to the Netscape FastTrack Server to exist), then create a Group object to which you assign Read and File Scan rights for the restricted directory you just created.
11. Add those users who are to have access to the restricted directory as Members of the Group object you just created.
12. Locate the **Sys:** volume object for the Netscape FastTrack Server, locate the restricted directory you created, then add the Group object as a trustee.

13. Right-click the container object where the Netscape FastTrack Server is located, click **Details**, click **Trustees of this object**, then restrict access from flowing down the Directory tree by unchecking the **Read** and **File Scan** access rights in the Access Rights area.

Set Server Performance Parameters

If file size or content is not the cause of performance problems on the network, you may want to consider reconfiguring various server performance parameters. For example, you can restrict the number of simultaneous requests for service that your Netscape FastTrack Server handles (the default is 48). By doing so, the server will not become so congested with requests that it functions sluggishly for everyone.

In addition to changing this parameter to improve server performanc, you can also modify the following parameters, procedures for which are included in this section:

- Domain name system lookups
- Size of the Listen queue
- HTTP persistent connection timeout
- Maximum Packet Receive Buffers and Maximum Physical Receive Packet Size

CHANGING THE MAXIMUM NUMBER OF SERVICE REQUESTS

Change the maximum number of service requests using Server Manager as follows:

1. Click **Server Preferences**. The left frame expands to show a link list of server preferences.
2. Click **Performance Tuning**. The Performance Tuning form opens (see Figure 8-6).
3. Change the default of 48 to another number.
4. Click **OK**.
5. Save and apply the changes, approving the change and save when prompted.

You will have to shut down and restart Netscape FastTrack Server before the change takes effect.

DISABLING DOMAIN NAME SYSTEM LOOKUPS

Domain Name System (DNS) lookups is a feature designed to let administrators see the domain name of each user requesting services from the Netscape FastTrack Server. The domain name is resolved to its IP address,

FIGURE 8-6 The Performance Tuning form used to set server performance parameters such as the maximum number of simultaneous requests for service the server is to handle.

and then the information is stored in a log. This can be useful if you need to track potential security breaches and for other potential reporting issues, but can substantially slow down user access to the server.

By default, DNS lookups is disabled. You can enable DNS lookups if you choose to do so, and if having done so is causing performance to be too slow, you can again disable it. To disable DNS lookups, complete the following steps:

1. Click **Server Preferences**. The left frame expands to show a link list of server preferences.
2. Click **Performance Tuning**. The Performance Tuning form opens.
3. Click **No** under Enable DNS.
4. Click **OK**.
5. Save and apply the changes, approving the change and save when prompted.

CONFIGURING THE HTTP PERSISTENT CONNECTION TIMEOUT

With HTTP 1.1, connections can be set to be persistent, but a timeout setting is still necessary to terminate an inactive connection. Otherwise, inactive connections can tie up all of the server's resources, making them unavailable to other users. To configure this parameter, you use the Server Manager, as follows:

1. Click **Server Preferences**. The left frame expands to show a link list of server preferences.
2. Click **Performance Tuning**. The Performance Tuning form opens.
3. In the **HTTP Persistent Connection Timeout** field, type the number of seconds of inactivity that will be allowed before the connection is terminated.
4. Click **OK**.

5. Apply the changes and save when prompted.

CONFIGURE LISTEN-QUEUE SIZE

The Listen-Queue Size parameter specifies how many incoming connections the server will accept for a given socket. The default setting is 100 incoming connections. If the server becomes overloaded with connections it cannot handle, modify this setting by completing the following steps:

1. Click **Server Preferences**. The left frame expands to show a link list of server preferences.
2. Click **Performance Tuning**. The Performance Tuning form opens.
3. Type the maximum number of connections to be handled for any given socket into the **Listen Queue Size** field.
4. Click **OK**.
5. Apply the changes and save them when prompted.

SETTING MAXIMUM PACKET RECEIVE BUFFERS AND MAXIMUM PHYSICAL RECEIVE PACKET SIZE

Packets are data encapsulated in coding, which makes it possible to transmit requests for service, data, and program files across the network. Workstation network boards, server network boards, and routers can't always handle the same size packet. Therefore, you should set the parameter that specifies the maximum size of acceptable network packets (Maximum Physical Receive Packet Size). Setting it to the smallest of the maximum packet sizes that the workstation, server, or router can handle will help improve the reliability of packet delivery.

You must set Maximum Physical Receive Packet Size and its companion setting, Maximum Packet Receive Buffers (which specifies how much memory is to be allocated for receiving and holding incoming packets until they can be processes) using the Monitor utility that ships with NetWare. You do not use the Administrative Server or Server Manager to set these two parameters. Instead, load Monitor at the NetWare server console, and complete the following steps to set these two packet-related parameters:

1. From Monitor's main menu, choose **Server Parameters**. The Server Parameters menu opens.
2. Choose **Communications**. The Communications screen opens.
3. Choose **Maximum Physical Receive Packet Size** and enter the maximum packet size that the workstations, server, and any routers on the network can handle.

4. Choose **Maximum Packet Receive Buffers** and enter the calculated number for this parameter. (To calculate this number, multiply the maximum physical receive packet size by the current maximum receive buffers. Then multiply the maximum physical receive packet size by the desired number of maximum packet receive buffers. Subtract the first answer from the second answer to determine memory requirements for the change.)

5. Press **Esc** twice, then choose **Exit Monitor**, answering **Yes** when prompted to exit.

6. Shut down and then restart the NetWare server.

Controlling User File Storage

Controlling user file storage is another way to help ensure the server functions at its best possible performance level. You have to depend on your users to implement this type of control, however, as there are no server parameters you can set to implement the types of control suggested here.

It is important, that your users cooperate, and restrict the size of and use of special features in their Web documents. The use of some HTML features in files such as CGI scripts and imagemaps, and very large files such as some video and audio clips, can reduce server performance and even make it difficult for network users to gain access to the server. As a rule, you may prefer not to ask the users to restrict the size of files they store on the network. However, if special file features or large files start to cause performance degradation, you may have to consider setting some restrictions, and rely on the users to implement them.

Although you can't use Server Manager or Administrative Server to set restrictions on file size and content, you can restrict the actual size of the user's home directory space if you need to by using NetWare Administrator. In the User Space Limits page for the related volume object, restrict the size of the user's home directory space or other space where you let them put their Web files.

Installing and Configuring FTP Services for NetWare

Enabling FTP Services for NetWare allows your network users access to Internet servers and the ability to transfer files across the Internet. To take advantage of the provided services, you must:

■ ensure the server meets minimum requirements
■ install the FTP server

- configure, tune, and troubleshoot (if needed) FTP

Minimum Requirements

To take advantage of Novell FTP Services, you install the Novell FTP Server. Because Novell FTP Services are automatically installed as part of NetWare NFS Services, your server must meet minimum requirements for loading and running NetWare NFS Services. Once your server meets the minimum requirements for NetWare NFS Service, it also will have met the minimum requirements for Novell FTP Services.

The minimum requirements which the server must meet in order to run Novell FTP Services are:

- NetWare 4.1 or later must be installed and running
- Minimum RAM requirements for NetWare operating system, plus an additional 12 MB of RAM for Novell FTP Services
- 8 MB minimum of available space on the **Sys** volume
- TCP/IP configured on the NetWare server

Installing FTP Server

Because it is installed as part of NetWare NFS Services, installing the FTP Server requires that you start by adding the NFS name space support driver to the volume on which the FTP Server will be functioning. To load name space support on the NetWare server, complete the following steps:

1. Type **NFS** at the server console prompt and press **Enter**. The NFS.nlm loads.
2. Load the NFS name space at the server console by typing **Add name space NFS to volume_name** and pressing **Enter**. When you use this command, replace **volume_name** with the name of the volume the FTP Server will be using.

 Since the command to add the NFS name space only has to be run once on any NetWare server, do not put the **Add name space** command in the **Autoexec.ncf** file, or attempt to manually enter it again unless it did not actually load this first time.

NOTE

To install NetWare NFS Services, you must:

- Mount the NetWare CD-ROM as a NetWare volume.
- Load the NetWare configuration utility **Nwconfig**.

- Install a Local Network Information Services (NIS) distributed database.
- Start Novell FTP Services.

The following steps walk you through this process.

1. Insert the NetWare 5 CD into the file server's CD-ROM drive, then type **CDROM** and press **Enter**. Wait while the NetWare 5 CD is mounted as a NetWare volume.
2. Type **Nwconfig** at the console prompt and press **Enter**. The Nwconfig utility opens.
3. Choose **Product Options**.
4. Choose **Install a product not listed**. You are prompted to install from drive **A:** or to press **F3** to specify a different path (see Figure 8-7).
5. Press **F3**, then enter the path to the CD-ROM volume as **server_name\NetWare5:\Products\Nwuxps**, replacing *server_name* with the actual name of the server.
6. Choose whether to read the readme file, then continue.
7. When prompted for the path to the server's boot files, enter **C:\Nwserver**. The files are then copied to the server.
8. When the Server Login screen opens, authenticate to the server as user Admin (or other user with the same rights as user Admin).
9. When prompted to choose a name service option (Local NIS or Remote NIS), choose **Local NIS**. The Setup Name Services screen opens.
10. Press **Esc** so that no settings are changed, then choose **Yes** when prompted to continue name services installation. The process to convert the text files runs.
11. Press **Esc**. The Product Initialization States screen opens. When it is complete, press **Esc**.

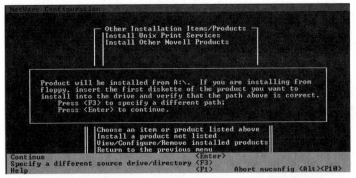

FIGURE 8-7 The Nwconfig utility prompting you to specify the path from which the new product installation is to be run.

12. Press **Ins**, then choose **FTP Server**.

13. Press **Esc** to complete the installation, then press **Esc** again to exit the Unicon utility.

14. Press **Esc** twice more to exit Nwconfig.

15. Bring the server down and restart it.

Default configuration settings exist for various FTP server parameters, but you may want to change those default settings. You change those settings using the Unicon utility, instructions for which can be found in the following section.

Configuring and Troubleshooting FTP Servers

Configuring FTP servers requires that you modify one or more configuration parameters, depending on your company's requirements. Properly configuring your FTP server can help head off potential problems, but won't prevent all problems. To configure your FTP server to meet your company's needs and resolve problems when they occur, you must learn:

- what parameters you can set on FTP Servers
- how to set those parameters
- what problems you are most likely to encounter with your network's FTP servers
- how to handle problems when they do occur

CONFIGURING FTP SERVER PARAMETERS

As part of the installation process (or later if you want to make changes), you can configure several parameters for your FTP server. For example, if you want your FTP server to be an anonymous FTP server, you must configure the Anonymous User Access parameter (allows or prevents access by users without an authorized login name and password) and Anonymous User's Home Directory parameter (home directory into which anonymous users can place files). Other parameters you can configure by running the Unicon utility at the server are:

- **Default Name Space.** The default name space (DOS or NFS) for users.
- **Default User's Home Directory.** Where users' files will be placed when they do not have their own home directory on the server.
- **Detection Reset Interval.** The length of time during which multiple unsuccessful login attempts will be allowed before this login attempt is logged as an intruder.

- **Idle Time Before FTP Server Unloads.** The length of time the server remains loaded in memory if no active sessions exist.
- **Intruder Detection.** Whether intruder detection is enabled or disabled, determining whether unsuccessful login attempts will be recorded to the Intruder log file, and an SNMP alert message sent to the Network Management Console.
- **Log Level.** What types of login information will be recorded in the log. Options are None (no information), Logins (only login information), Statistics (login information and the number of files copied to or from the FTP server), and File (login and statistics information as well as a description of all FTP transactions).
- **Maximum Number of Sessions.** How many FTP sessions are allowed to run concurrently. The valid range is 1 to 64.
- **Maximum Session Length.** How long an individual session can remain open.
- **Number of Unsuccessful Attempts.** How many times within a given time frame a user is allowed to try to log in without a matching user name and password, before the login attempt is recorded as an intruder detection event.

To set or modify FTP server parameter settings, complete the following steps:

1. From the server console prompt, type **Unicon** and press **Enter**. When prompted, provide the context. (It should match that shown in the new NDS Context area at the bottom of the screen.)
2. Also provide the complete typeful user name for the Admin user or other user with the same rights as user Admin, and the password, then press **Enter**. The Unicon main menu opens.
3. Choose **Manage Services**.
4. Choose **FTP Server**. The FTP Administration menu opens.
5. Choose **Set Parameters**. The FTP Server Parameters screen opens (see Figure 8-8).
6. Modify parameters as needed, then exit the Unicon utility and save your changes.

TROUBLESHOOTING FTP SERVERS

All networks and their servers have occasional problems. FTP Servers are no exception. Experienced network administrators, particularly those experienced with FTP servers, will tell you that there are certain types of problems that typically occur, and standard ways of verifying and resolving the problem. Typical problems and suggestions for verifying and, where applicable, resolving them include:

FIGURE 8-8 The FTP Server Parameters window.

- **Network failure.** Enter **Ping ftp_server_ip_address** at the DOS prompt to verify whether there is a problem on the network. If you cannot ping the FTP Server, you will need to troubleshoot possible network problems.
- **Server down or overloaded.** If there is no response from the server, it may be down. Check it using the **Start/Stop Services** option in Unicon. If the server is up, it simply may be congested. Unusually slow file transfers or clients receiving messages indicating that the server has no available connections are symptoms of a down or overloaded server.
- **Server configuration.** If a user cannot connect even though there are available connections, the user's account at the server might be configured to restrict their access. You will have to modify the user's restrictions to correct this problem. In addition, if a user has trouble downloading a file, it may be because the file is flagged to be Read-Only. Either change the file's attribute, or tell the user this file is not available for download.
- **Client configuration.** Inability to connect to the server may be the result of network failure, or the FTP Server being down or overloaded. If these are ruled out, then it may be that the user's workstation is not properly configured. To access an FTP Server, the workstation must have the TCP/IP protocol stack properly loaded and configured. In addition, the network board must be configured with the proper frame type.
- **User error.** Common user errors which cause problems accessing and transferring files from an FTP server are: incorrectly specifying the FTP server name, mistyping the user's login name or password, or lack of rights to the directory into which the user wants to copy files.

Chapter Summary

The purpose of using Netscape FastTrack Server for Novell is to make those documents and other files your company wants to publish to the Internet available to users accessing the Internet. The purpose of using Novell FTP Services for NetWare on your network is to allow your company's users fast and easy access to published documents and other files on remote computers, across the Internet.

In order for remote users to access the documents you publish on your Web server, those document requests must be in a format (protocol) the Web server can understand and translate, or communication and transfer of files across the Web is not possible. Two common protocols used on the Internet are:

- **HTTP (HyperText Transfer Protocol).** A protocol used to transfer hypertext files across the Internet. To use HTTP, both the computer requesting the file (the client) and the computer responding to the request (the server) must have special HTTP server software on them. HTTP is one of the most important and commonly used protocols on the Web. When you enter a URL (Uniform Resource Locator)—Web site address—that begins with http:// (such as **http://www.novell.com**), you are specifying that the **www.novell.com** Web server is one which uses HTTP.
- **FTP (File Transfer Protocol).** This is another common protocol for transferring files across the Internet. FTP is a special way to log in to a Web site. Web sites that support this protocol may require that you have a special user account (user name) to log in with, but many FTP Web sites allow access to some of their files (public repositories) using an anonymous user name. These sites are called *anonymous FTP servers.*

Netscape FastTrack Server for NetWare is software run on a NetWare file server which gives that NetWare server the capabilities of a Web server. When Netscape FastTrack Server for NetWare is installed, configured, and running on a NetWare server, it makes it possible for that NetWare server to publish HTML documents and other types of files on the Web.

To make your Netscape FastTrack Server available to Web users, you must:

- ensure the server meets minimum requirements
- install Netscape FastTrack
- understand how to use the Administrative Server and Server Manager
- configure, tune, and troubleshoot (if needed) your Netscape FastTrack Server

Novell FTP Services for NetWare is software run on a NetWare file server which gives that NetWare server's users the ability to transfer (send or receive) files between a remote host computer and the local (NetWare) computer across a TCP/IP network. The FTP server establishes the connection to a remote server on the user's behalf, then sends or receives files when the user requests them.

Once running, FTP provides:

- The ability to log in to a remote network
- The ability to view a list of directories and files on the remote network
- The ability to copy files to or from the remote network

Novell FTP Services for NetWare can handle up to 65 simultaneous active client sessions. It provides file transfer services through two modules:

- **Inetd.nlm.** The agent module responsible for accepting the connection and loading the Ftpserv.nlm to service the connection. The Inetd.nlm loads the Ftpserv.nlm when an FTP client (a network workstation with the needed files loaded and configured) initiates a session with the NetWare server running Novell FTP Services for NetWare software.
- **Ftpserv.nlm.** The server module responsible for enabling the connection and providing the requested services. This module only resides in server memory as long as there is at least one active session.

As with any software, you must install and configure Netscape FastTrack Server for NetWare and Novell FTP Services for NetWare before you can take advantage of the services they provide.

During the installation of Netscape FastTrack, several NLMs are copied to the Netscape FastTrack Server. These NLMs make various features and utilities available. When the FastTrack Server is started, the following NLMs are loaded into server memory:

- **Admserv.nlm.** Provides the Netscape Administration Server.
- **Btrieve.nlm.** Provides the client/server database.
- **Cron.nlm.** Provides the NetWare scheduler utility.
- **Cssysmsg.nlm.** Enables system messages on Netscape FastTrack.
- **Netdb.nlm.** Enables network database access.
- **Nshttpd.nlm.** Loads the Netscape FastTrack Server for NetWare.
- **Nslcgi.nlm.** Provides the LCGI support library.

The installation of Netscape FastTrack Server makes several modifications to your NetWare 4 or NetWare 5 server. First, two new files are created: **Nsweb.ncf** and **Nswebdn.ncf**. These two files contain the commands to load and unload the Netscape FastTrack Server, respectively.

The NetWare server's **Autoexec.ncf** file is modified during installation. The line to run the **Nsweb.ncf** file is added to **Autoexec.ncf** so that the Netscape FastTrack server will be automatically loaded each time the NetWare server is started. In addition, the command to run the Administration Server utility by which you can configure and manage the FastTrack Server is also added to this file, and run automatically whenever the NetWare server is started. (If you later choose to unload this utility, you can start it again manually by typing **Admserv** at the NetWare server console.)

To configure Netscape FastTrack Server you use the Administration Server which you run from a browser, after the needed NLMs are loaded at the file server. The command to load those NLMs was added to the **Autoexec.ncf** file. To start the Administration Server, open the browser at your workstation and enter the URL to the Netscape FastTrack Server, logging in as the Admin user when prompted. You can configure Netscape FastTrack Server from the Administration Server and the Server Manager, which provides forms for you to use to make configuration changes to various parameters.

Some of the parameters you can modify using Server Manager are:

- The server's port number
- Which directories are to be document directories
- Access to Web server documents
- Performance parameters

Enabling FTP Services for NetWare allows your network users access to Internet servers and the ability to transfer files across the Internet. To take advantage of the provided services, you must:

- ensure the server meets minimum requirements
- install the FTP server
- configure, tune, and troubleshoot (if needed) FTP

Installing the FTP server, because it is installed as part of NetWare NFS Services, requires that you start by adding the NFS name space support driver to the volume on which the FTP server will be functioning. To install NetWare NFS Services, you must:

- Load name space support on the NetWare server
- Mount the NetWare CD-ROM as a NetWare volume
- Load the NetWare configuration utility Nwconfig
- Install a Local Network Information Services (NIS) distributed database
- Start Novell FTP Services

Default configuration settings exist for various FTP server parameters, but you may want to change those default settings. Once you install Novell FTP Services, you change those settings using the Unicon utility. To start this utility, type **Unicon** at the server console then press **Enter**. From the menu that opens, choose **Manage Services**, then choose **FTP Server**. You can now change a variety of parameters including:

- **Default Name Space.** The default name space (DOS or NFS) for users.
- **Default User's Home Directory.** Where user's files will be placed when they do not have their own home directory on the server.
- **Detection Reset Interval.** The length of time during which multiple unsuccessful login attempts will be allowed before this login attempt is logged as an intruder attempt.
- **Idle Time Before FTP Server Unloads.** The length of time the server remains loaded in memory if no active sessions exist.
- **Intruder Detection.** Whether intruder detection is enabled or disabled, determining whether unsuccessful login attempts will be recorded to the Intruder log file, and an SNMP alert message sent to the Network Management Console.
- **Log Level.** What types of login information will be recording in the log. Options are: None (no information), Logins (only login information), Statistics (login information and the number of files copied to or from the FTP server), and File (login and statistics information as well as a description of all FTP transactions).
- **Maximum Number of Sessions.** The number of FTP sessions allowed to run concurrently. The valid range is 1 to 64.
- **Maximum Session Length.** How long an individual session can remain open.
- **Number of Unsuccessful Attempts.** How many times within a given time frame a user is allowed to try to log in without a matching user name and password, before the login attempt is recorded as an intruder detection event.

As needed, troubleshoot and fine tune FTP services on your network.

Practice Test Questions

1. Which two NLMs provide file transfer services for Novell FTP Services for NetWare?
   a. Inetd.nlm
   b. Ftpserv.nlm
   c. Admserv.nlm
   d. Unicon.nlm

2. What is the maximum number of simultaneous active client sessions that any one Novell FTP Services server can handle?
   a. 32
   b. 65
   c. 98
   d. There is no maximum

3. Which of the following statements about Netscape FastTrack Server is *not* true?
   a. Long name space support must be loaded on volume **Sys** and other volumes that will hold Web server files
   b. DNS must be running if host names will be used
   c. 64 MB or more of RAM is required to install Netscape FastTrack server
   d. Installation is run from the **Products\FastTrack directory**.

4. For the server to automatically load Netscape FastTrack Server, which file must be modified?
   a. Install.nlm
   b. Config.sys
   c. Autoexec.ncf
   d. Startup.ncf

5. Which Netscape FastTrack Server NLM loads the Netscape FastTrack Server for NetWare?
   a. Admserv.nlm
   b. Cssysmsg.nlm
   c. Netdb.nlm
   d. Nshttpd.nlm

6. To access the Administration Server to configure Netscape FastTrack Server, you:
   a. Type **Admserv.nlm** at the file server and press **Enter**.
   b. Launch NetWare Administrator and choose **Configure FastTrack Server** from the Tools menu.
   c. Run a browser and provide the server's URL.
   d. Click the associated server's name icon on the desktop once you have installed its related workstation software.

7. What is the standard port number used for an unsecured Web server?
   a. 64
   b. 80
   c. 443
   d. 65535

8. Which of the following is *not* one of the parameters you can modify using Server Manager?
   a. Port number
   b. Document directories
   c. User file storage
   d. Performance

9. Which form do you use to set the maximum number of connections to be handled for any given socket?
   a. Listen Queue Size
   b. Performance Tuning
   c. Packet Delivery
   d. Content Management

10. What do you specify in order to control what the user sees when they log in to your Netscape FastTrack Server?
    a. Index filename
    b. Default directory
    c. Content management
    d. Listen Queue Size

11. Which two files are default index filenames?
    a. Index.html
    b. Start.html
    c. Home.html
    d. Main.html

12. Which two tasks must you perform to control which documents users can see when they access your Netscape FastTrack Server?
    a. Bind the Netscape FastTrack server to NDS
    b. Establish local settings
    c. Specify indexing to be Fancy
    d. Create access restrictions

13. What is the minimum amount of RAM that your server must have in addition to that needed for the NetWare operating system in order to run Novell FTP services?
    a. 4
    b. 6
    c. 8
    d. 12

14. Which of the following statements about FTP server is *not* true?
    a. It is installed as part of NetWare NFS Services.
    b. It requires that NFS name space support be added to the volume on which FTP server will be functioning.
    c. The command to load NFS name space support must be placed into the **Autoexec.ncf** file to ensure it is loaded each time the server is started.
    d. The installation is run using the Nwconfig utility.

15. Which FTP server parameter would you consider modifying if most network users access the server early in the morning, and don't release the connection for others to use until they go home at night?
    a. Intruder Detection
    b. Idle Time Before FTP Server Unloads
    c. Maximum Number of Sessions
    d. Maximum Session Length

Answers to Practice Test Questions

1. a, b	6. c	11. a, c
2. b	7. b	12. a, d
3. d	8. c	13. d
4. c	9. b	14. c
5. d	10. a	15. d

CHAPTER 9

Maintaining and Optimizing a NetWare 5 Network

I nstalling the NetWare 5 server, creating user accounts and various NDS objects, setting up printing, and the host of other tasks you must do as a network administrator gets your network up and running. Default configuration settings implemented when the server is installed establish a baseline from which your NetWare 5 server and network can function. As the needs of your network's users grow and change, and network traffic and processing demands increase, you may want to optimize your network, and you will occasionally need to troubleshoot and repair problems. To ensure your NetWare 5 network performs at its best possible level, you will benefit from an understanding of how a NetWare server performs some of its basic tasks such as:

- Memory allocation and memory management
- Disk space usage
- Network communications
- NDS maintenance

This chapter provides you with basic information about how NetWare 5 implements such things as memory allocation, CPU time allocation, and disk usage. It also explains how NetWare 5 maximizes network communications, using features such as Packet Burst protocol and Large Internet Packets. In addition, it provides you with information about the types of tasks you can perform to help maintain a stable, consistent, and responsive NDS database.

Understanding Memory and Memory Management

Just like our children, NetWare has grown up over the years. If you have any experience with previous versions of NetWare such as versions 2, 3, or 4, you will recognize the many improvements in NetWare 5. For example, NetWare 5's GUI (Graphical User Interface) installation is much easier to run and configure than was the DOS, text-based installation programs used in earlier versions.

For those network administrators doing the actual installations or working with utilities to manage the network, changes such as a GUI instead of a text-based installation are obvious. Much of the growing up that NetWare has done, however, is less obvious; it has occurred on the inside. Basic functionality, how NetWare handles memory, and a variety of other less-noticeable improvements contribute substantially to enabling an effective, stable network.

For you to successfully manage the network, you need a basic understanding of NetWare 5's memory management architecture. NetWare 5's memory management architecture and how it handles memory allocation and utilization not only makes for a more efficient server operating system, but makes it much easier for companies to develop specialty NLMs to run on NetWare 5 servers. The more NLMs available and loaded on your server, the more important it becomes that memory management and allocation function efficiently. Parameter settings help ensure that proper utilization and efficient processing occur on the NetWare server. While default parameters settings deemed to be optimal for the NetWare server are created during server installation, it is up to you as the network administrator to modify those settings when changes such as network growth make those settings less than optimal. Of course, that also means you have to know how to determine when the settings are no longer optimal, and what effect making changes to those settings will have on your network.

Memory Management Architecture

Memory management architecture is what makes memory allocation and efficient utilization possible. NetWare 5's memory management architecture is designed to meet four specific goals:

- Efficient performance
- Efficient memory allocation
- Simple memory environment
- Secure memory environment

Memory allocation is probably the most important memory architecture goal over which you can have some influence. Once you understand what memory allocation is and how NetWare 5 implements it, you will be able to see what configuration changes you can make to optimize memory allocation in your networking environment.

> Memory allocation in the NetWare 5 server is accomplished by using *paging*. Each 4 KB block of RAM in a NetWare 5 server's memory is a page. Regardless of where any two or more pages of memory are physically located, NetWare can treat them as if they were contiguous. This allows NetWare to load files and program instructions larger than 4 KB in size anywhere it needs to in memory, and still access it all as if it was one continuous file or program process.

KEY CONCEPT

While NetWare can put these files and instructions anywhere it wants to, it is more efficient to put collections of data and instructions contiguously together when possible. For some programs, such as the NetWare 5 operating system software, it is crucial that the software be placed in an area of memory where a certain amount of protection from other programs and files can occur. Even if only one 4 KB page of NetWare OS software were to be overwritten by an application program or data file, disastrous results could occur.

To protect important software such as the NetWare OS, and to ensure that other processes and data files don't become corrupted or corrupt other processes and data files in memory, NetWare 5 reserves specific memory location in RAM for processes, instructions, and data. These areas in memory are referred to as *pools*. The NetWare 5 network operating system (NOS) gives each process its own allocation pool. When a process needs memory, it is given memory from its assigned allocation pool. When it has finished using that memory, the memory is returned to the allocation pool and made available for other processes.

This process is similar to what travel agencies do for a group of conventioneers. The travel agency reserves a block of hotel rooms. When each conventioneer arrives at the hotel, they are randomly assigned a room, but only within that block of rooms that have been reserved for their group. If a conventioneer is staying only for one night of a three night stay, another conventioneer who is staying for the other two nights can be allocated the same room once the first conventioneer has turned in the key. (That way, the conventioneers only trip over each other at brunches and conferences.)

When a process or file releases the space in memory that was allocated to it, NetWare uses memory deallocation and garbage collection to collect unused segments of memory and return them to the common memory pool. This is somewhat similar to what the hotel employees must do when one or more conventioneers checks out of their room.

Like the hotel employees who know as soon as you check out that the room needs to be cleaned and put back into the list of available rooms, NetWare has to be notified that the allocated memory is now available. A check of the usage of *virtual memory* (data storage on the disk in which the processor can temporarily store data needed back in memory within a short period of time) is the trigger which determines whether garbage collection happens immediately (on heavy virtual memory usage), or if it happens according to a predefined interval (on light virtual memory usage). That predefined interval is established by configuring the Set Garbage Collection Interval parameter.

KEY CONCEPT

When garbage collection is initiated, an API (Application program Interface) named Free identifies the pages in memory as deallocated. The garbage collection process then gathers those areas of deallocated memory and returns them to the memory pool. This garbage collection routine is run automatically by NetWare 5 as a background process so that it does not interfere with regular work. Garbage collection can be interrupted to allow tasks with higher priority to be performed. For best memory allocation efficiency, garbage collection should be run frequently.

Virtual Memory

As noted, virtual memory is a NetWare system that allows data currently in RAM that is not being used frequently to be moved temporarily to storage in one or more volumes on the hard disk. The storage area is referred to as a *swap file*. You only can have one swap file on each NetWare volume.

This storage space (swap file) is as accessible to the processor as RAM, although somewhat slower to access. Virtual memory gives NetWare the ability to work more efficiently when multiple processes are required than it would otherwise be able to were it limited to the available physical RAM—even though some additional resources are required to manage virtual memory.

During the installation of NetWare 5, a swap file is automatically created on the Sys volume. Swap files are approximately 2 MB in size, although they are *dynamic* (changing in size as data is swapped in and out of the file).

Although an initial swap file is created on the **Sys** volume, you may prefer to create a swap file on another volume and delete the one that

■ **Swap Parameter volume parameter=value.** Replacing *volume* with the actual name of a volume, and *parameter=value* with a parameter name and value, an existing swap file's parameter values are modified to this specified setting.

You can also view information about swap files currently in use by completing the following steps:

1. Load the Monitor utility at the server by entering **Monitor** at the server console prompt. The Monitor utility Available Options menu opens.
2. Choose **Virtual Memory**.
3. Choose **Swap Files**.
4. Select a swap file, then press **Tab**. Swap file information displays (see Figure 9-1).

If only one swap file displays, pressing **Tab** only switches between the Swap files list and the window displaying swap file information.

NOTE

Even though virtual memory gives NetWare the ability to work more efficiently when multiple processes are required, there is such a thing as too much of a good thing when it comes to virtual memory. Time is required to transfer data in and out of RAM and virtual memory. If doing so takes up too much of the processor's time, there's little time left for the processor to do the tasks for which it was designed.

Insufficient server memory causes excessive use of virtual memory. This condition is known as *disk thrashing*. While even disk thrashing is

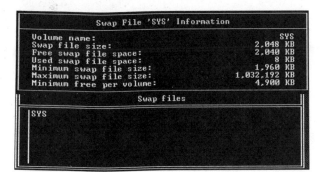

FIGURE 9-1 An example of the swap file information that the Monitor utility displays.

exists on **Sys**. Whenever data needs to be swapped out of me
into a swap file, the data can be put into any swap file on an\
depending on where the software decides to put it. Therefore,
file on the **Sys** volume could actually be used too frequently. Ke
Sys volume free of extraneous data and limited in access
results in better network server performance.

A swap file is deleted from the volume on which it resides w
volume is dismounted, with the exception of the swap file on the
ume. Part of the process of bringing down the server is that of di\
ing volumes. Therefore, when you create swap files on other volun
need to put the commands to create the swap file into the **Autoe**
file so that the files are created whenever the server is started.

To create a swap file, put the following command in
Autoexec.ncf file: **Swap add volume [parameter=value]** or ty
the server console. Replace *volume* with the name of the volu
which you want the swap file created, and *parameter=value* with
the following parameters and their value:

- **Min=.** This parameter allows you to specify the minimum size
  swap file. If not specified, the default is 2 MB. For example, to us
  parameter type: **Min=5**.
- **Max=.** This parameter allows you to specify the maximum size o
  swap file. If not specified, the default is all free space on the vol\
  For example, to use this parameter type: **Max=Free volume spac**
- **Min Free=.** This parameters allows you to specify how much
  space must remain on the volume, the balance of which can ther
  given to the swap file. If not specified, the default is 5 MB. For ex\
  ple, to use this parameter type: **Min Free=6**.

NOTE

When specifying a parameter, specify the parameter's name f\
lowed without space by the equal sign, then again without spa\
by the value. For example, create a swap file on volume **Dat**
which sets a minimum size of 4 MB by typing: **Swap Add Dat**
Min=4.

Other commands you can use regarding swap files are:

- **Swap.** Typed at the server console prompt, it displays information
  about all swap files currently in use.
- **Swap Del volume.** Replacing *volume* with the actual name of a server
  volume, this command deletes the swap file from the volume, transferring any current data it contains to another swap file.

better than having processes fail due to lack of memory, response time is drastically reduced.

To correct disk thrashing, you must add RAM to your NetWare server. Then the virtual memory will be able to better do what it was intended to do—make more efficient use of sufficient memory and improve server performance. The fact that applications loaded into virtual memory also provide a certain amount of protection means that server reliability is improved as well.

Protected Memory

In a perfect NetWare world, all NLMs developed by other companies would be as conscientious of memory usage as the NOS itself. But sometimes NLMs run a little wild and tromp on memory that has not been allocated to them. When this occurs, corruption of the memory space into which the NLM trespassed, as well as of the NLM itself can cause the NetWare server to ABEND (suffer an abnormal end), the only solution to which can require a cold boot of the server. Any of the NLMs may end up with corrupted files as well, requiring that some or all of the system and NLM files be reinstalled.

To prevent this kind of occurrence, NetWare provides protected memory, also called protected address space. *Protected address space* is an area of memory that is carefully controlled. Any software loaded into protected memory is not allowed to read or write to a memory location outside of its assigned protected memory. In effect, it is prevented from using any memory except protected memory, or virtual memory. Both the NLM and the data it needs can be swapped to virtual memory.

When a module is loaded into protected memory, even its communication with the server operating system is carefully controlled. The Syscalls.nlm and the memory protection subsystem that NetWare 5 provides act as the interface between the protected address spaces and the server operating system (which runs in its own space called the *OS address space* or the *kernel address space*), preventing modules in protected space from passing calls to the OS. Faulty or corrupted calls passed to the NetWare OS could also corrupt the OS and unexpectedly bring down the NetWare server.

As the network administrator, you have control over whether protected memory space is used (created) and what modules are loaded into or unloaded from it. Like many server configuration implementations, you enter one or more commands at the server console to set or modify configuration related to protected address spaces. There are ten protected address space-related commands you can enter at the console prompt. Before you use any of them, however, consider the following:

- If you load a module into protected memory space and it must communicate with other modules in addition to the NOS (NetWare Operating System), the other modules with which it must communicate must also be loaded into the same protected memory space. (If loading an NLM that autoloads other NLMs, all of the NLMs will be automatically loaded into the same protected memory space.)
- A single module (even one that is designed to be loaded only once) can be loaded multiple times if each load instance places the module into a different protected address space. In addition, if a module is loaded into multiple protected address spaces, the code for that module can be shared among the different protected address spaces into which the module was loaded. The software for the module then is not duplicated. Extra space is only required for the data that is unique to each protected address space.
- While no single protected address space can be larger than 512 MB, within that maximum, the amount of space expands or contracts as needed for the module.

The ten protected address space-related commands you can enter at the server console prompts are:

- **Load Address space=address_space_name module_name.** When used more than once with a different module name (in place of *module_name*), but with the same address space name (in place of *address_space-name*), loads multiple modules into the same address space.
- **Load Protected module_name.** Loads a module into a new protected address space. (Replace *module_name* with the name of the NLM.)
- **Module.** Lists all NLMs and the address space in which they are loaded.
- **Protect NCF_file_name.** Creates a protected address space with the same name as the NCF file, and loads all of the modules specified in the .NCF file into this protected address space.
- **Protection.** Displays all address spaces and the modules they contain.
- **Restart module_name.** Loads a module into protected address space with the restart option. If the module ABENDS, the system automatically shuts down, restarts the protected address space, and reloads the module.
- **SET Memory Protection Fault Cleanup=On.** If the module in a protected address space ABENDs, this parameter causes the server to remove the space and its modules, and returns the resources to the system. Otherwise, the cleanup is left to the ABEND recovery mechanism.

- **Unload Address Space=address_space_name.** Removes the address space and returns the resources to the system after first unloading any modules that currently reside in the specified address space.
- **Unload Address Space=address_space_name module_name.** Unloads the module from this address space without removing the address space.
- **Unload Kill Address Space=address_space_name.** Removes the address space and returns the resources to the system without first unloading any modules currently residing in the specified address space.

To create a protected address space and load a module into it:

1. From the server console prompt, enter **Load Protected module_ name**, replacing *module_name* with the actual name of the module. For example, to load Unicon.NLM into protected address space, enter: **Load Protected Unicon**.

2. At the server console prompt, verify that the load was successful by entering **Protection**. A list of address spaces displays (see Figure 9-2).

Optimizing Disk Space and Usage

Optimizing RAM is one way to maintain your network, but hard disk space is important as well, particularly when it affects the **Sys** volume. Preventing the **Sys** volume from filling up is key to keeping the NetWare server running efficiently. Optimizing hard disk storage space not only makes better, more cost-effective use of file server storage, but also helps to ensure that **Sys** volume continues to have enough space to function properly.

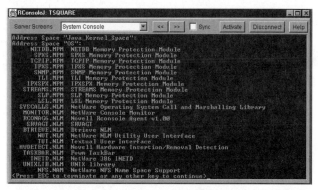

FIGURE 9-2 A list of address spaces retrieved by entering the Protection command at the server console prompt.

To optimize hard disk storage space, you can use two NetWare features:

- Block suballocation
- File compression

Block Suballocation

Just as NetWare divides memory into usable chunks (pages), it also divides hard disk space into usable chunks (blocks). One commonly used block size is 4 KB, although larger sizes (16 KB or larger, referred to as *large disk allocation blocks*) can be allocated, depending on how much hard disk storage space the server has available.

When NetWare saves a file to the hard disk, it saves it into these blocks, using as many or as few blocks as needed. For an 8 KB file, NetWare will use two blocks of storage space. For a 7 KB file, NetWare still uses two blocks of storage space, and the same is true for files sized 6 KB, 5 KB, 4.75 KB, and so on. In other words, if a file is even a fraction larger than 4 KBs, NetWare requires two full blocks of space to store the file. Any file smaller than 4 KBs in size still requires that an entire 4 KB block space be set aside for its use. On a network where most files are quite large, the wasted hard disk space is much less than on a network where many files are relatively small.

NetWare's block suballocation capability allows NetWare to subdivide individual blocks into chunks as small as 512 bytes. Each 512 byte of hard disk space is called a *suballocation block*. Each 4 KB block can be subdivided into multiple 512 byte suballocation blocks. With suballocation, any time a file is less than 4 KB in size, or is larger than any increment of 4 KB, the leftover bytes can be stored in one or more suballocation blocks.

NOTE The beginning of each 512 byte maximum piece of file that needs to be stored in a suballocation block is stored at the beginning of the suballocation block. If the file fragment or small file does not fill the entire 512 byte suballocation block, then the remainder of that block will be wasted space. However, any percentage of a 512 byte suballocation block that is wasted is substantially less than it would be if a portion of an entire 4 KB block were to be wasted.

The process of suballocation is a little like packing to move. Boxes come in preset sizes. However, your dishes, clothing, collectibles, and so on don't come in the same sizes as the boxes. It would be inefficient and more costly for you to simply put one item in each box, as a tremendous amount of space would be left over. Consequently, you generally pack the larger items into boxes first, then tuck the smaller items into those same boxes, wherever they will fit.

Suballocation works basically the same way. Initially, files are stored in whichever blocks are available, then NetWare later determines whether a file or file fragment is taking up a full 4 KB block of space it does not need. If the file or file fragment is not using a full 4 KB block, NetWare moves the file or file fragment into one or more suballocation blocks. Although we pack our little items into whatever leftover space exists in the box, not concerning ourselves with whether or not those little items are put at the beginning of the box, NetWare must put each file or file fragment at the beginning of each 512 byte suballocation block so that it can find it later.

NOTE

By default, block suballocation is enabled when NetWare is installed. If you want to disable block suballocation, you must recreate the volume. Doing so, of course, destroys all data on the existing volume, so be sure to back up that data first so you can restore it later.

File Compression

Have you ever used a file compression utility such as WinZip? The concept of file compress in NetWare is very similar, but the control you have over it is much greater in NetWare than with products such as WinZip. When running a file compression utility such as WinZip, about the only thing you get to specify is which files get compressed, and the name of the path to the zip file which results from the compression process.

In addition, if you want WinZip (or other similar software) to compress one or more files, you must tell it to do so. With NetWare, however, once file compress is set to on (file compression is enabled on each volume by default unless you turned compression off during installation), compression of files is automatic. You do not have to even worry about whether the files get compressed.

NOTE

Once file compression is enabled for a volume, you cannot disable it without recreating the volume. However, you can prevent the automatic compression of some or all files on the volume from occurring, even though compression is enabled for the volume. To prevent compression from occurring on a volume in which file compression has been enabled, enter the following command at the server console: **Set Enable File Compression=off**.

On the average, compressing files on a volume saves approximately 63% of storage space over not compressing the files on a volume. This is referred to as the *file compression ratio*. As long as the minimum required compression ratio will be met, NetWare compresses files quickly, with minimum overhead, and only when the files have not been accessed for a period of time. This ensures that compression and subsequent decompression (done when the files once again need to be accessed) have no noticeable effect on system performance. Figure 9-3 shows you the process that the NetWare OS goes through in order to determine whether a file should be compressed, then to compress, validate, and restore the file.

With NetWare's file compression, you get to specify not only whether it runs, but also several other features of file compression. To specify settings for those features, you use Set commands stored in the **Autoexec.ncf** file. Features (settings) you can modify, and the accompanying **Set** command you use, include:

- When the NOS should start looking for files to compress (Compression Daily Check Starting Hour)
- When the NOS should stop looking for files to compress (Compression Daily Check Stop Hour)
- Whether the compressed version of a file that has been decompressed and committed to disk should: 0= always be left on the disk, 1=should be left on the disk for a limited period of time (default), or 2=should be changed to the uncompressed version (Convert Compressed to Uncompressed Option)
- How many days after a file was last accessed should the system wait before compressing a file (Days Untouched Before Compression)

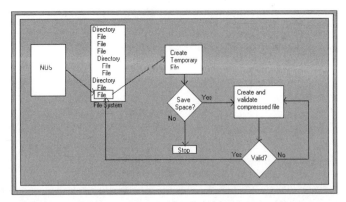

FIGURE 9-3 The file compression decision making and completion process.

- How often warning alerts should be displayed when insufficient free disk space exists for decompressing files (Decompress Free Space Warning Interval)
- What percentage (10% is the default) of free disk space should be available before an uncompressed file can be committed to disk (Decompress Percent Disk Space Free To Allow Commit)
- How unpurged deleted files should be compressed: 0=never, 1=compress next day (default option), or 2=compress immediately (Deleted File Compression Option)
- What percentage smaller in size a file must be after compression for the system to compress the file at all (Minimum Compression Percentage Gain)
- How many volumes (2 is the default) can simultaneously compress files (Maximum Concurrent Compressions)

You can view compression statistics for any server on which compression is enabled by using any of the following utilities:

- **NetWare Administrator.** Right-click the volume object, click **Details**, then click **Statistics** (see Figure 9-4).
- **Windows Explorer.** Run **Explorer**, right-click a drive mapped to the volume, click **Properties**, then click the **NetWare Volume Statistics** tab (see Figure 9-5).
- **NDIR.** In a DOS box or at a DOS prompt, type **Ndir /Vol** (see Figure 9-6).
- **Filer.** Run Filer, choose **View Volume Information**, then choose **Statistics** (see Figure 9-7).

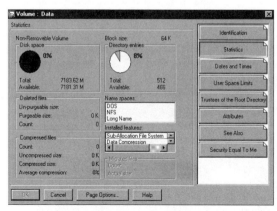

FIGURE 9-4 View of volume compression information using NetWare Administrator.

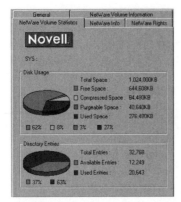

FIGURE 9-5 View of volume compression information using Windows Explorer.

To maximize disk space savings on your NetWare 5 file server, consider enabling suballocation, compression, and the use of large disk allocation blocks when appropriate.

Improving Communications Using Packet Burst and Large Internet Packets

While suballocation and compression concern themselves with making the most use of disk space and efficiently handling small files or file fragments, LIP and Packet Burst are designed to deal with larger files and the transmission of packets (data encapsulated in transmission information

```
⌐⌐ Command Prompt                                                    _ □ ✕
E:\PUBLIC>ndir /vol

Statistics for fixed volume  SSSCO\SYS:
Space statistics are in KB (1024 bytes).

Total volume space:                          1,024,000  100.00%
Space used by 20,653 entries:                  338,688   33.08%
Deleted space not yet purgeable:                     0    0.00%
                                             ---------
Space remaining on volume:                     685,312   66.93%
Space available to ADMIN:                      685,312   66.93%

Maximum directory entries:                      32,768
Available directory entries:                    12,115   36.97%

Space used if files were not compressed:       199,168
Space used by compressed files:                 84,480
                                             ---------
Space saved by compressing files:              114,688   57.58%

Uncompressed space used:                       294,848

Name spaces loaded: OS/2

E:\PUBLIC>
```

FIGURE 9-6 View of volume compression information using Ndir /Vol.

```
                      Volume statistics
Total space in KB(1024 bytes):        1,024,000  100.00%
Active space used:                       338,752   33.08%
Deleted space not yet purgeable:              64    0.01%
Space remaining on volume:               685,248   66.92%

Maximum directory entries:                32,768
Directory entries available:              12,105   36.94%

Space used if not compressed:            199,168
Total space compressed:                   84,480
Space saved by compressing data:         114,688   57.58%
Uncompressed space used:                 294,912
```

FIGURE 9-7 View of volume compression information using Filer.

such as where the data is to be delivered, who sent the packet, what protocol is being used, and so on).

Packet Burst Protocol

Imagine trying to carry on a telephone conversation that mandated that after you said a single sentence, you couldn't speak again until you received an acknowledgment from the party on the other end. Network communication use to be like that. The Packet Burst protocol has changed that so that network communications now functions more like normal conversation. The Packet Burst protocol is a NetWare Core Protocol (NCP) that helps to ensure the quick and successful delivery of multiple read or write requests in a single transmission. Packet Burst makes it possible for up to 64 KB of data to be transmitted at a time. Using Packet Burst, the client or server can transmit multiple packets without having to wait for a response between each packet from the receiving client or server.

NOTE

The Packet Burst protocol has proven to be quite effective, increasing communication performance anywhere from 10% to 300%. Before NetWare 4.11 was released, network administrators had to set parameters in the workstation's **Net.cfg** file and load the Pburst.nlm on the file server to take advantage of Packet Burst. Since NetWare 4.11 (and thus in NetWare 5), Packet Burst is enabled by default.

When a workstation establishes its initial connection with a NetWare server, it sets up a Packet Burst connection, providing the workstation has sufficient memory to use Packet Burst. If it does not, or if Packet Burst has been turned off at the workstation (it cannot be turned off at the server) a regular NCP connection is established.

During setup, the workstation and client negotiate as to the largest Packet Burst size to be used (it doesn't have to be the full 64 KB in size, since the workstation may not be able to handle packets that large). Once established, the Packet Burst connection remains open for as long as the connection exists to the server.

Like other aspects of NetWare, Packet Burst parameters can be set to configure some aspects of Packet Burst. For example, you can set a parameter that specifies how many packets should be sent in a single burst (burst window size), and how much time should exist between individual packets in the burst so that the buffers don't become flooded with packets before they can each be processed (burst gap time).

 You can set the burst window size to a theoretical maximum of 128, since each packet is 512 bytes in size, and the maximum that can be sent in a single burst is 64 KB.

KEY CONCEPT

Even when the burst window size and burst gap time are set to what seems to be optimal, packets can still sometimes get dropped during transmission. This happens on networks that are particularly busy. However, because the Packet Burst protocol also includes a packet monitoring capability, it knows when a packet was not successfully delivered. It then resends the dropped packet without having to resend the other packets that were contained in the burst.

To modify Packet Burst parameters at a Windows 95 or Windows NT workstation, you right-click Network Neighborhood, then complete the following steps:

1. Click **Properties**.
2. Click the **Client Configuration** tab.
3. Click **Novell NetWare Client**.
4. Click **Properties**.
5. Click the **Advanced Settings** tab.

You can then scroll to see the parameters associated with Packet Burst.

Large Internet Packets (LIP)

By default, the typical packet size is 512 bytes. This size accommodates sending packets on networks where not all workstations can handle larger packets, or where *routers* (devices—often NetWare servers—running software that handles the exchange of packets between different network cabling systems) exist that are restricted in the maximum packet size that they can handle. However, if the network has neither of these packet size limitations, the Large Internet Packet (LIP) feature of NetWare lets the workstation and server negotiate the size of packets, based on the size of the workstation's and server's buffers. By default, LIP is enabled at the server when NetWare is installed, and at the workstation when the Novell Client is installed.

Those routers capable of handling larger packets are often set to the more restricted size of 512 KB. If this is the case and you want to take advantage of LIP, you will need to configure the routers to handle the larger packet size. You add the following command to the server's **Startup.ncf** file to enable routers to handle larger packets: **Set Maximum Physical Receive Packet Size = size** (replacing *size* with the maximum packet size you want to use). The default size is 4202 bytes. However, the maximum packet size cannot exceed the maximum size that NetWare can handle, and that size is determined by the topology (the physical connection of servers and clients) of your network. Those maximum sizes based on topology are:

- On an Ethernet network: 1514 bytes
- On a 4 Mbps Token Ring network: 4202
- On a 16 Mbps Token Ring network: 4202

When used together, the Packet Burst protocol and LIP improve the exchange of packets on the network, reduce the number of packets that need to be exchanged, and improve the overall performance of your network.

Using Applications

NetWare 5 memory management and its use of virtual memory help to protect processes running on the server, improve performance, allow multiple processes to run and use resources simultaneously, and provide overall better service to your network users. Of course, what network users care about the most is how quickly they can get what they need, including how quickly any processing they request can be accomplished. You know that NetWare 5 automatically allocates CPU time to processes, but it can also allocate CPU time to applications.

Applications (sometimes referred to as *virtual machines*), like NLMs and other modules, function because they contain strings of code which cause various tasks to be performed. These strings of code are referred to as *threads*. A single thread has a beginning, an end, and often has multiple paths that it can take in between. Each of these threads is also called a *routine*.

Applications consist of groups of threads. When a thread that needs CPU time requests it, a share of CPU time is allocated to it. When a routine is given its turn at using the CPU, if it gets in, does its job, then releases the CPU to service other threads, other routines can then be given the same consideration. Sometimes, however, threads take up more CPU time than they should. When this occurs, the thread is said to have *gone to sleep*. When a thread is in sleep time, NetWare suspends the thread. The CPU time is then allocated to another thread. (It's a bit like waiting in line at the checkout for a price check on a product someone in front of you is buying. You don't know how long it will take, so you're grateful when another check stand is opened and you get to finally check out.)

While NetWare makes allocation of CPU resources available, it lets you decide how long a thread is allowed to tie up the CPU before it must release the resource. You do this by first specifying programs as applications, then assigning a share value to the application.

You don't have to specify all programs as applications, however, since some programs create their own applications when they are loaded. For example, all of the NetWare services are provided by the NetWare Application, and all the threads run by NLMs are assigned to this application. Also, programs which don't create their application are assigned by default to the NetWare Application. If you want a program to be assigned to its own application so that you can then assign a larger share of CPU time, you can do so.

To manually define an application, load the NLM using the following special format: **Load -A=app_name NLM_name**. Replace *app_name* with the name you want to assign to the application, and *NLM_name* with the name of the NLM to be loaded. For example, to load the FastTrack Web Server, type **Load -A=FastTrack nsweb.ncf**.

To adjust the share value of an application, complete the following steps:

1. From the file server console, load the Monitor utility by typing **Monitor** and pressing **Enter**. The Available Options menu opens.
2. Choose **Kernel**. The Kernel Options menu opens.
3. Choose **Applications**. The Applications menu opens.
4. Select the application for which you want to modify the share value, then press **F3**. The New Share Value window opens.
5. Enter the share value you want to set for this application.
6. Press **Esc** repeatedly to save the change and return you to Monitor's Available Options menu, then Exit Monitor.

KEY CONCEPT

It is the ratio between the application's share value and the share values assigned to other applications on this server that determines how much CPU time this application will receive, not the actual number you assigned as the application's share value. For example, if only one other application exists and it has a share value of two, assigning a share value of one to this application will allot it half as much CPU time as the other application receives. If you want this application to have twice as much CPU time as the other application, you'd have to assign it a share value of four. To allot an equal amount of CPU time to both applications, set both applications to the same number. In this case, both applications would have a share value of two.

Maintaining NDS

Although by now you should be quite familiar with the terms NDS and Directory, a brief review of these terms, and information on how NDS updates, tracks, and maintains the Database may help you to better understand how to maintain NDS. This section provides a review of these terms, and gives you a brief overview of how the Database is organized, managed, and updated in a NetWare 5 network. This section also explains what you as a network administrator can do to help maintain NDS and thus the efficient functioning of your network.

Overview of NDS and the Directory

NetWare's NDS is a network service like printing, security, or electronic messaging, responsible for organizing and providing access to all information related to other network services and how to access them. NDS stores this information in a database called the Directory, which is made up of three named items:

- **Objects.** Represent resources available on the network. Every resource, whether physical like a printer or logical like a group of users, is represented by an object. An object is a record of information about that resource.
- **Properties.** For every object on the network, there is a defined set of information that can be stored about that object. For example, a User object's defined set of information includes such properties as a user's name, address, telephone number, login ID, and so on. The list of properties for an object is its list of what types of information can be stored for that object. (This is similar to the names of fields that have

been defined as information to be collected about each record in a database.)

- **Values.** The actual information associated with each property is the value of that property. For example, the user's actual name is the value associated with the User object's User Name property.

NDS uses the Directory to verify an object's rights to perform an action and to authenticate users to the network. Unlike a directory on a PC, this Directory does not contain information about the file system, except that it does contain Server and Volume objects and information related to those objects. In order to store information about all objects in the Directory tree, NDS stores the information in a database.

That database, although it actually consists of multiple files, is treated as a single database in NetWare: its associated database files are stored on one or more NetWare file servers. However, because that database is arranged in a logical hierarchy using container objects, it can be logically divided into smaller segments of information (referred to as *partitioning the database*) for purposes of storing the database information. Even though the information can be divided into smaller, logical segments called *partitions*, each partition is still a logical part of the whole database and is treated as such.

Because each partition can keep its own associated information about the objects contained within it in its own set of interrelated files, the partition can be copied out to multiple file servers in the network. This process is known as *replication* and the copy of the partition is known as a *replica*. Any replica of a given partition can be stored on several different file servers. Storing replicas on multiple file servers provides network fault protection, load balancing, and easier user access. It also requires that NetWare ensures that these replicas all keep updated with the most current information (objects, properties, and values) stored in the replica's related set of database files. Ensuring that all replicas are kept updated is known as *synchronization*. Replicas on the network must be periodically synchronized to ensure the latest information is available. Replica synchronization is done automatically by NetWare, and is affected by:

- Whether the change is simple (such as making a change to the value of a User object's Address property) or complex (such as combining two partitions into one).
- The size of the partition (smaller partitions take less time to synchronize than do larger partitions).
- The number of servers holding a copy of the replica, as each copy of the replica, except possibly the subordinate reference replica (defined below), must be updated.

Replica synchronization is determined by the type of replica, of which there are four:

- **Master.** A complete copy of the partition. Only one master replica can exist for each partition. It is responsible for original requests to make changes to the partition and the objects it contains.
- **Read/write.** Also a complete copy of the partition. It can fill original requests for object changes. However, it passes all requests for partition changes to the master replica. The network can have multiple read/write replicas for any given partition.
- **Read only.** Also a complete copy of the partition. It passes all request for original changes to either the master replica or to one of the read/write replicas. As with read/write replicas, each partition can have multiple read only replicas.
- **Subordinate reference.** This type of replica is not a copy of the partition. It is only a pointer used to direct NDS to replicas that contain a copy of the partition.

How to Maintain NDS

Maintaining NDS means that you are doing your part to monitor and maintain the integrity of the NDS database. NetWare 5 provides you with three specialized tools to help you do just that:

- **Set command.** Enter **Set NDS Trace to Screen = On** at the server console prompt to enable a console display of network activity. This is a tool to help you view and monitor activity, rather than to help you affect activity.
- **Dsrepair utility.** Enter **Dsrepair** at the server console to repair and correct problems in the NDS database. Dsrepair can correct problems within records, the schema, and other areas. To run Dsrepair, enter **[path]DSREPAIR [-U]**. Replace *[path]* with the path to this NLM if you moved it from its default path of **Sys:System**. Include the -U option if you want Dsrepair to exit and unload from server RAM when it has finished running. When you enter the Dsrepair command, the Available Options menu opens (see Figure 9-8). Choose what you want Dsrepair to do. For more information about the options on this menu, press **F1** for help.
- **NDS Manager utility.** This is the utility you will use the most for managing your Directory. (It is also the utility that the NetWare 5 Advanced Administration course manual concentrates on, so it's the one discussed the most here as well.) With NDS Manager (a replacement for the Partition Manager you ran from the Tools menu in NetWare Administrator for NetWare 4.11), you can work with parti-

FIGURE 9-8 The Available Options menu for Dsrepair.NLM.

tioning and replication, repair the NDS database from a client workstation, update NDS with a newer version of DS.nlm, print partition information, and run diagnostics to determine the general condition of the Directory tree.

To use NDS Manager, run it from a Windows workstation by completing the following steps:

1. Click **Start**, then click **Run**.
2. Use the browse button and locate the **Ndsmgr32.exe** file at the following path on the file server: **Sys:\Public\Win32**, then double-click the file.
3. Click **OK** to launch NDS Manager. The NDS Manager utility opens. (If no view displays by default inside the utility, click **Window** in the menu bar, then click **New Window**. A view similar to that shown in Figure 9-9 displays.
4. If necessary, change your context in NDS Manager to ensure the server you want to manage is displayed in the Server window on the right. Once the context is set, you can use NDS Manager to perform several tasks.

NOTE

The NetWare 5 CNE Advanced Administration course does not cover each of the tasks listed below. It only introduces you to the NDS Manager, shows you how to start it, and has you perform an exercise using it. Other information you learn about NDS Manager comes from those features of NDS Manager that the course instructor chooses to show you and explain. NDS Manager is a very useful tool. You should run NDS Manager in your own network (or at least in a lab environment so that you can make changes without causing temporary network problems), and become familiar with its capabilities, screen views, and usefulness.

Using NDS Manager, you can:

■ **View a server's replica information.** In the right window pane, double-click the name of the server. (You can also choose **Object** from the

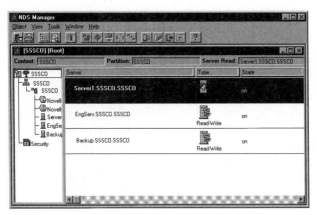

FIGURE 9-9 The main window that displays in NDS Manager.

menu bar, then choose **Information**.) The Replica Information window opens. It provides information such as the partition and server on which the replica is stored, the type of replica, and the last date and time it was successfully synchronized.

- **Add a replica.** Choose **Object** on the menu bar, then choose **Replica**. The Add Replica window opens. Specify the partition, name of the server to hold the replica, and the type of replica, then click **OK**.
- **Check synchronization for the tree.** This requires that you have the tree selected in the left window pane, then you can choose **Object** from the menu bar, and then choose **Check Synchronization**. The Check Synchronization window opens. Identify whether all partitions or just the selected partition is to be checked, click **OK**, and follow any additional prompts.
- **Merge or move a partition, or abort the process if one has already been chosen.** To do these tasks, choose **Object** from the menu bar, and choose **Partition**. You can then choose to **Merge**, **Move**, or **Abort Operation**.
- **Establish partition continuity.** Partition continuity involves various tasks such as synchronizing partition information, sending or receiving updates, verifying remote server IDS, assigning a new master, and removing a server. It also allows you to run a repair on replicas, network addresses, the local database, or volume objects. You access the separate partition continuity window and menu options by choosing **Object** from the NDS Manager window, then choosing **Partition Continuity**.
- **Manage the NDS schema.** By choosing **Object** from the menu bar, then choosing **NDS Schema**, the NDS Schema Manager window

opens. From the Object option on its menu bar, you can choose to perform such tasks as creating a new object class, deleting a class, adding optional attributes to an object class, run class manage, show inheritance, manage attributes, manage schema extension, run a schema compare or report, and set up printing so that you can print schema information.

- **View and update the NDS version.** Choose **Object** from the menu bar to display these two options. Choose to update the NDS version when the version of NDS running on your NetWare 5 network needs to be updated to a more recent version.
- **Set up printing, and print using the Object option on the menu bar.**
- **Set preferences.** You can determine how you want the default and replica display to look, what NDS update options you want to use (such as whether DS Repair should be unloaded when servers are being updated), and the location and file name to be used for the NDS update log, along with whether the log should be overwritten or have log files appended to one another.
- **Modify the view used to display information in NDS Manager.** Using the **View** option on the menu bar, you can change typical Windows options such as whether to show Hints and Quick Tips, but you can also select view options specifically for NDS Manager. For example, you can set your context, expand or collapse the view, choose between a view emphasis of Tree or Partitions and Servers, or choose how to split the view.
- **Load Remote Console.** By choosing **Remote Console** from the Tools option on the menu bar, you can load the Remote Console utility if the program files are set up in the default path.
- **Perform other basic Windows tasks** such as refreshing the window's contents (choose **Window**, then choose **Refresh**) or changing to a different window by choosing from the list of open windows in the Window menu.
- **View help information for NDS Manager.** Choose the **Help** option on the menu bar.

BASIC NETWORK MANAGEMENT TASKS

You can use the NDS Manager to perform some basic network management tasks. The important thing to concentrate on in this section is learning what types of network management tasks you should perform as a network administrator, and some basic information about those tasks.

Basic tasks a network administrator can do to monitor and manage their network include:

- **Regulate partition management rights.** Changes to partitions can have a profound affect on the database. Therefore, it is important that you be cautious when working with partitions, using only one workstation at a time from which you create or merge partitions (partition locking prevents simultaneous changes to multiple partitions anyway). In addition, you should regulate who manages partitions, limit their Supervisor right to only the partition root object they are administering, and grant only Create, Delete, Rename, and Browse object rights to container administrators for specific containers, but not to the partition.

- **Plan replica placement carefully.** Too many replicas of a partition increases network traffic, because synchronization affects more servers and can result in a less stable NDS. Too few can make it more difficult for users to authenticate to the network and access its resources, provide insufficient fault tolerance, and be problematic if the master and all of its replicas are damaged. Planning replica placement, however, is part of the design of your network, and not a management task you will perform once its design and setup (usually before the network is even installed) has been completed.

- **Back up the Directory on each server.** When you run regular network backups, you are backing up the file system. As a rule, you are not backing up the NDS tree. You should back up the NDS tree, however, when you first install and set up the directory tree, after major changes have been made, before creating or merging a partition, to ensure you have a current backup in case synchronization errors make it necessary to restore the NDS tree, or any other time you consider it important to have a more current backup of the NDS tree. Although Enhanced Sbackup software is provided with NDS which lets you back up the NDS tree, you can use any NDS-compliant backup set up that you have implemented.

- **Maintain a standard version of NDS.** When Novell provides an updated version of DS.nlm, you should implement it on your network's NetWare 5 servers in your NDS tree. (See the Novell Support Connection Web page at **http://support.novell.com** for updated versions). NDS problems are fixed by these updates, and functionality is often improved as well. However, your Directory tree can't take advantage of the updates unless all servers in a partition's replica list are running the new version.

- **Maintain sufficient disk space on the Sys volume.** Your network can experience difficulties if the **Sys** volume does not have enough space to perform its tasks. One thing that occurs when **Sys** runs out of space is that the Transactional Tracking System (TTS) of NetWare is turned off, and no changes to the Directory (which is stored on the **Sys** volume) can then be made. (TTS ensures each transaction is performed to full completion before committing it to the Directory so that if something happens in the middle of the process, either all of the transaction is recorded, or none of it is recorded.)

Some ways you can keep the **Sys** volume from running out of space include storing print queues and user files on other volumes, adding replicas only to servers with a plenty of space on **Sys** volume, and ensuring that if the server has a CD-ROM drive, you have an average of 8 MB of additional space the **Sys** volume can donate to the index (Cdrom$$.rom) the CD-ROM creates when it is mounted as a volume.

In addition, set minimum space requirements so that you receive a warning alert when the **Sys** volume is almost out of space (has only 256 blocks left). You do this with the following command: **SET VOLUME LOW WARNING THRESHOLD=number**, replacing *number* with a numeric from 0 to 1000000.

- **Prepare servers for scheduled downtime.** If you have to bring down a server or WAN link for an extended period of time (including permanently), you have to replace the hard disk in the server, or this server contains the only replica of the partition, first back up NDS, then remove NDS from the server using Nwconfig.nlm. If you have to bring down a server temporarily to perform a partition operation, make a large number of replica changes, or move the server, remove all replicas on the server first.

Some of these management tasks are done using NDS Manager. Brief descriptions and basic steps required of the majority of tasks you can perform using NDS Manager were discussed earlier in this chapter, so they are not repeated here.

DIAGNOSE AND RESOLVE NETWORK PROBLEMS

Your goal is to maintain an efficient, consistent network with no problems and limited downtime. Maintaining the NDS database is an important key to accomplishing that. The NDS database can occasionally experience problems, and sometimes become inconsistent (partition replicas are not synchronized so shared information is dissimilar or corrupted). If the NDS database does become inconsistent, you can use any error codes that have been generated as a result of the problem to help with troubleshooting. You can also use the online help or documentation to develop a strategy for resolving the error. If these two initial approaches are insufficient, you will need to do additional troubleshooting to determine and resolve the problem.

If you recognize the following symptoms, they may be an indicator that your network is having problems due to inconsistencies in the database:

- **Unknown objects display in NDS.** They show a question mark instead of their regular icon next to them.
- **NDS error messages display.** Look these up for more information about the problem and what to do to try to resolve it.
- **Users complain about problems** such as being prompted for a password when none exists for the user, login taking significantly longer than usual, changes that were made to the Directory are no longer there, NDS rights they had before they don't have now, and these and other problems are hard to duplicate (especially when they have you standing there looking over their shoulder).

As mentioned earlier, another problem you can have on the network is running out of space on the **Sys** volume. As this volume contains required NetWare operating system and associated files, problems with the **Sys** volume can cause problems on more than just that single server. If the **Sys** volume fails, you will need to remove the server from the Directory and replica lists, restore NDS, and re-add replicas to the server.

Whenever a NetWare server is unable to complete the synchronization process with another server, NDS displays error messages. You can view these messages with NDS Manager (use partition synchronization and continuity), or by entering the **SET NDS TRACE TO SCREEN=ON** command at the server console and watching the replicas synchronize with each other. Common synchronization error messages which occur when two servers are having difficulty synchronizing replicas are: **SYNC: failed to communicate with server <CN=FS2> ERROR -625** and **SYNC: End sync of partition < name>. All processed = NO.**

Chapter Summary

Default configuration settings implemented when the server is installed establish a baseline from which your NetWare 5 server and network can function. As the needs of your network's users grow and change, and network traffic and processing demands increase, you may want to optimize your network, and you will occasionally need to troubleshoot and repair problems. To ensure your NetWare 5 network performs at its best possible level, you will benefit from an understanding of how a NetWare server performs some of its basic tasks. This chapter discussed those basic tasks, and provided information about how NetWare 5 implements such things as memory allocation, CPU time allocation, and disk usage. It also explained how NetWare 5 maximizes network communications using features such as Packet Burst protocol and Large Internet Packets. In addition, it provided you with information about the types of tasks you can perform to help maintain a stable, consistent, and responsive NDS database.

To protect important software such as the NetWare OS, and to ensure that other processes and data files don't become corrupted or corrupt other processes and data files in memory, NetWare 5 reserves specific memory location in RAM for processes, instructions, and data. These areas in memory are referred to as *pools*. The NetWare 5 network operating system (NOS) gives each process its own allocation pool. When a process needs memory, it is given memory from its assigned allocation pool. When it has finished using that memory, the memory is collected (garbage collection routine is initiated) returned to the allocation pool, and made available for other processes.

When garbage collection is initiated, an API (Application program Interface) named Free identifies the pages in memory as deallocated. The garbage collection process then gathers those areas of deallocated memory and returns them to the memory pool. This garbage collection routine is run automatically by NetWare 5 as a background process so that it does not interfere with regular work.

Virtual memory is a NetWare system that allows data currently in RAM that is not being used frequently to be moved temporarily to storage in one or more volumes on the hard disk. The storage area is referred to as a *swap file*. You only can have one swap file on each NetWare volume.

NetWare also provides another kind of memory: *protected memory*, also called *protected address space*. Protected address space is an area of memory that is carefully controlled. Any software loaded into protected memory is not allowed to read or write to a memory location outside of its assigned protected memory. In effect, it is prevented from using any memory except protected memory or virtual memory. Both the NLM and the data it needs can be swapped to virtual memory.

Memory allocation and memory management are important aspects of an efficiently functioning NetWare network. So too is optimization of hard disk storage space. To optimize hard disk storage space, you can use two NetWare features:

- Block suballocation
- File compression

Just as NetWare divides memory into usable chunks (pages), it also divides hard disk space into usable chunks (blocks). One commonly used block size is 4 KB, although larger sizes (16 KB or larger, referred to as *large disk allocation blocks*) can be allocated, depending on how much hard disk storage space the server has available. When NetWare saves a file to the hard disk, it saves it into these blocks, using as many or as few blocks as needed.

File Compression is the reduction in the amount of space a file uses by eliminating as much as possible the unused storage area, similar to the way a program such as WinZip compresses files. On the average, compressing files on a volume using NetWare's file compression capabilities saves approximately 63% of storage space over not compressing the files on a volume. This is referred to as the *file compression ratio*. As long as the minimum required compression ratio will be met, NetWare compresses files quickly, with minimum overhead, and only when the files have not been accessed for a period of time. This ensures that compression and subsequent decompression (done when the files once again need to be accessed) have no noticeable effect on system performance.

While suballocation and compression concern themselves with making the most use of disk space and efficiently handling small files or file fragments, LIP and Packet Burst are designed to deal with larger files and the transmission of packets (data encapsulated in transmission information such as where the data is to be delivered, who sent the packet, what protocol is being used, and so on).

Packet Burst is the ability to send multiple packets across the network in a single transmission (burst) without waiting for a response from the receiving station between each packet. When a workstation establishes its initial connection with a NetWare server, it sets up a Packet Burst connection, providing the workstation has sufficient memory to use Packet Burst. If it does not, or if Packet Burst has been turned off at the workstation (it cannot be turned off at the server), a regular NCP connection is established.

During setup, the workstation and client negotiate as to the largest Packet Burst size to be used (up to 64 KB). Once established, the Packet Burst connection remains open for as long as the connection exists to the server, and transmission of packets can occur in bursts.

By default, the typical packet size is 512 bytes. This size accommodates sending packets on networks where not all workstations can handle larger packets, or where routers are restricted in the maximum packet size that they can handle. However, if the network has neither of these packet size limitations, the Large Internet Packet feature of NetWare lets the workstation and server negotiate the size of packets, based on the size of the workstation's and server's buffers. By default, LIP is enabled at the server when NetWare is installed, and at the workstation when the Novell Client is installed.

If your network has routers that can handle larger packet sizes and you want to take advantage of LIP on your network, you will need to configure the routers to handle the larger packet size. However, you cannot set the maximum packet size above the maximum size that NetWare can handle, and that size is determined by the topology (the physical connection of servers and clients) of your network. Those maximum sizes based on topology are:

- On an Ethernet network: 1514 bytes
- On a 4 Mbps Token Ring network: 4202
- On a 16 Mbps Token Ring network: 4202

NetWare 5 memory management and its use of virtual memory help to protect processes running on the server, improve performance, allow multiple processes to run and use resources simultaneously, and provide overall better service to your network users. Of course, what network users care about the most is how quickly they can get what they need, including how quickly any processing they request can be accomplished. You know that NetWare 5 automatically allocates CPU time to processes, but it can also allocate CPU time to applications.

Applications (virtual machines) like NLMs and other modules function because they contain strings of code (threads) which cause various tasks to be performed. Applications consist of groups of threads. When a thread that needs CPU time requests it, a share of CPU time is allocated to it. Each thread requesting CPU time is in turn allocated some of the CPU's time. When a routine is given its turn at using the CPU, if it gets in, does its job, then releases the CPU to service other threads, other routines can then be given the same consideration. Sometimes, however, threads take up more CPU time than they should. When this occurs, NetWare suspends the thread and reallocates the CPU time to another thread.

You can configure how much of the CPUs time certain applications can receive. This is known as *share value*. When you assign share value, it is the ratio between one application's share value and the share value assigned to other applications that determines how much CPU time the application gets, not the actual number you assign as the value.

Many of these NetWare features work with little or no attention from you as a network administrator. The NDS database, however, needs you to design, configure, implement, and manage it. Managing the NDS database means that you must consider and implement the best division of the database into logical groupings called *partitions*. You must then ensure that a sufficient number of copies of each partition (replicas) exist on the network, and on the right file servers. Doing so makes for easy user authentication and access to resources, effective distribution of the database, fault tolerance, and accuracy of the database's content.

Synchronization of replicas is important to database integrity. Each partition must have only one master partition to handle original requests and make changes to the partition, but it can have multiple read/write, read only, and subordinate reference replicas.

Synchronization of replicas once they are established is automatically handled by NetWare. You as the network administrator, however, must create those replicas to begin with, decide where they go, and monitor and manage them as needed. The NDS Manager utility is provided to let you handle a large variety of partition-related tasks.

Partition monitoring and maintenance is one of your tasks as a network administrator. There are other basic network managements tasks for you to perform as well, including:

- Regulating partition management rights
- Planning placement of replicas
- Backing up the Directory on each server
- Maintaining a standard version of NDS on each server
- Maintaining sufficient disk space on the **Sys** volume
- Preparing servers for scheduled downtime

In addition, you are responsible for diagnosing and resolving network problems. Certain symptoms such as unknown objects displaying in NDS and users being prompted for passwords when no password is required on their user account are symptoms of possible inconsistencies in your network's database. Some other symptoms are more obvious and even help you determine the problem and resolution. The display of error messages is one of the more obvious and helpful. Error messages can be looked up in documentation to determine their possible causes, and get suggestions for correcting it. In addition, whenever a NetWare server is unable to complete the synchronization process with another server, NDS displays error messages. One way you can view these messages is with NDS Manager.

Another problem you can have on the network is running out of space on the **Sys** volume. As this volume contains required NetWare operating system and associated files, problems with the **Sys** volume can cause problems on more than just that single server. If the **Sys** volume fails, you will need to remove the server from the Directory and replica lists, restore NDS, and re-add replicas to the server, a time consuming task. The best medicine in this case is prevention: take care to ensure the **Sys** volume always has plenty of space.

Practice Test Questions

1. What is another name for a 4 KB block of RAM used to store files?
   a. Process
   b. Page
   c. Program
   d. Pool

2. Which of the following identifies that area in server memory where processes and files that need to be protected are located?
   a. Process
   b. Page
   c. Program
   d. Pool

3. What two do NetWare use to collect and prepare unused segments of memory for use by another program or file?
   a. Virtual memory
   b. Memory deallocation
   c. Common memory pool
   d. Garbage collection
   e. Swap file

4. What is the trigger that determines when unused segments of memory can be gathered up and made accessible for other programs or data to access?
   a. Virtual memory
   b. Memory deallocation
   c. Common memory pool
   d. Garbage collection
   e. Swap file

5. What is another name for the storage area on the hard disk which the NetWare server can use as if it were RAM?
   a. Virtual memory
   b. Memory deallocation
   c. Common memory pool
   d. Garbage collection
   e. Swap file

6. What is the maximum number of swap files you can have on the Sys volume?
   a. Sys volume cannot have a swap file
   b. 1
   c. 2
   d. Unlimited

7. What must you do if your server is suffering from disk thrashing?
   a. Limit the number of swap files on each volume to 1
   b. Increase the number of swap files on each volume
   c. Add memory to the server
   d. Provide protected memory for all processes

8. What is the largest size a single protected address space can be?
   a. 1024 bytes
   b. 64 KB
   c. 512 MB
   d. 1 GB

9. What two NetWare features are designed to help you optimize hard disk space?
   a. Swap files
   b. Block suballocation
   c. File compression
   d. Paging

10. In block suballocation, what is the smallest size that a page of RAM can be divided into?
    a. 512 bytes
    b. 4 KB
    c. 512 KB
    d. 1 MB

11. Which of the following *cannot* be used to view compression statistics?
    a. NetWare Administrator
    b. Explorer
    c. Monitor
    d. Filer

12. What NetWare feature allows transmission of multiple packets without having to wait for a response between each packet from the receiving server or workstation?
  a. Compression
  b. Swap file
  c. LIP
  d. Packet burst

13. What is another name for an application running on a NetWare server?
  a. Packet
  b. Procedure
  c. Virtual machine
  d. Virtual memory

14. When adjusting how much CPU time a given application can have, what is the most important factor?
  a. Whether the application has 512 threads or fewer
  b. If a kernel option is available
  c. What the ratio of the new share value is to existing share values
  d. Whether block suballocation is enabled on the server

15. If you need to add a replica to your network, what utility can you use?
  a. NetWare Administrator
  b. NDS Server
  c. NDS Manager
  d. Monitor

Answers to Practice Test Questions

1. b	6. b	11. c
2. d	7. c	12. d
3. b, d	8. c	13. c
4. a	9. b, c	14. c
5. e	10. a	15. c

CHAPTER 10

Enhancing the Network with Other Novell Services

ccess to applications is of key importance to network users. So too is access to printers, electronic mail, and other network services. Users want to choose what services they use and, in many cases, expect the network administrator to ensure the network supports various operating systems so that the users don't have to keep duplicate information on different systems or login to multiple networks to get at what they need.

In today's environment, Internet access has also become important to many network users, as well as to many businesses. Some businesses exclusively use the Internet for commerce, or at least are heading that way. Egghead Software is a good example. Until just this year, Egghead Computers had retail stores in many locations. It closed many if not all of those locations, and now depends heavily on the Internet for its sales.

In addition, fulfilling users' needs may also mean adding to the network's inventory of software products. But every product you add to your network can also add a layer of potential problems. To keep problems to a minimum, network administrators need to be sure they are purchasing and installing products that are compatible with their existing networking software and with the other products on their network. Sometimes, the quickest way to do that is to buy all of their software from the same manufacturer, or to at least be sure the other software they do buy has been certified to run on their networking software.

Novell attempts to provide both options to businesses. Through their Yes program, partnerships, and other key implementations, Novell accomplishes that task. In addition, Novell makes available other Novell products to enhance your network's usefulness and your companies productivity. This chapter discusses four specific products that Novell provides:

- BorderManager
- NDS for NT
- GroupWise
- ManageWise

Although you may not currently be interested in any of these four products for your company, you may find it helpful to at least know what they are and what services they provide. In addition, if you are a NetWare 5 CNE candidate, you must pass tests for various electives in addition to passing the NetWare 5 Administration and NetWare 5 Advanced Administration tests. These four products all have available Novell Certified courses and their associated certification tests qualify as CNE elective credit. Therefore, this chapter provides information to give you a better understanding of how these products function once integrated into your NetWare network.

NOTE

The information in this chapter only gives you an introduction to and brief overview of these four products. You should not assume that the information included in this chapter provides you with sufficient knowledge to pass the associated Novell certification elective test.

For more information on these and other Novell products, see the corporate Web site at **http://www.novell.com**.

Integrating BorderManager Services

BorderManager is a set of NLMs which protects your private network from unauthorized access by individuals on the Internet. BorderManager is named for that "border" area between your network (Intranet) and the public Intranet.

When you implement BorderManager, you make it possible to accelerate Internet-related performance, as well as user, service, and content access control. In addition, you increase security on your network because BorderManager lets you monitor and control inbound (traffic moving from the Internet to an Intranet) access, as well as outbound (traffic moving from an Intranet to the Internet) traffic.

Because security and privacy for your Intranet is a key reason for using BorderManager, a brief understanding of how that security is provided (using a firewall) may be useful. A firewall is similar in nature to the firewall that building codes require between a house and an attached garage. Its purpose is to inhibit entry. In the case of a house's firewall, prevention of fire into the house from the garage is its main purpose. In BorderManager, the purpose of the firewall is to place both outbound and inbound access control limits. Outbound access control limits can be set to restrict what Web sites your network users can access. Inbound access control limits can be set to restrict unauthorized external Internet users from accessing servers on your Intranet. BorderManager firewalls accomplish this using:

- **Routers that can filter packets.** Packet-filtering routers (also called *screening routers*) restrict incoming traffic by filtering on the IP address and port number from which the packet originated. They can also use network address, node address, or a combination of all four to filter incoming packets. Because of this diversity, they function at the Data Link, Network, and Transport layers of the OSI model. (The OSI model is a standard designed to help companies develop communications methods that would provide compatibility and interoperability. Figure 10-1 shows the layers of the OSI Model and which layer each of the firewall components are implemented.)
- **Circuit gateways.** These circuit-level proxies accept Intranet user requests for access to the Internet, validate the TCP or UDP session, substitute their own IP address for that of the requester (this hides the requester's actual IP address), and implement routing policies based on HTTP protocols. They are implemented at the Session layer of the OSI model.
- **Application gateways.** These application-level proxies are the most secure. They are implemented at the Application and Presentation layers of the OSI model.

When you implement the following major BorderManager components, you create a firewall that protects your Intranet:

- **Novell Internet Access Server (NIAS) 4.1 software.** Provides multi-protocol routing and WAN support, packet filtering, Network Address Translator (NAT—for translating individual user's IP addressed to registered addresses), IPX mapping gateway (does the same for IPX that NAT does for IP), and inbound and outbound remote access.
- **Remote Access.** Enables modem-based remote connection to your Intranet.
- **IP Gateway software.** Enables the use of TCP/IP on the Intranet and still retain compatibility with the Internet. (Translates IPX to IP, and IP to IP).

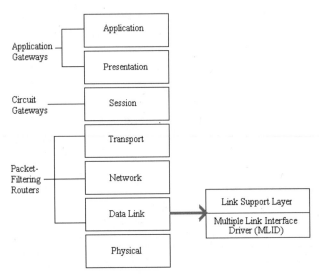

FIGURE 10-1 Firewall components and how they correspond to the OSI model.

- **Virtual Private Network (VPN) encryption software.** Uses tunneling and multiple layers of encryption to make the link look like a single point-to-point link which can be used at full speed over T1 and T3 lines. It is cost effective and lets private networks share information over the Internet without that information being accessible to the public. The initial connection is made using Diffie-Hellmand public-key, private-key encrypted authentication.
- **Proxy cache software.** Improves browser performance by allowing communications to occur with a local server containing a cache (Web proxy cache) of the Web content, instead of requiring access to a more delayed (higher latency) Web (origin) server. There are three types of proxy caches:
  - **Standard proxy cache.** Stores frequently-accessed Web pages on a local server so users spend less actual time waiting for information to be delivered from the Web. (The standard proxy cache is also referred to as a *client accelerator.*)
  - **HTTP accelerator.** Contains a dedicated cache of the majority (95 to 100%) of your network's Web server content to reduce Intranet bottlenecks. (The HTTP accelerator is also referred to as a *Web server accelerator* or *reverse proxy*).
  - **Hierarchical proxy cache.** Places multiple caches in strategic areas throughout your Intranet (on proxy servers) to further increase access speed for users.

Working with NDS for NT

NDS for NT lets you place Windows NT domains in your network's NDS tree. NT Domains are well-suited for small workgroup structures, but in larger, more integrated networks, managing domains is a complex task. You cannot move objects between domains without deleting and recreating the object and there is no rights inheritance model such as in NDS. In addition, you must maintain multiple databases for domains and applications and create complex trust relationships between domains so that users have access to the resources they need.

NDS for NT allows you to administer mixed Windows NT and Novell networks from one access point without the complexity of trust relationships. To do so, it extends the NDS schema so that you can manage all components of your network from a single Directory. Your management capabilities are extended, and your management costs reduced as well because all network management support is now through a single point of administration and is provided using Novell's Directory administration tool—NetWare Administrator.

You can move Windows NT domain information into your NDS database using the NDS for NT Domain Object Wizard (see Figure 10-2).

Once you have moved NT domain information into NDS, you then manage domains as NDS group objects (see Figure 10-3). You do not have to create and maintain separate Windows NT and NetWare user accounts to give users access to applications (such as Exchange) and network resources (such as printers and servers). With NDS for NT, users log in only once to access all the resources and applications they need on both NetWare and Windows NT servers.

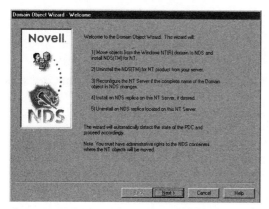

Figure 10-2 The Domain Object Wizard Welcome screen.

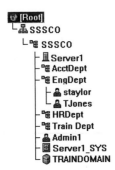

FIGURE 10-3 NetWare Administrator showing Domain Object.

When NDS is added to a Windows NT Server, in addition to single-source administration, there are several management capabilities that you do not have in a Windows NT domain network without NDS for NT:

- Trust relationships, complex and difficult to administer, can be eliminated when NDS for NT is added. Instead, all you have to do is make NDS users members of NDS groups with access rights to multiple domains. Doing so then gives those users access to multiple domains.
- Because NDS is implemented as a single database, you only create one user account to give that user all of the network access you want them to have. You do not have to create user accounts in multiple domains. When you want to remove a user, you just remove their one account. In the meantime, the user only has to log in to the network one time to access all resources for which they are authorized.
- One simple step inside the NetWare Administrator utility is all that is needed to move a user from one container to another, thus effectively changing their access to domains, if the container's access is to a different domain. In NT, you have to write down the user account information, delete the user account out of the one domain, then recreate it in another domain.
- Greater control over user's access rights is possible in NDS for NT because a user can be given rights to a single object. In NT, the equivalent requires that rights be granted to a type of object within a domain. For example, you give a user access to all printers in an NT domain, or to no printers. In NDS, you can give a user access to a single printer, and restrict access from all other printers in that same container.

NDS for NT provides five components which allow Windows NT domains to be managed from the NDS database:

- **Domain Object Wizard.** After NDS for NT is installed, the Domain Object Wizard runs the first time you startup the Windows NT server. This program is a user-friendly graphical utility designed to associate domain users with NDS users, and let you specify where to put the Windows NT domain in the NDS tree. You only run this program once, unless you want to uninstall NDS for NT. This program can be run for that purpose. One other important function performed by the Domain Object Wizard is that it renames the existing **Samsrv.dll** file to **Mssamsrv.dll**. This makes room for the **Samsrv.dll** file provided by NDS for NT.

- **Samsrv.dll file.** The NDS for NT **Samsrv.dll** file redirects domain access calls to NDS so that NDS can fulfill domain requests made by Windows NT Servers, Windows NT Workstations, and applications. If NDS for NT did not replace the **Samsrv.dll**, the original Windows **Samsrv.dll** would continue to access the Windows NT Security Accounts Manager (SAM) containing the domain database to perform whatever task had been requested of it. As every domain controller in the Windows NT domain contains a copy of the Windows **Samsrv.dll**, you must install the NDS for NT version of **Samsrv.dll** on every domain controller in the Windows NT domain. Installing NDS for NT first on the Primary Domain Controller (PDC), then on every Backup Domain Controller (BDC) accomplishes this tasks.

- **Novell Client.** This software is installed on every Windows NT Server automatically when NDS for NT is installed. It lets the client access NDS running on any platform to which NDS has been ported.

- **NetWare Administrator.** This is the Novell utility used for single point network administration of Windows NT domains and NDS. It is used on regular NDS networks, but with the snap-ins provided by NDS for NT, you can administer Windows NT domain objects using NetWare Administrator once you have migrated them to the NDS tree.

- **Mailbox Manager for Exchange.** This is also a NetWare Administrator snap-in. It lets you use NetWare Administrator to create, edit, and delete Exchange mailboxes. Although you must perform these tasks manually to ensure changes made in Microsoft's Exchange Manager are also made to NDS, these tasks are relatively easy to do in NetWare Administrator.

Taking Advantage of GroupWise

Communication on a network is of key importance. GroupWise 5 is a messaging system that is integrated with NetWare. GroupWise 5 provides:

- Calendaring
- Internet access
- Remote access
- Scheduling
- Shared folders
- Task management
- Threaded conferencing

This integration of GroupWise and NetWare lets GroupWise be centrally administered using the NetWare Administrator utility. A snap-in module also called the GroupWise administration module allows you to administer GroupWise using NetWare Administrator. As with many of the other products Novell provides, GroupWise integration lets you continue to manage your network through a centralized utility—NetWare Administrator.

When you install the GroupWise 5 administration software, the installation process extends the NDS schema to accommodate GroupWise objects. Then, you just have to add the GroupWise administration module (snap-in) to NetWare Administrator, and you will be able to perform the following GroupWise-related tasks using NetWare Administrator:

- Configure and modify the GroupWise system (including its six components: client, message transfer system, administration program, message store, directory store, and document store)
- Manage GroupWise user properties and user preferences
- Manage and maintain the message store (a server-based storage area for user messages, the method of which is known as *store-and-forward*)
- Run diagnostics on the GroupWise system
- Manage client software (the interface users see and use to create, send, and receive messages, manage incoming and outgoing messages as well as personal calendars, access documents in a GroupWise library, and schedule meetings with other GroupWise users)

Message transferring is an important task of GroupWise 5. It is responsible for taking messages that a user sends (a copy of which is kept in a storage area on a NetWare server called the *message store*), and through the message transfer agent (MTA), deliver them to the recipient (see Figure 10-4). Two types of message stores are used. One holds the E-mail messages, the other holds attached files. The receiving user can then retrieve the message. As gateways are used to deliver messages when users exist in different geographical locations and don't share the same server, gateways can also be an important part of the message transfer system.

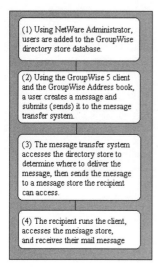

(1) Using NetWare Administrator, users are added to the GroupWise directory store database.

(2) Using the GroupWise 5 client and the GroupWise Address book, a user creates a message and submits (sends) it to the message transfer system.

(3) The message transfer system accesses the directory store to determine where to deliver the message, then sends the message to a message store the recipient can access.

(4) The recipient runs the client, accesses the message store, and receives their mail message

FIGURE 10-4 The GroupWise process involved in the successful delivery of an E-mail message.

You cannot use GroupWise 5 or any other program to send E-mail if you don't know how to address that E-mail. In addition, the GroupWise system will not accept mail delivery for an E-mail user who is not part of its E-mail directory (the GroupWise directory store). Just as NDS' database is distributed and replicated, so too is the GroupWise directory store database. It is kept constantly updated with information such as the name, location, and other relevant number of each GroupWise user. The Message Transfer System uses the information contained in the directory store to help ensure proper delivery of messages. The GroupWise directory store also provides information for the Address Book that users access when they need to look up another user's mailing address or other related information.

Implementing ManageWise on the Network

ManageWise allows you to manage your varied network components, and keep control of such necessary management tasks as asset inventory and management. Using ManageWise, you can inventory your existing network system, monitor network devices, gather relevant information so that you can analyze and evaluate the network's performance, and print gathered information (see Figure 10-5). If you find problems or potential problems, you can gather needed information about the real-time problems that are occurring and be prepared to perform preventative maintenance. Using ManageWise, you can perform these tasks from a remote location so that you don't have to travel from site to site or workstation to workstation to get the information and the answers you need.

ManageWise is right at home in a multi-operating system, desktop, application networking environment. It helps you to feel more at ease as well with some of your network management tasks because it assists you in:

- maintaining and managing a network's asset inventory
- monitoring and managing network servers
- managing user's desktops
- analyzing and managing network traffic
- providing network-wide virus protection

ManageWise helps you maintain and manage a network's asset inventory because it can:

- automatically discover network devices regardless of which protocol is being used
- display graphical maps (internetwork—network topology, segment—all stations on a single segment, and custom—geographical location of sites and devices)
- gather component information (processor type, memory, etc.) from each network node
- list assigned IPX and IP addresses and identify duplicate addresses

ManageWise helps you monitor and manage network servers by letting you compare multiple servers from a central site to optimize configura-

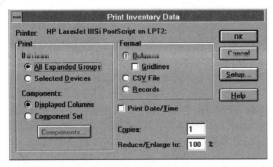

FIGURE 10-5 The screen from which you configure what inventory data to print.

tion and performance. It also performs unattended monitoring, notifying you when thresholds (such as high file activity) that you set are exceeded. You can also track server performance trends and print queue activity because of GroupWise's automatic information gathering and reporting capabilities.

Because ManageWise monitors workstations as well as servers, and includes a copy of Z.E.N.works, you can also manage users' desktops.

ManageWise also provides network traffic analysis to help you identify overloaded network devices or segments and head off trouble before it begins. It also provides more detailed troubleshooting information, such as identifying potential network errors. And, ManageWise is useful in a multi-protocol environment because it supports:

- Common hardware standards
- Ethernet, Token Ring, and variants of these standards
- Common protocols including IPX, NetWare/IP, TCP/IP, AppleTalk, and Systems Network Architecture (SNA)

ManageWise provides virus protection for both NetWare servers and workstations because it has comprehensive, intelligent, rule-based scanning capabilities that help it to identify virus-like behavior. It also checks for infected files anytime a file is transferred to or from the server, as well as when users login (even when that login is from a mobile computer). It also performs a regular workstation scan, and can be run manually whenever you choose to run a scan. In addition, it can scan at prescheduled times, and automatically quarantine, rename, delete, or clean infected files that it finds.

It probably seems unlikely that any single ManageWise component could do all of the tasks just described. Well, it is. ManageWise utilizes five software components to perform all of the described tasks, the first one of which has already been mentioned:

- **Z.E.N.works** (see Figure 10-6), which allows remote control and management of workstations. Components are located on both servers and workstations.
- **NetExplorer**, which creates and manages the asset inventory database. It must be run on at least one network server.
- **NetWare Management Agent (NMA)**, which allows remote management of network servers. Runs on each server.
- **NetWare LANalyzer Agent**, which gathers statistics and packet information. Runs on one server of each network segment.
- **Virus Protect**, which provides the network-wide virus protection. Components run on both workstations and servers (see Figure 10-7).

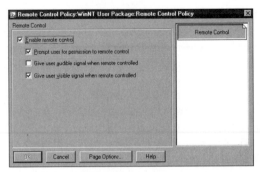

FIGURE 10-6 Z.E.N.works remote control policy used to set up remote workstation control.

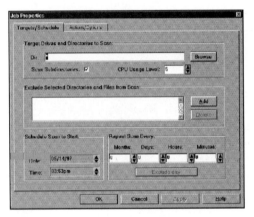

FIGURE 10-7 The dialog from which you add or reschedule a virus scan job
(request to run a virus scan).

Chapter Summary

This chapter introduced you to four Novell products designed to
enhance your network's usefulness and your companies productivity:

- BorderManager
- NDS for NT
- GroupWise
- ManageWise

BorderManager is a security implementation which protects your private
network from unauthorized access by individuals on the Internet. When
you implement BorderManager, you increase security on your network

because BorderManager makes it possible for you to monitor and control inbound (traffic moving from the Internet to an Intranet) access, as well as outbound (traffic moving from and Intranet to the Internet) traffic. BorderManager's firewalls provide this protection using one or more of the following:

- Packet-filtering routers
- Circuit gateways
- Application gateways

NDS for NT lets you place Windows NT domains in your network's NDS tree. To do so it extends the NDS schema, which also extends your management capabilities and reduces your management costs. It also improves user and application support because NDS' extended schema allows NDS to fulfill Windows NT domain requests made from Windows NT servers and Windows NT workstations, and provides users access to the entire network with only one login.

GroupWise 5 is a messaging system that is integrated with NetWare and thus can be centrally administered. GroupWise 5 provides:

- Calendaring
- Internet access
- Remote access
- Scheduling
- Shared folders
- Task management
- Threaded conferencing

ManageWise is a network asset tracking and inventory system that helps you manage your varied network components. Using ManageWise, you can inventory your existing network system, monitor network devices, and gather relevant information. You can then analyze that information to evaluate the network's performance, find potential problems before they become serious, and maintain your network at as close to peak performance as possible. Because you can use ManageWise and perform these tasks from a remote location, you won't have to travel from site to site to monitor your network.

Practice Test Questions

1. Which Novell product might you choose if you wanted to provide electronic mail to your network users?
   a. BorderManager
   b. NDS for NT
   c. GroupWise
   d. ManageWise

2. Which Novell product is designed to protect your network from unauthorized access by Internet users?
   a. BorderManager
   b. NDS for NT
   c. GroupWise
   d. ManageWise

3. Which Novell product should you install if you want to manage domains from NDS?
   a. BorderManager
   b. NDS for NT
   c. GroupWise
   d. ManageWise

4. To find potential network problems, which Novell product can you use?
   a. BorderManager
   b. NDS for NT
   c. GroupWise
   d. ManageWise

5. Which one of the following is *not* used for firewall protection of your network?
   a. Packet-filtering routers
   b. OSI model
   c. Circuit gateways
   d. Application gateways

6. In which of Novell's products is the Novell Internet Access Server included to provide multiprotocol routing and WAN support, among other things?
   a. BorderManager
   b. NDS for NT
   c. GroupWise
   d. ManageWise

7. What is another name for the Web server accelerator?
   a. Standard proxy cache
   b. Reverse proxy
   c. Hierarchical proxy
   d. Origin server

8. What is the name of the file NDS for NT must replace in order to be able to redirect domain access calls to NDS?
   a. Wizard.dll
   b. Object.dll
   c. Serv.dll
   d. Samsrv.dll

9. Where does the GroupWise Message Transfer System get its information for delivering E-mail?
   a. Directory store
   b. GroupWise users
   c. Address book
   d. Message store

10. Which Novell product includes NetExplorer?
   a. BorderManager
   b. NDS for NT
   c. GroupWise
   d. ManageWise

Answers to Practice Test Questions

1. c	6. a
2. a	7. b
3. b	8. d
4. d	9. a
5. b	10. d

Index

ABOUT THE AUTHOR

DOROTHY CADY is fully Novell certified—CNA, CNE, MCNE, and CNI. She is the author of 12 books including *NetWare Training Guide: CNA Study Guide* (1994) and *CNE 4 Short Course* (1996). Dorothy is a Novell employee and has been working with NetWare since the development of version 2.2. She resides in Spanish Fork, Utah.